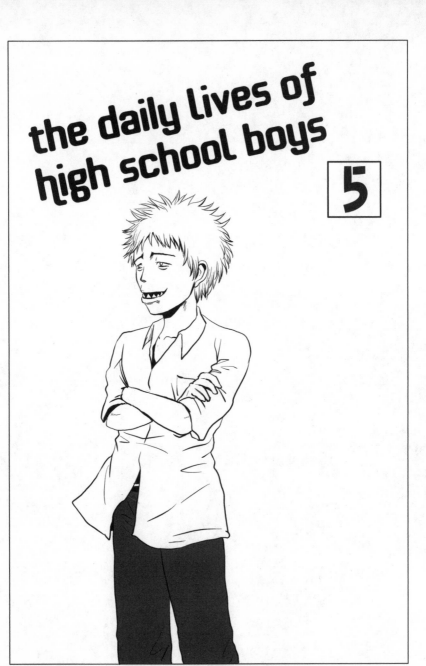

the daily lives of
high school boys

5

yasunobu yamauchi

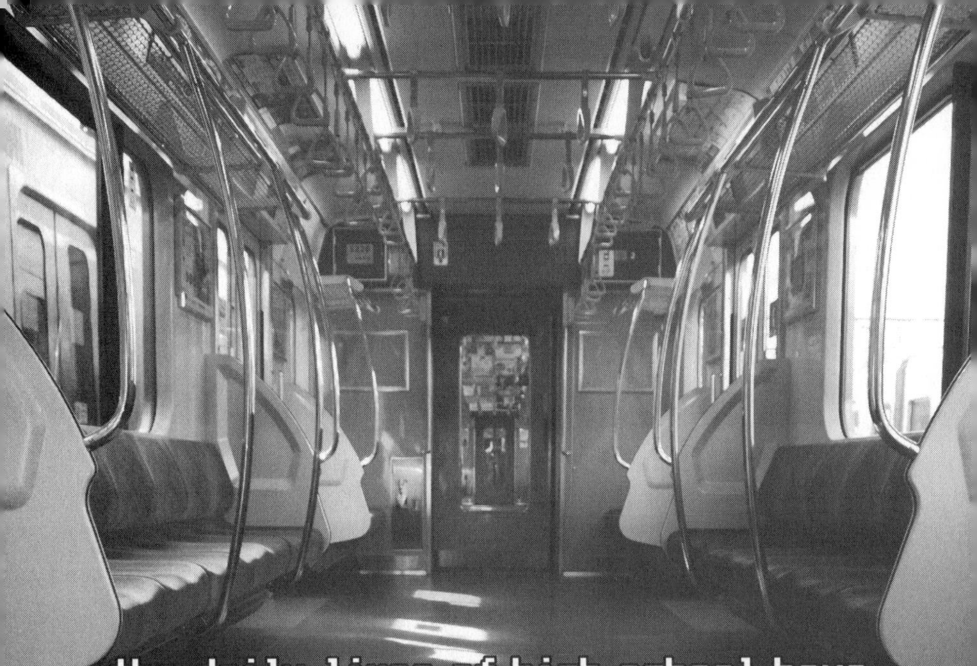

the daily lives of high school boys

5

CONTENTS

chapter 68:
high school boys and school

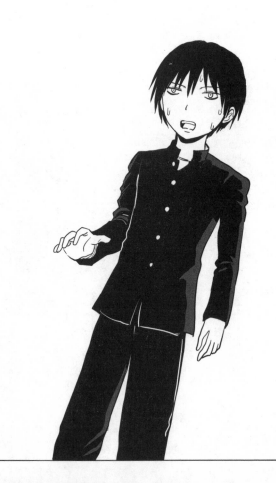

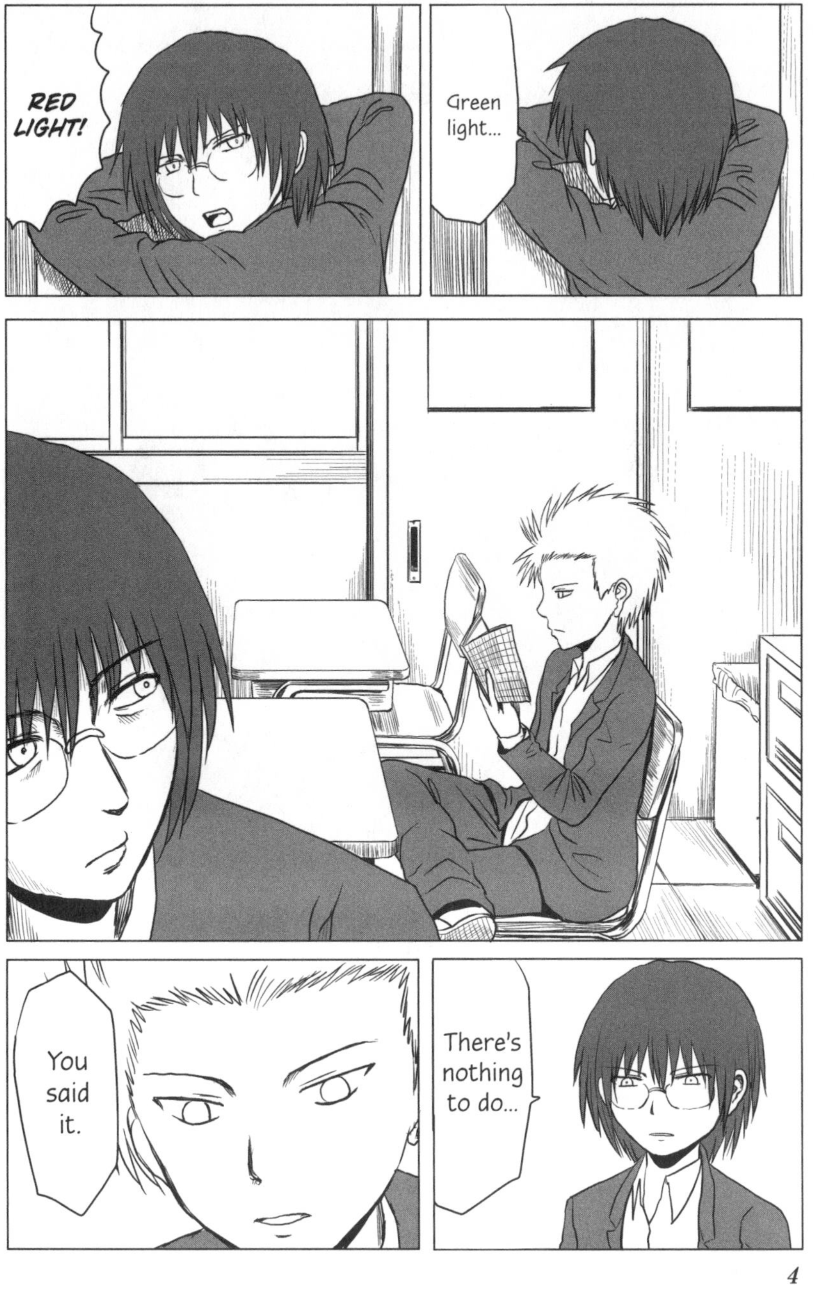
Green light...
RED LIGHT!
There's nothing to do...
You said it.

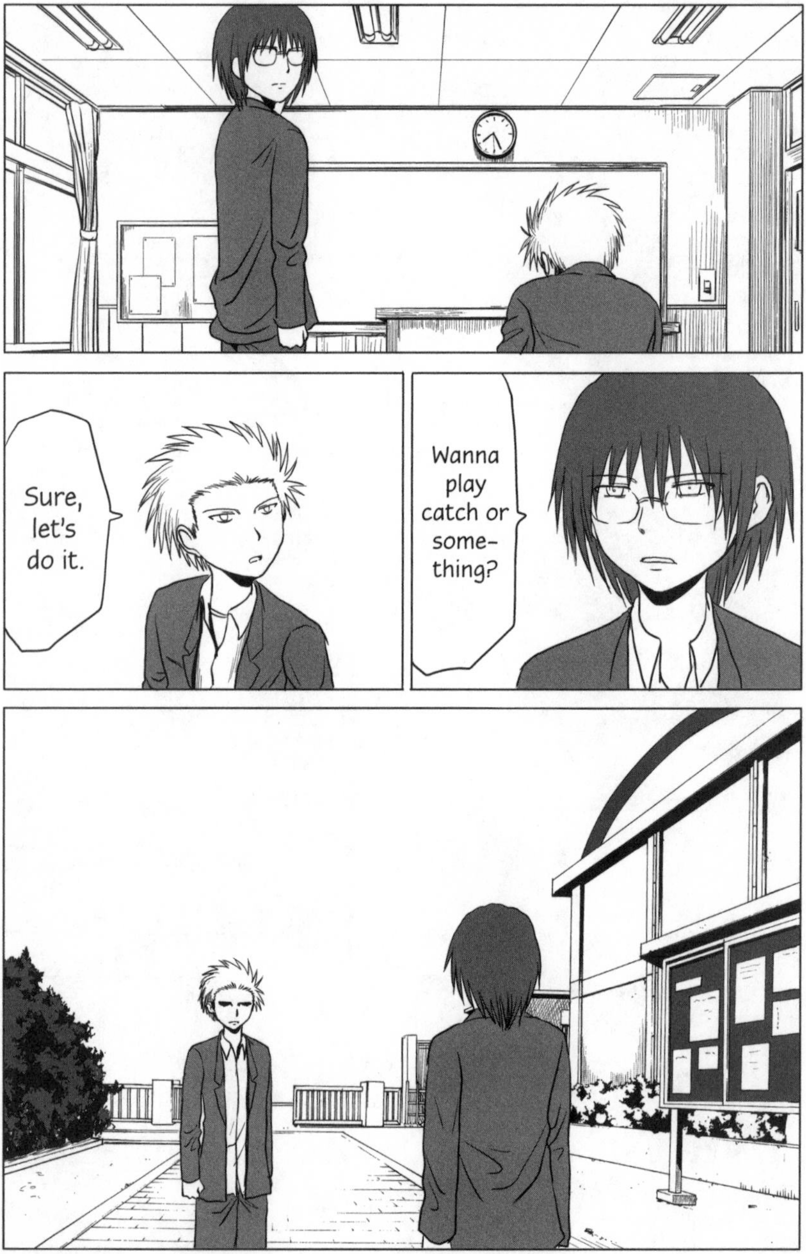
Wanna play catch or some-thing?
Sure, let's do it.

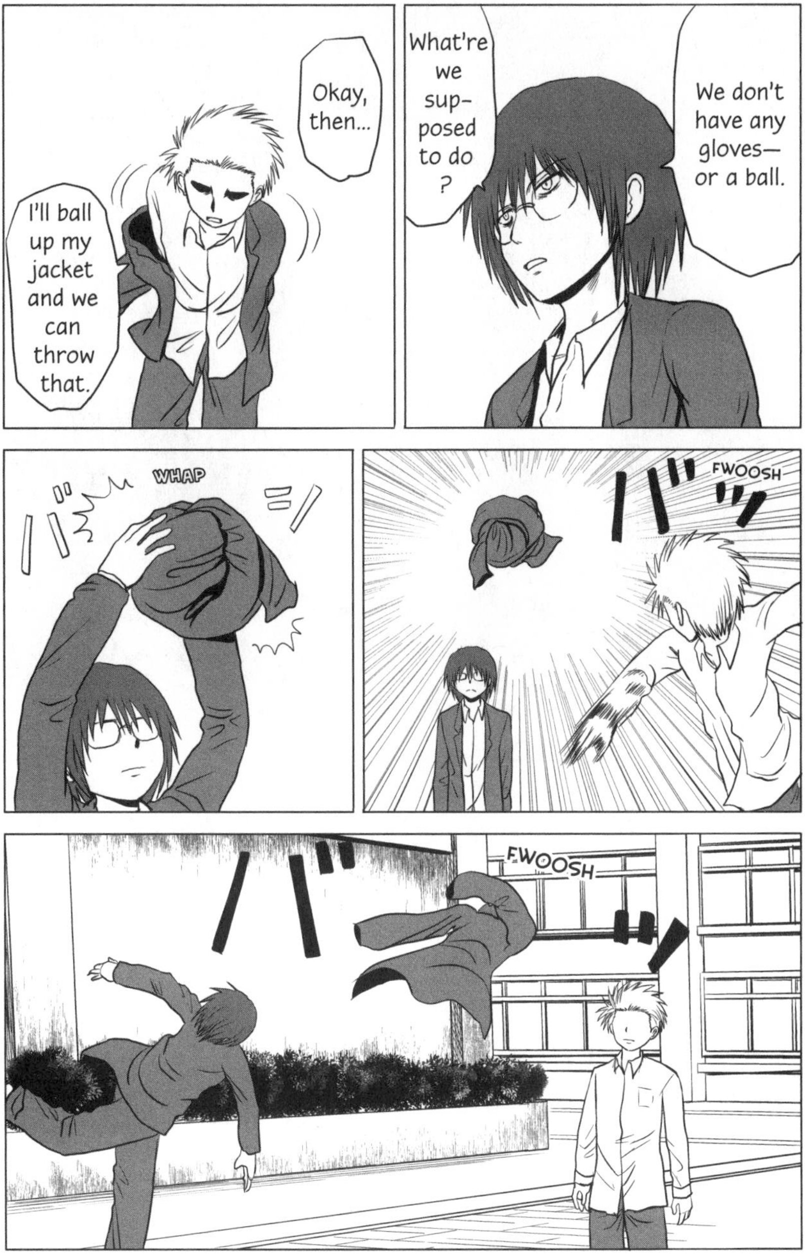
We don't have any gloves—or a ball.
What're we sup-posed to do ?
Okay, then...
I'll ball up my jacket and we can throw that.
FWOOSH
バッ
WHAP
バ
FWOOSH
バッ

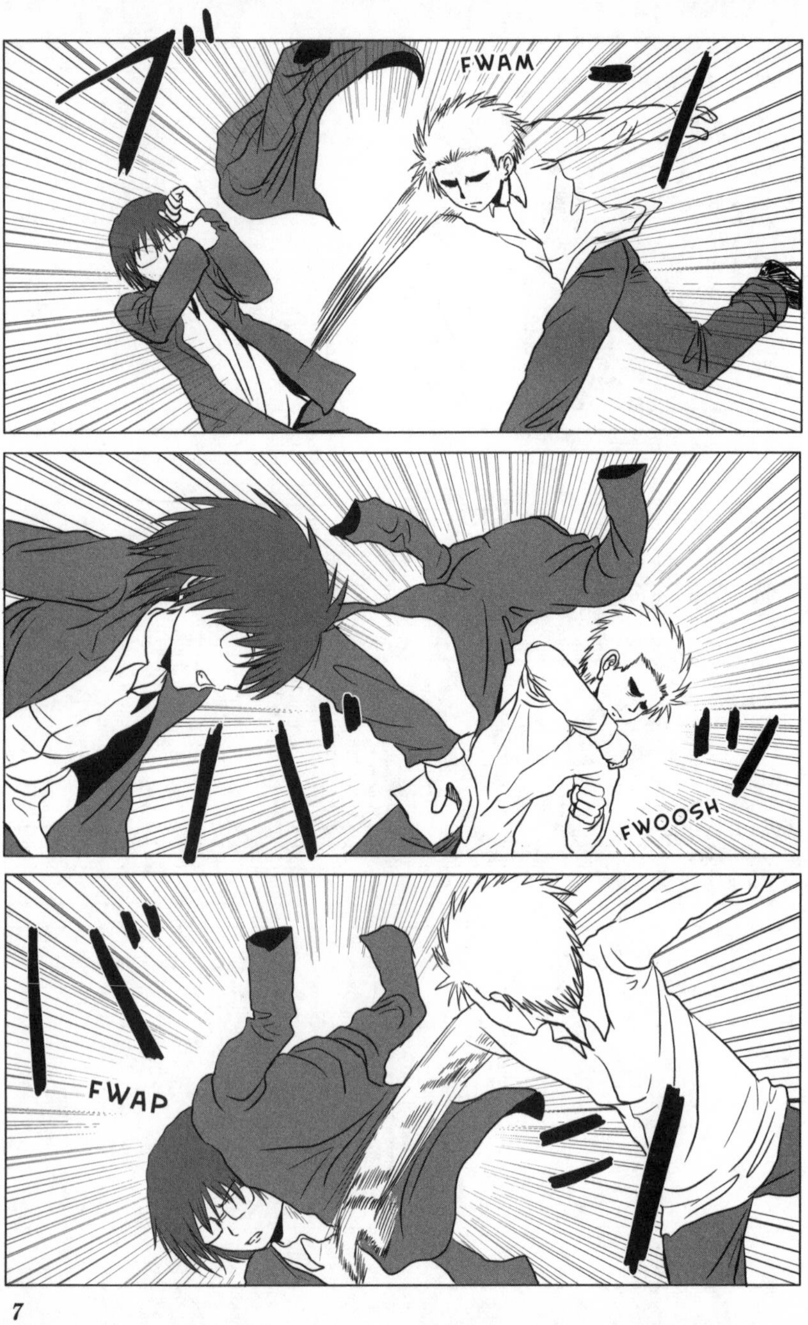
FWAM
FWOOSH
FWAP

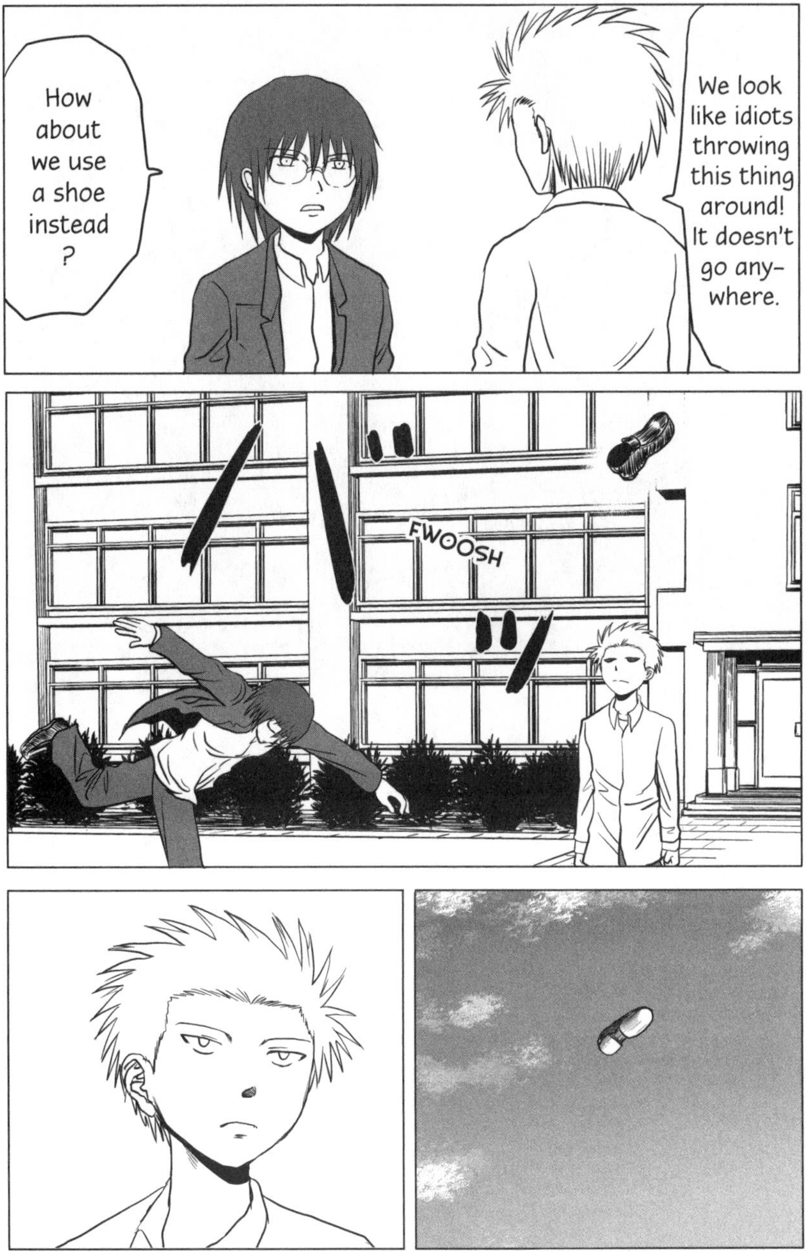
We look like idiots throwing this thing around! It doesn't go any-where.
How about we use a shoe instead ?
FWOOSH

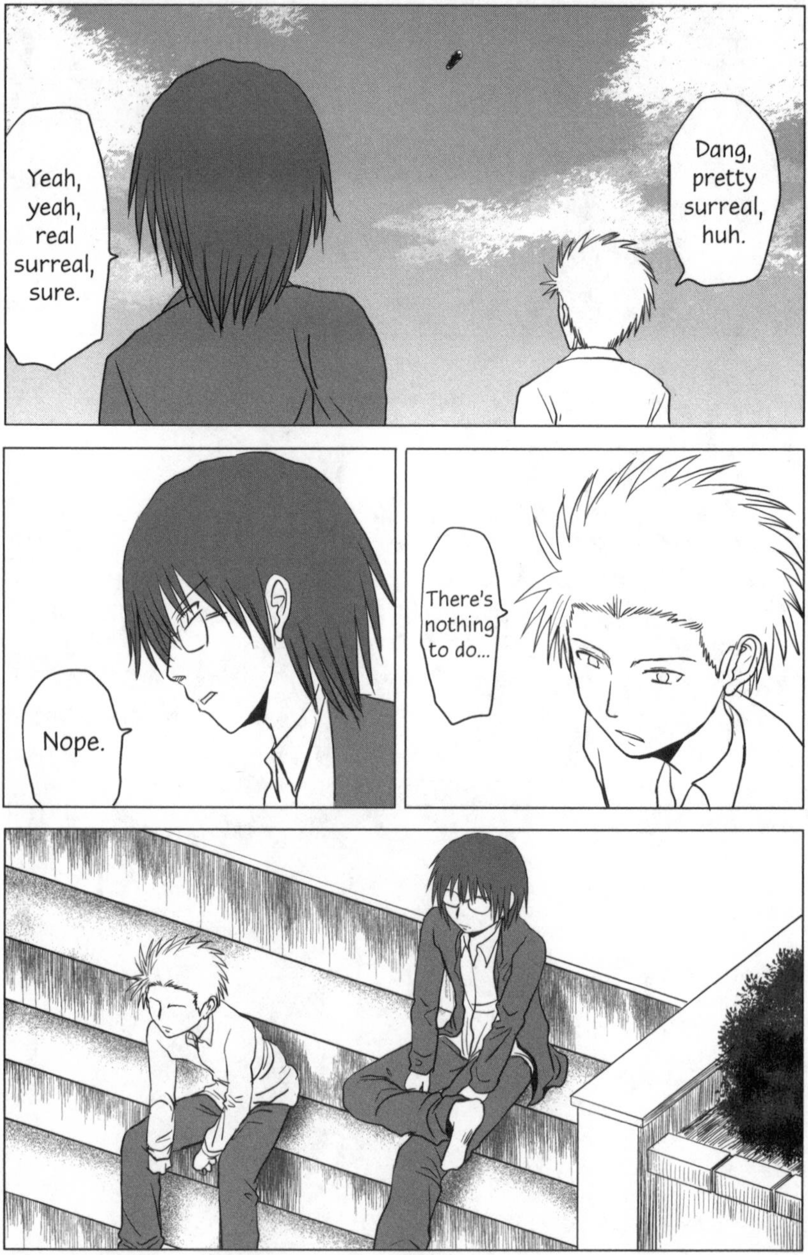
Dang, pretty surreal, huh.
Yeah, yeah, real surreal, sure.
There's nothing to do...
Nope.

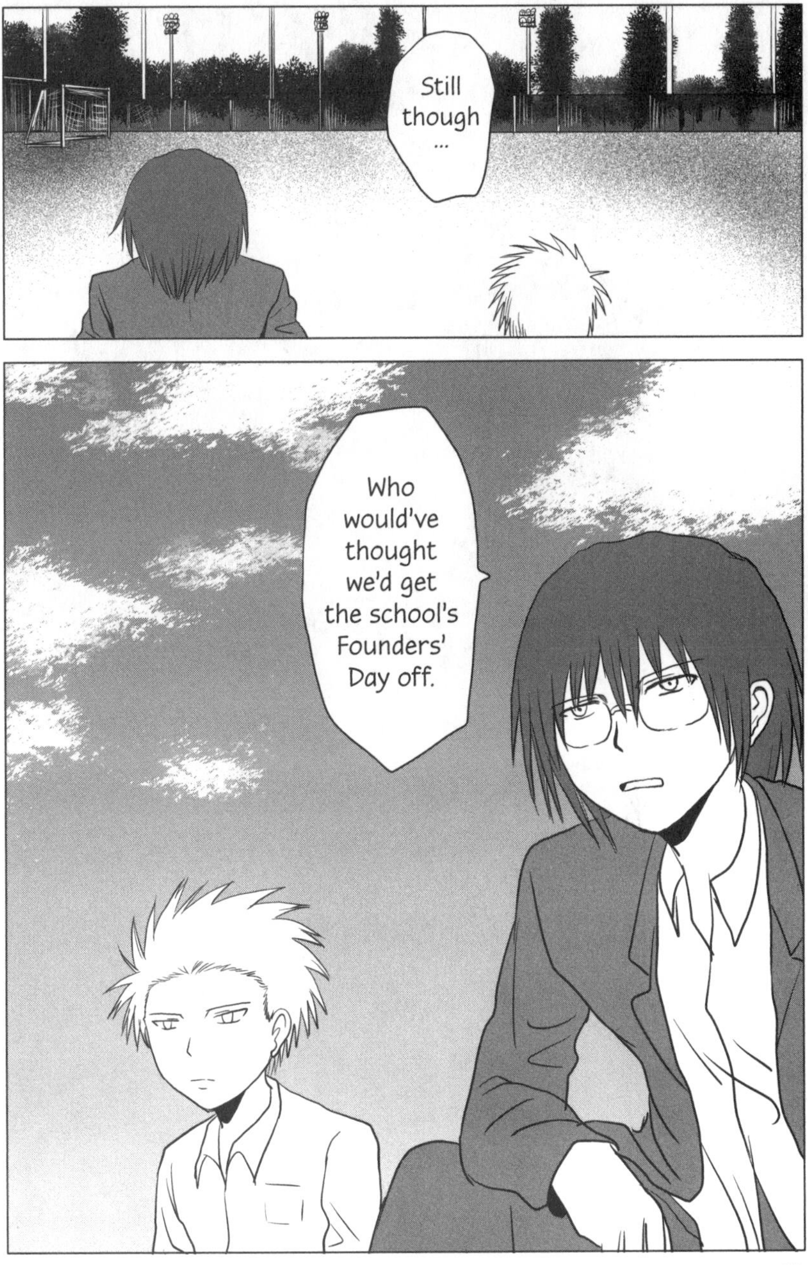
Still though ...
Who would've thought we'd get the school's Founders' Day off.

chapter 69:
high school boys and cooking

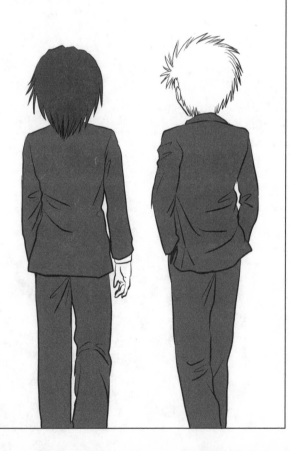

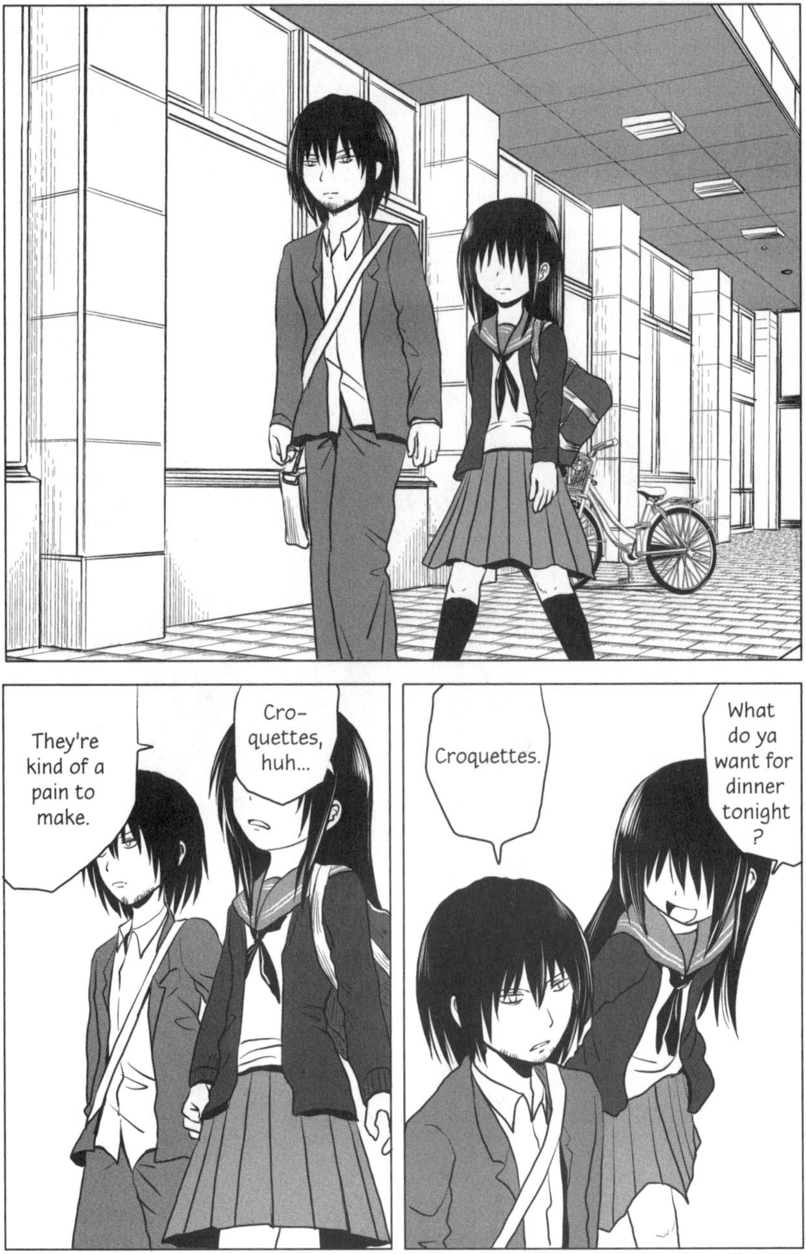
What do ya want for dinner tonight?
Croquettes.
Croquettes, huh...
They're kind of a pain to make.

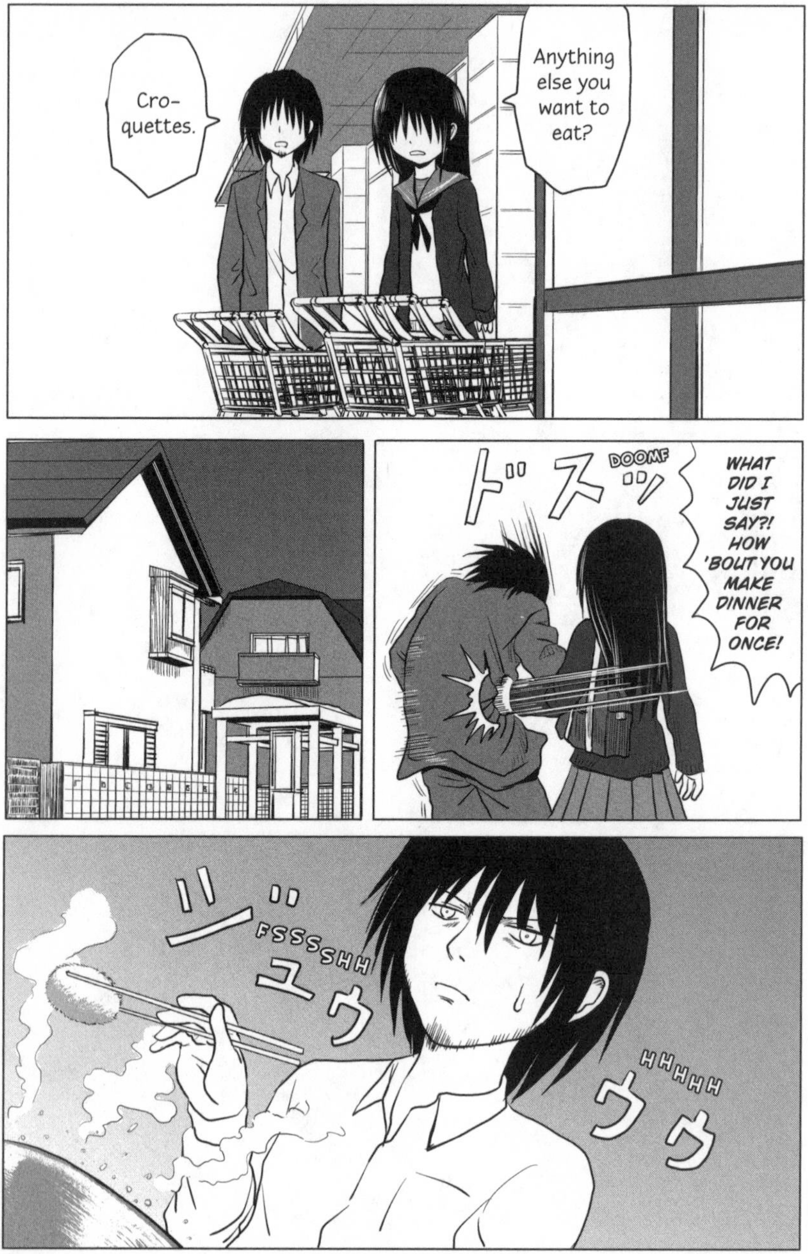
Anything else you want to eat?
Cro- quettes.
ドスッ
DOOMF
WHAT DID I JUST SAY?! HOW 'BOUT YOU MAKE DINNER FOR ONCE!
FSSSSHH
HHHHHH

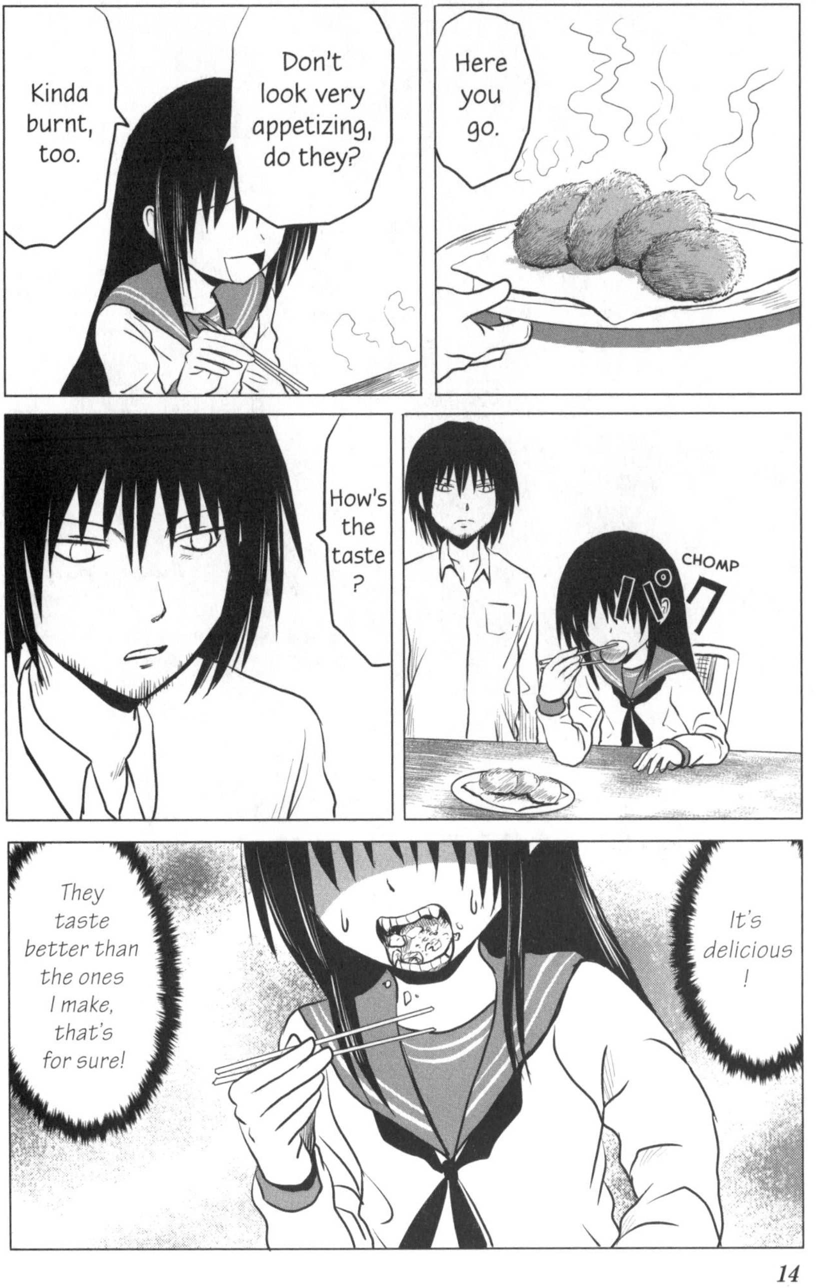
Here you go.
Don't look very appetizing, do they?
Kinda burnt, too.
パク
CHOMP
How's the taste?
It's delicious!
They taste better than the ones I make, that's for sure!

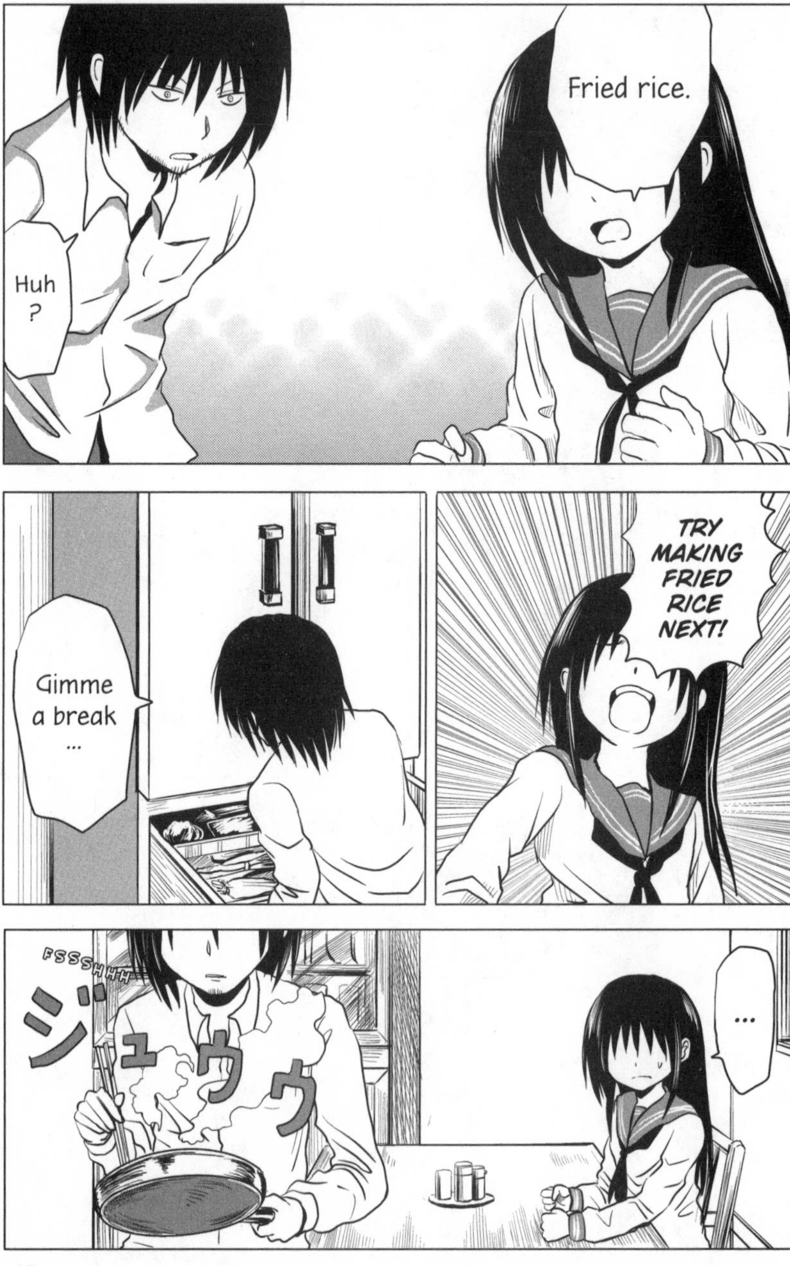
Fried rice.
Huh?
TRY MAKING FRIED RICE NEXT!
Gimme a break ...
...
FSSSHHH
ジュウウ

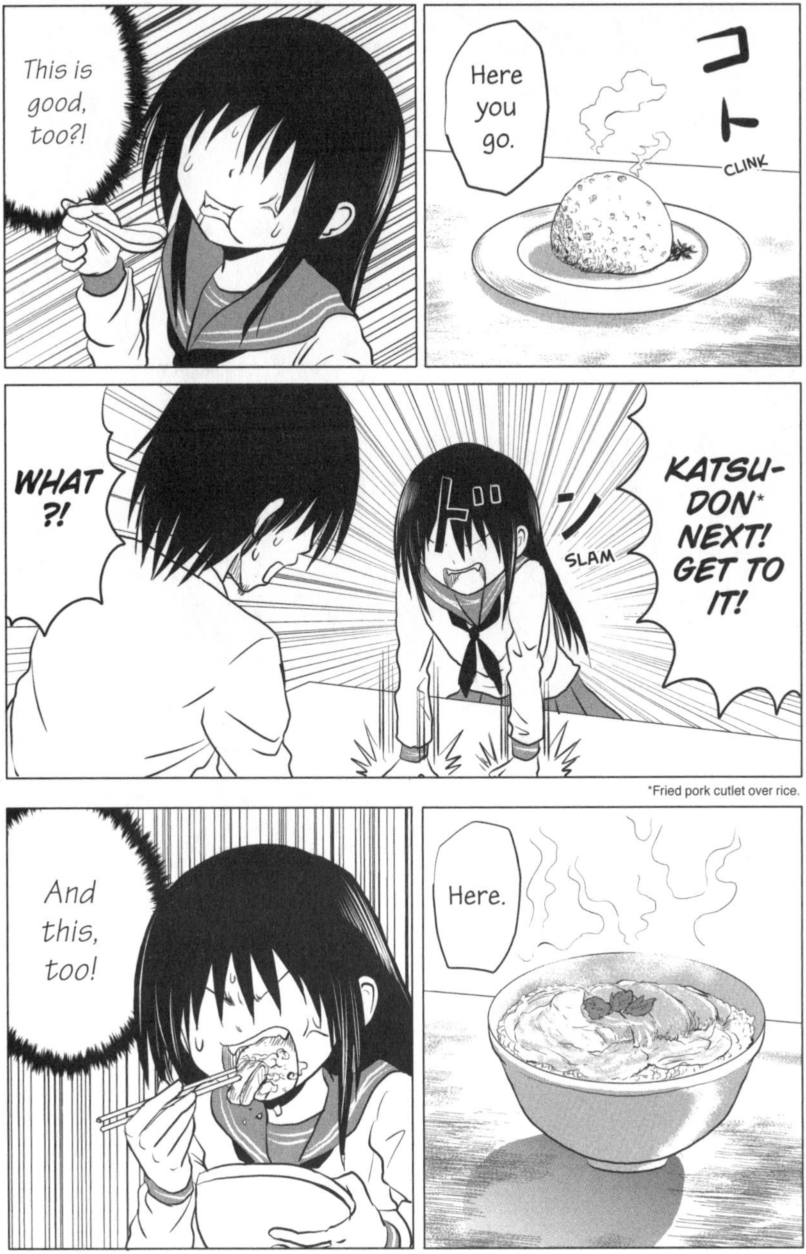
Here you go.
コト
CLINK
This is good, too?!
KATSU-DON* NEXT! GET TO IT!
ドーン
SLAM
WHAT?!
Here.
And this, too!

*Fried pork cutlet over rice.

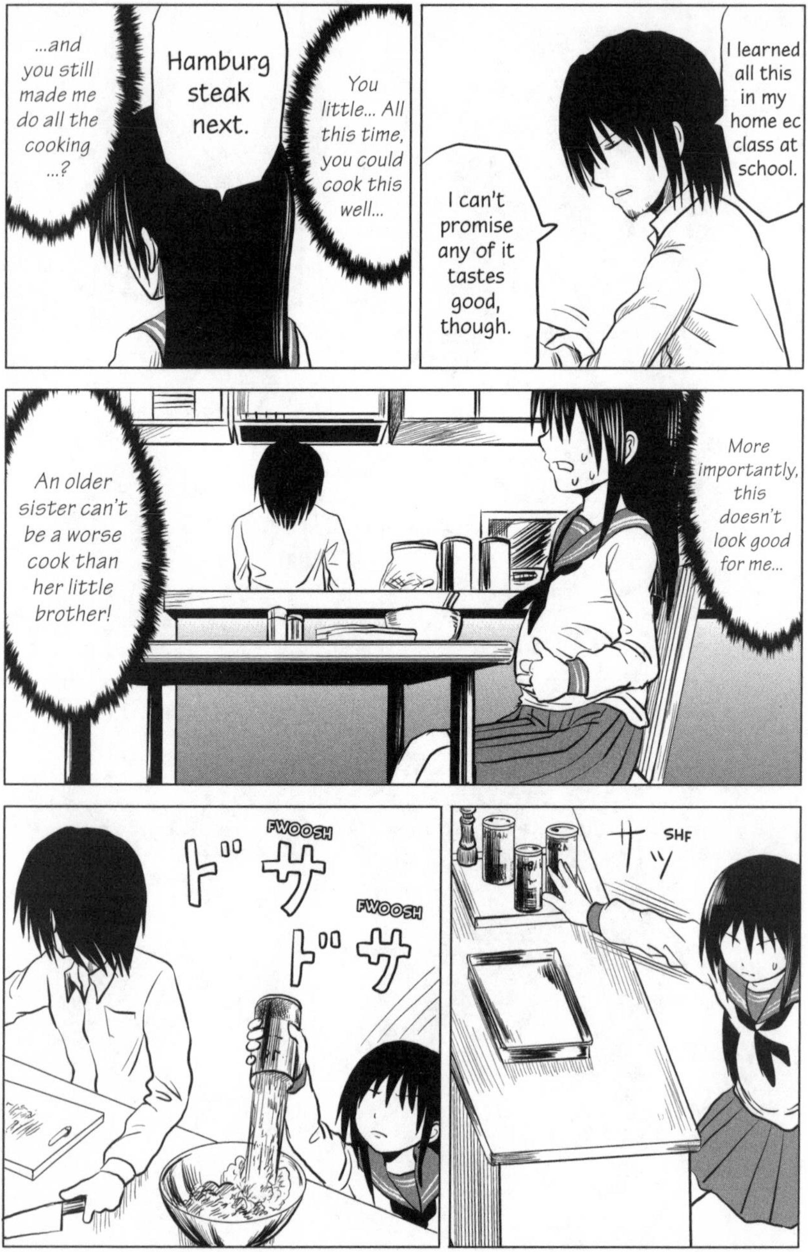
I learned all this in my home ec class at school.
I can't promise any of it tastes good, though.
Hamburg steak next.
You little... All this time, you could cook this well...
...and you still made me do all the cooking ...?
More importantly, this doesn't look good for me...
An older sister can't be a worse cook than her little brother!
サッ
SHF
ドサ
FWOOSH
ドサ
FWOOSH

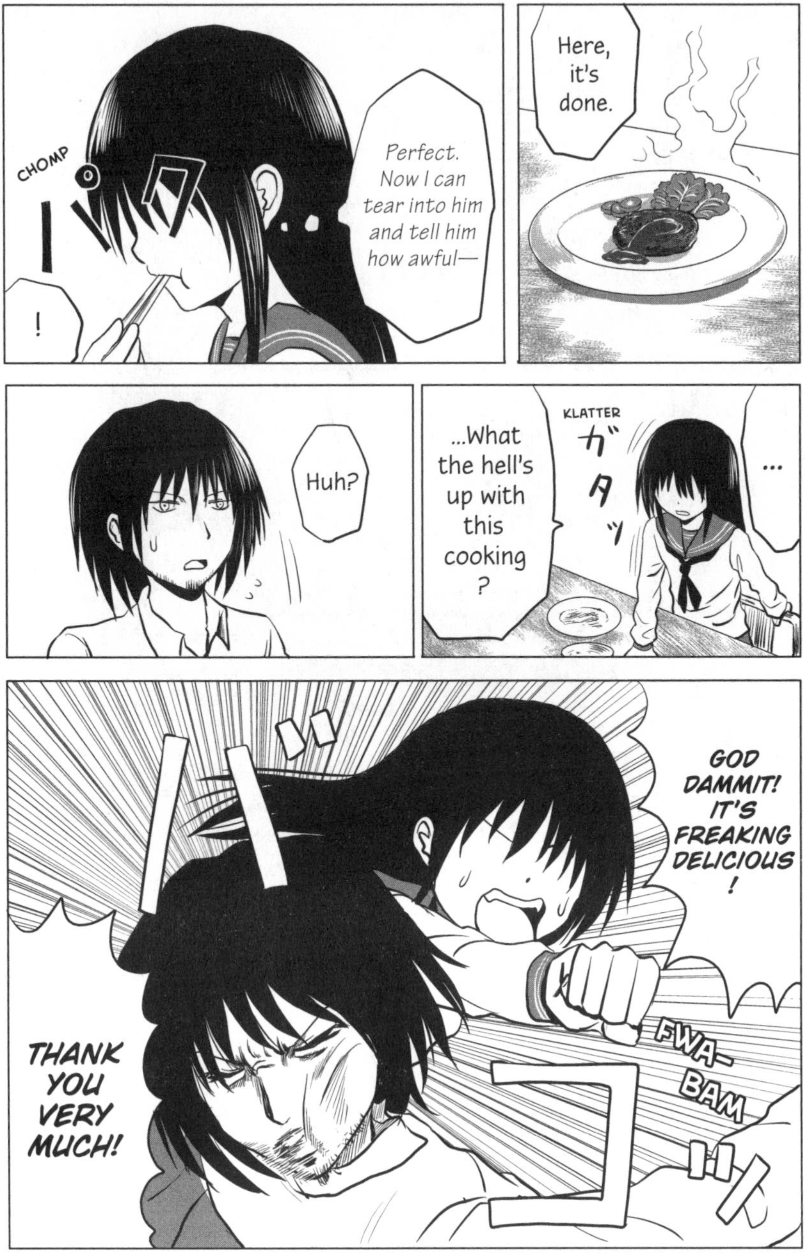

Here, it's done.
Perfect. Now I can tear into him and tell him how awful—
CHOMP
!
...
KLATTER
...What the hell's up with this cooking?
Huh?
GOD DAMMIT! IT'S FREAKING DELICIOUS!
FWA-BAM
THANK YOU VERY MUCH!

chapter 70:
high school boys and fathers

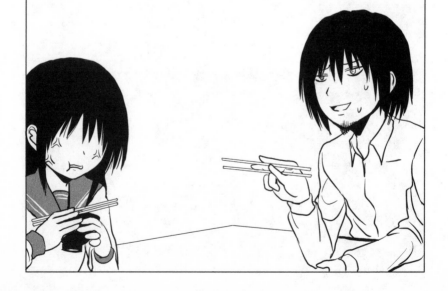

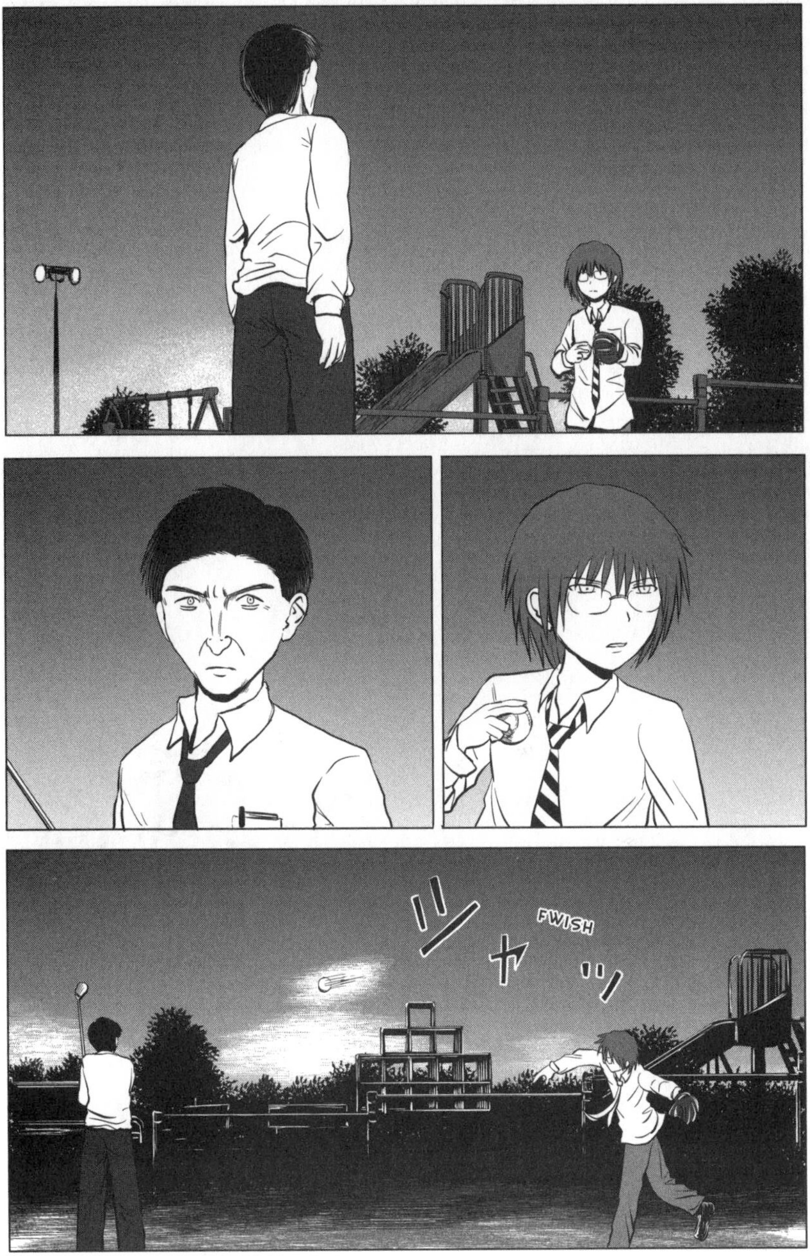
FWISH

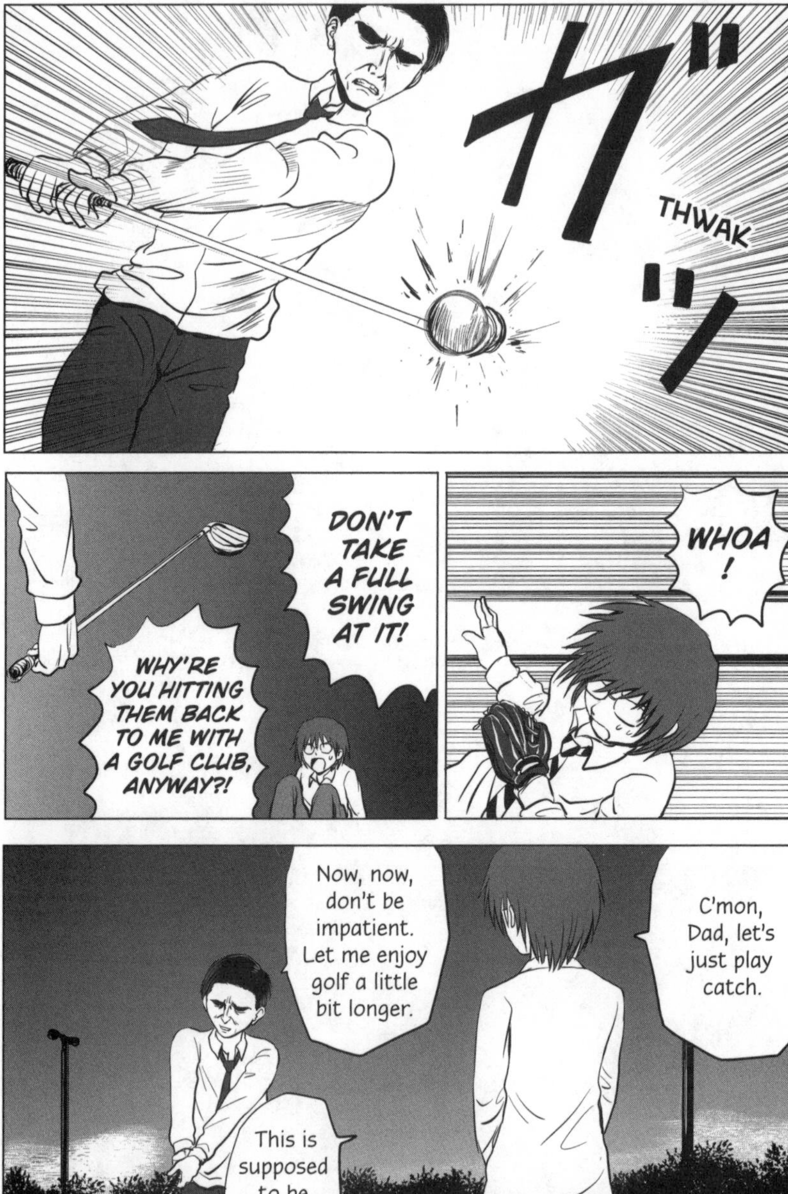
ガッ
THWAK
WHOA!
DON'T TAKE A FULL SWING AT IT!
WHY'RE YOU HITTING THEM BACK TO ME WITH A GOLF CLUB, ANYWAY?!
C'mon, Dad, let's just play catch.
Now, now, don't be impatient. Let me enjoy golf a little bit longer.
This is supposed to be golf?

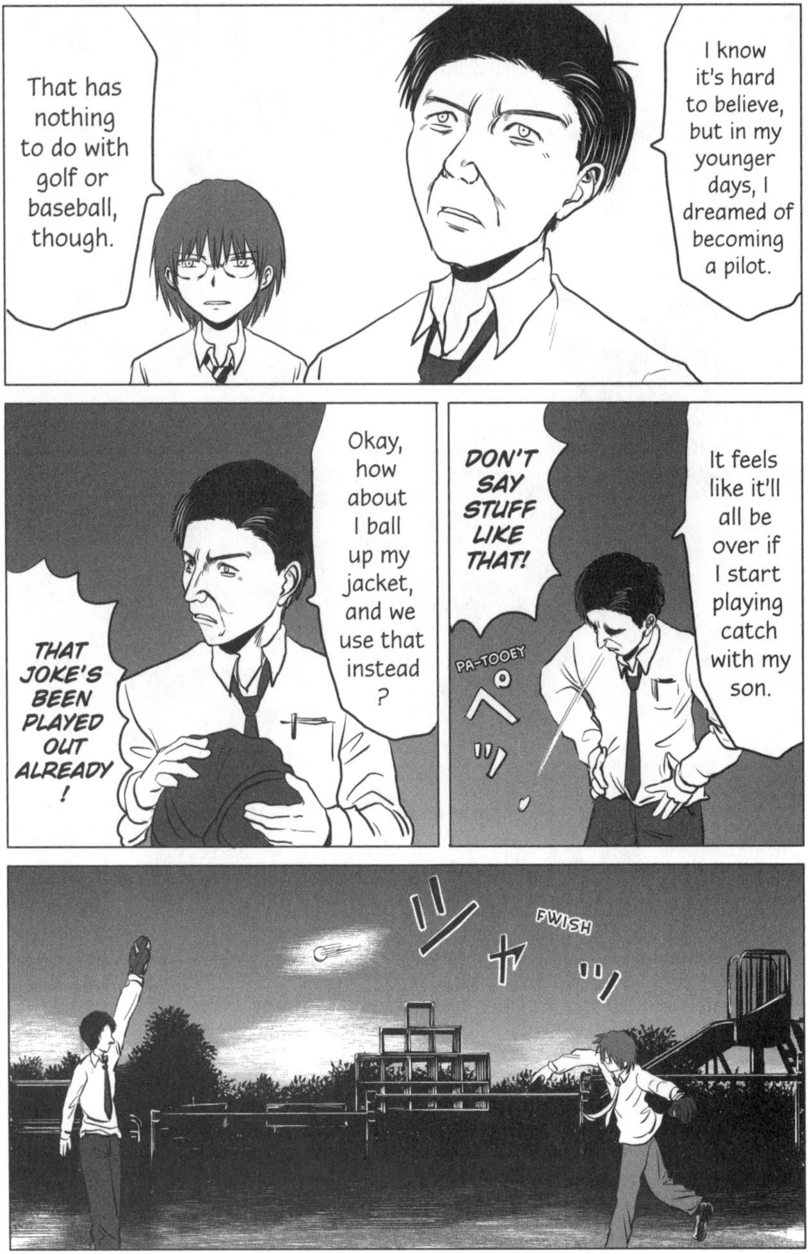
I know it's hard to believe, but in my younger days, I dreamed of becoming a pilot.
That has nothing to do with golf or baseball, though.
It feels like it'll all be over if I start playing catch with my son.
DON'T SAY STUFF LIKE THAT!
PA-TOOEY
Okay, how about I ball up my jacket, and we use that instead?
THAT JOKE'S BEEN PLAYED OUT ALREADY!
FWISH

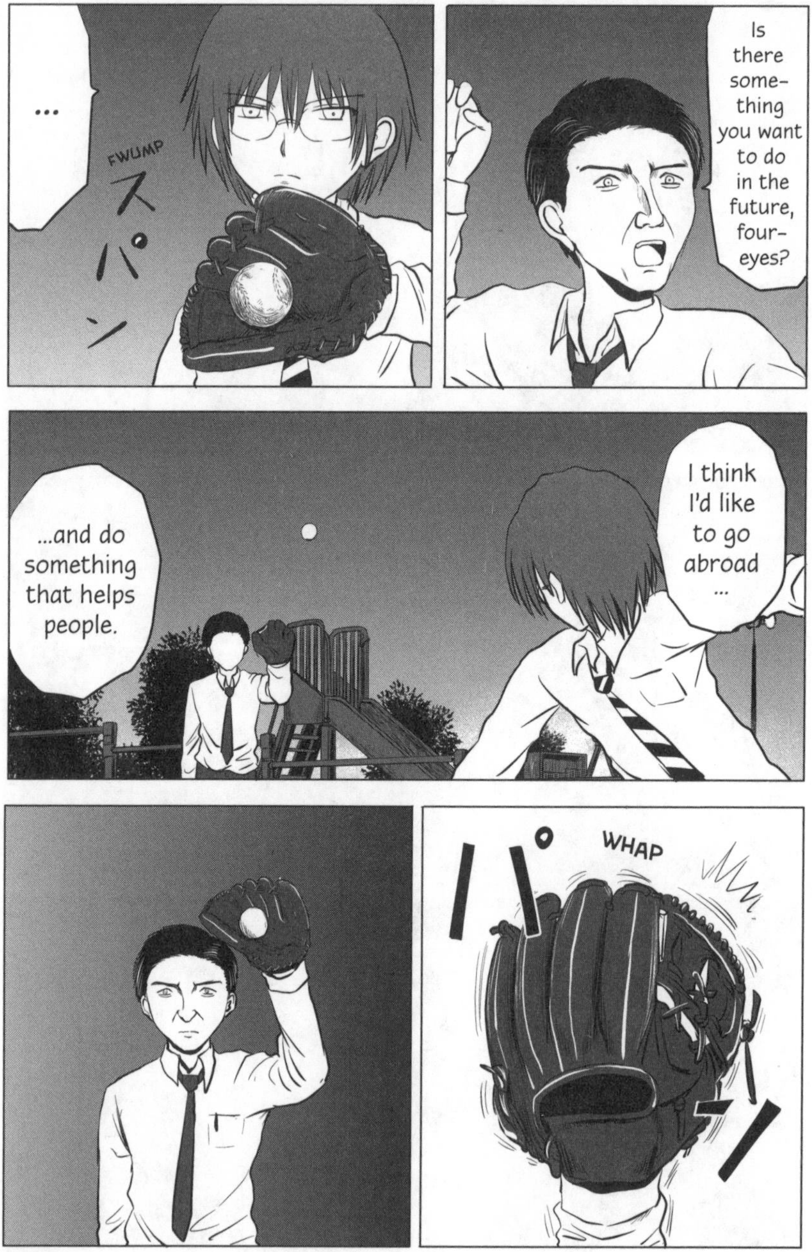
Is there some-thing you want to do in the future, four-eyes?
...
FWUMP
スパン
I think I'd like to go abroad ...
...and do something that helps people.
WHAP

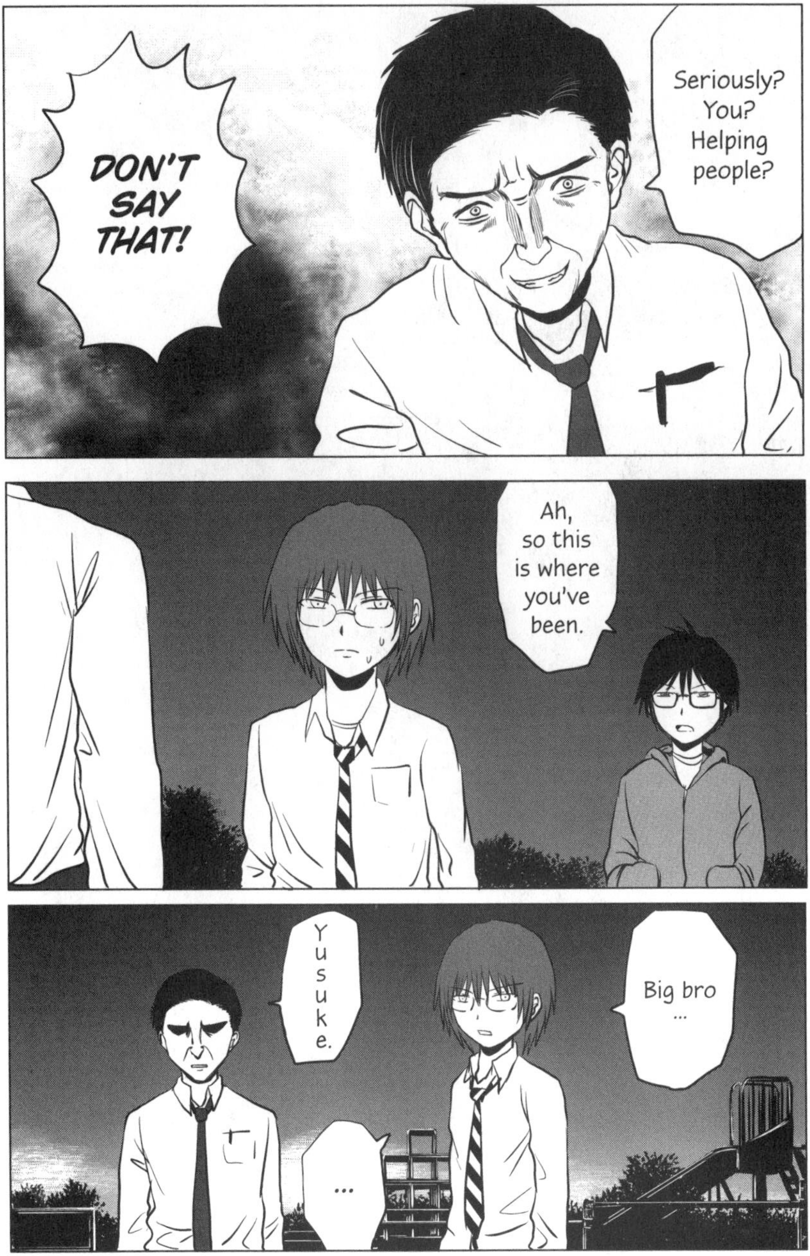
Seriously? You? Helping people?
DON'T SAY THAT!
Ah, so this is where you've been.
Big bro ...
Yusuke.
...

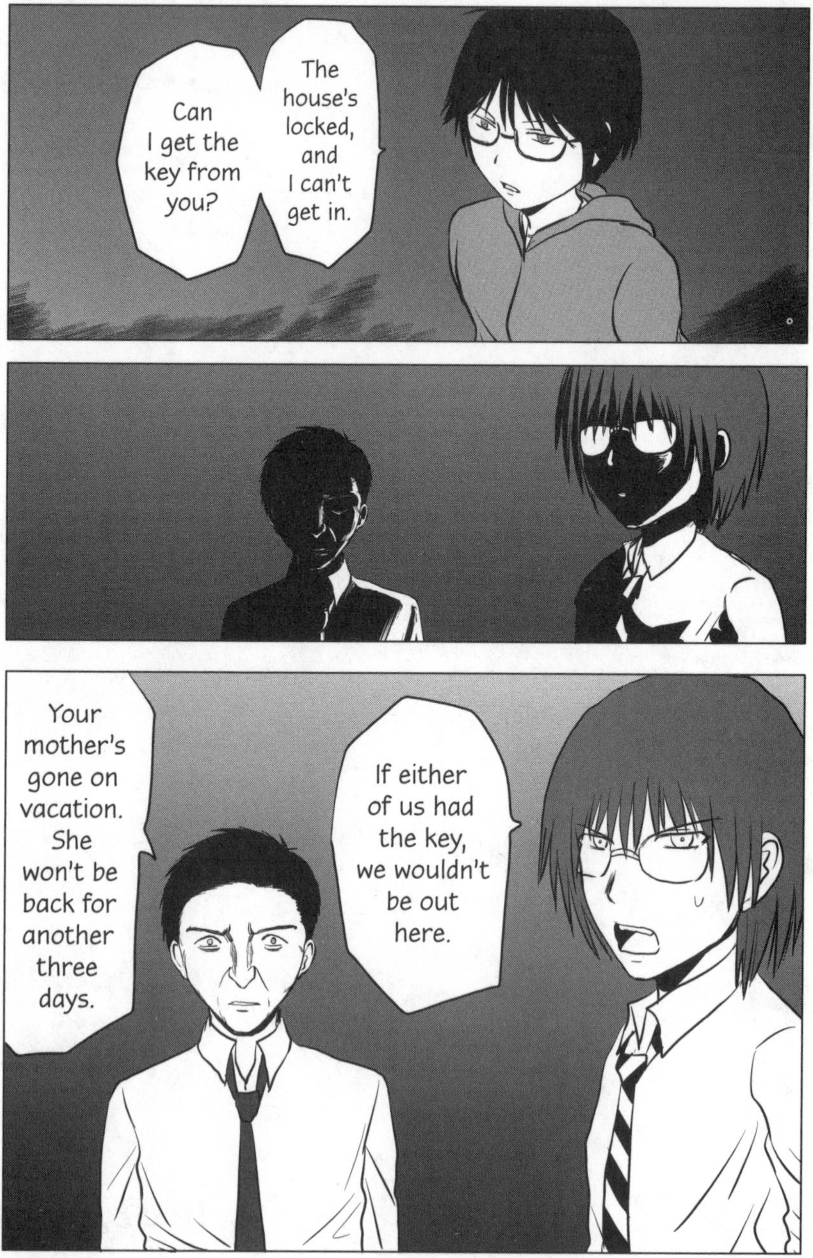
The house's locked, and I can't get in.
Can I get the key from you?
If either of us had the key, we wouldn't be out here.
Your mother's gone on vacation. She won't be back for another three days.

the

daily

lives

of

5 high school boys

chapter 71:
high school boys and literature girl. pt. 4

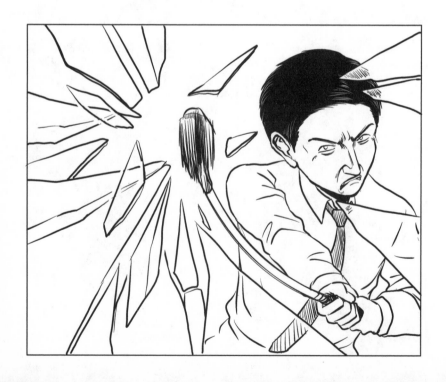

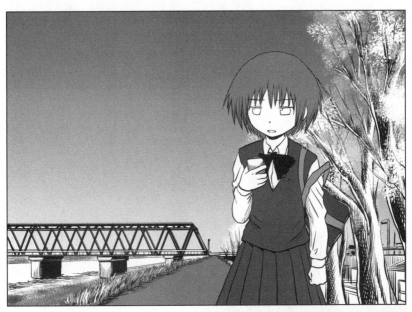

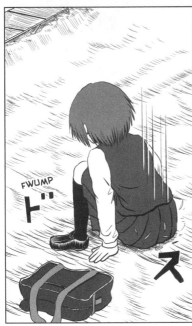

FWUMP
ド

ス

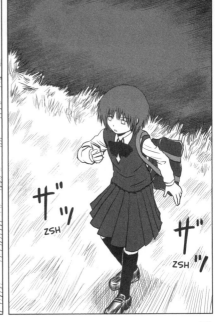

ザ
ッ

ZSH

ザ
ッ

ZSH

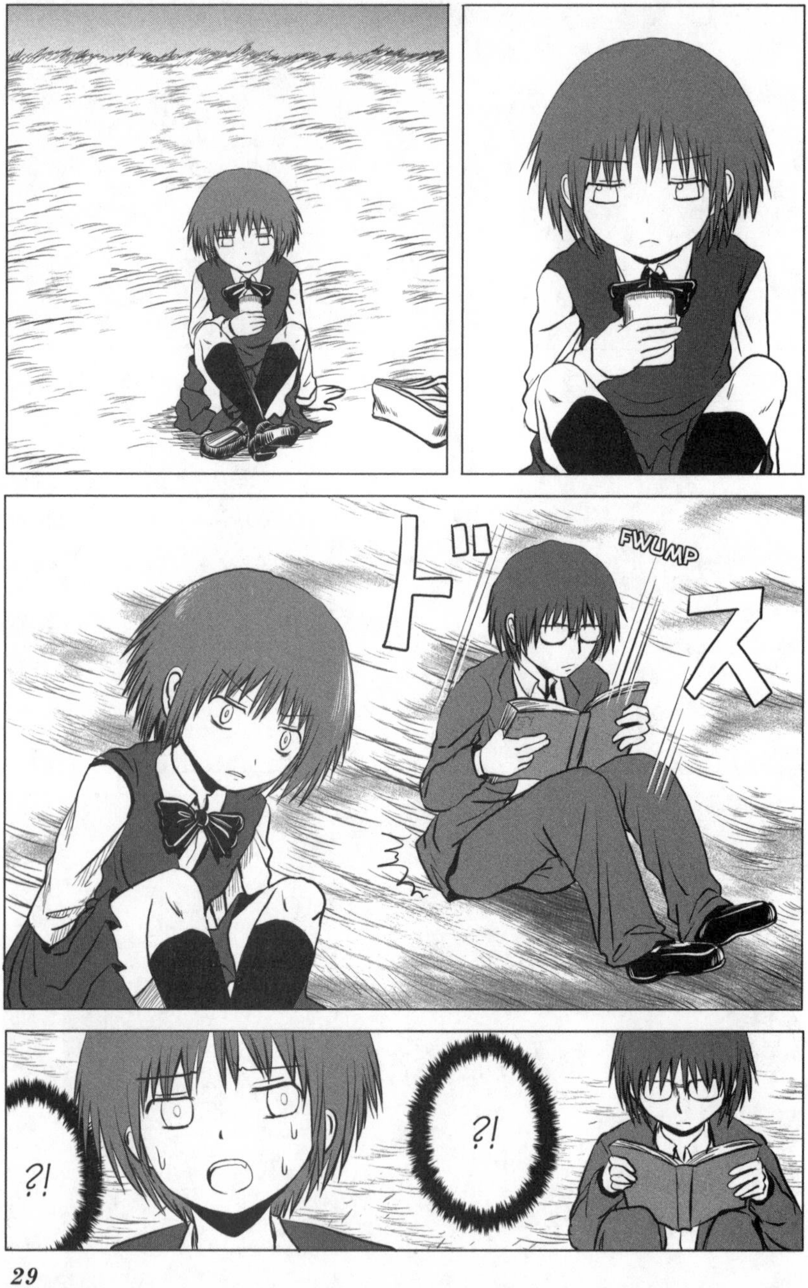
ドス
FWUMP
?!
?!

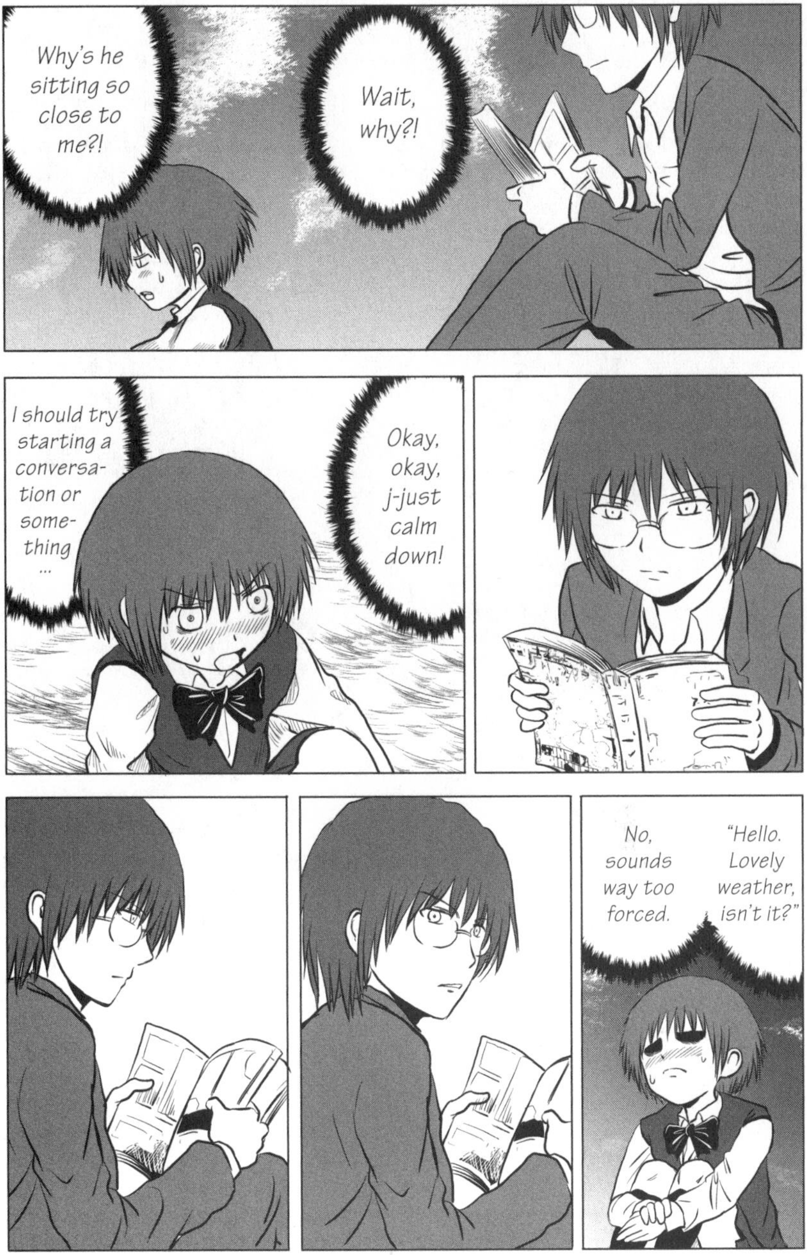
Wait, why?!
Why's he sitting so close to me?!
Okay, okay, j-just calm down!
I should try starting a conversation or something...
"Hello. Lovely weather, isn't it?"
No, sounds way too forced.

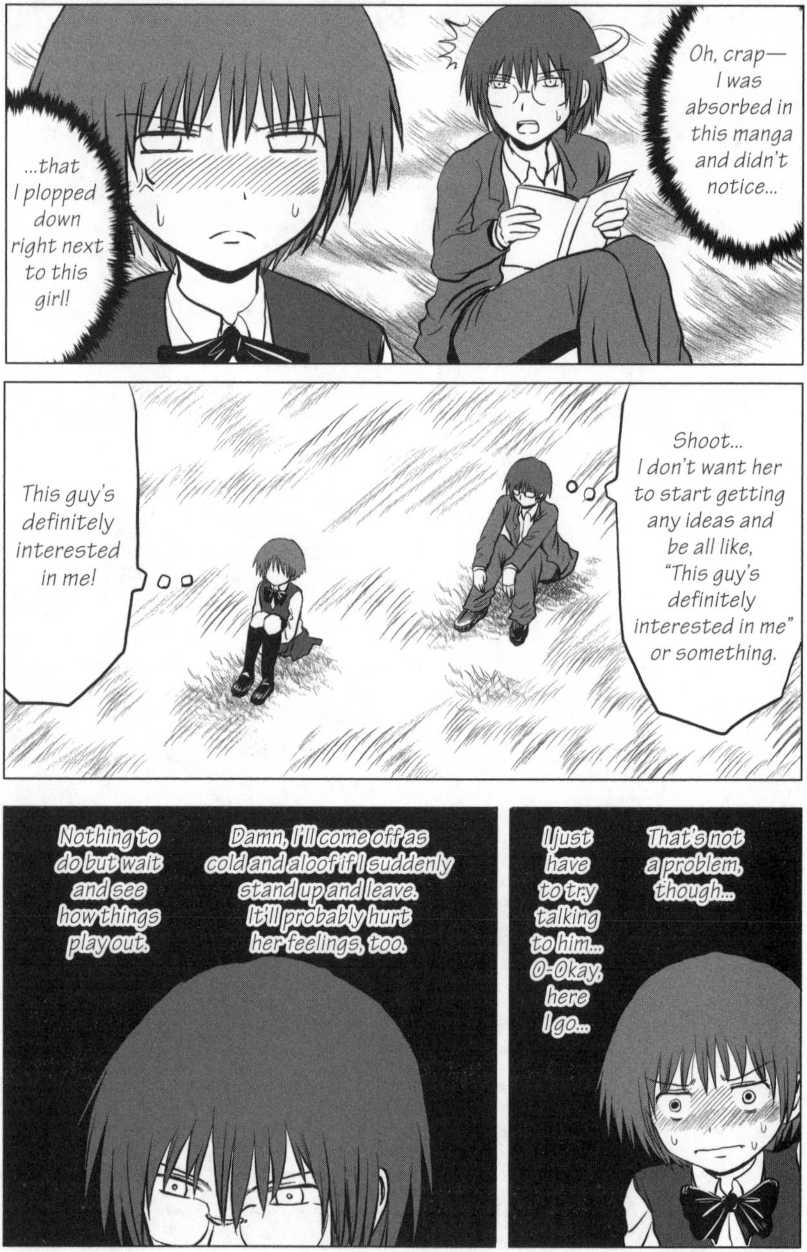
Oh, crap— I was absorbed in this manga and didn't notice...
...that I plopped down right next to this girl!
Shoot... I don't want her to start getting any ideas and be all like, "This guy's definitely interested in me" or something.
This guy's definitely interested in me!
That's not a problem, though...
I just have to try talking to him... O-Okay, here I go...
Damn, I'll come off as cold and aloof if I suddenly stand up and leave. It'll probably hurt her feelings, too.
Nothing to do but wait and see how things play out.

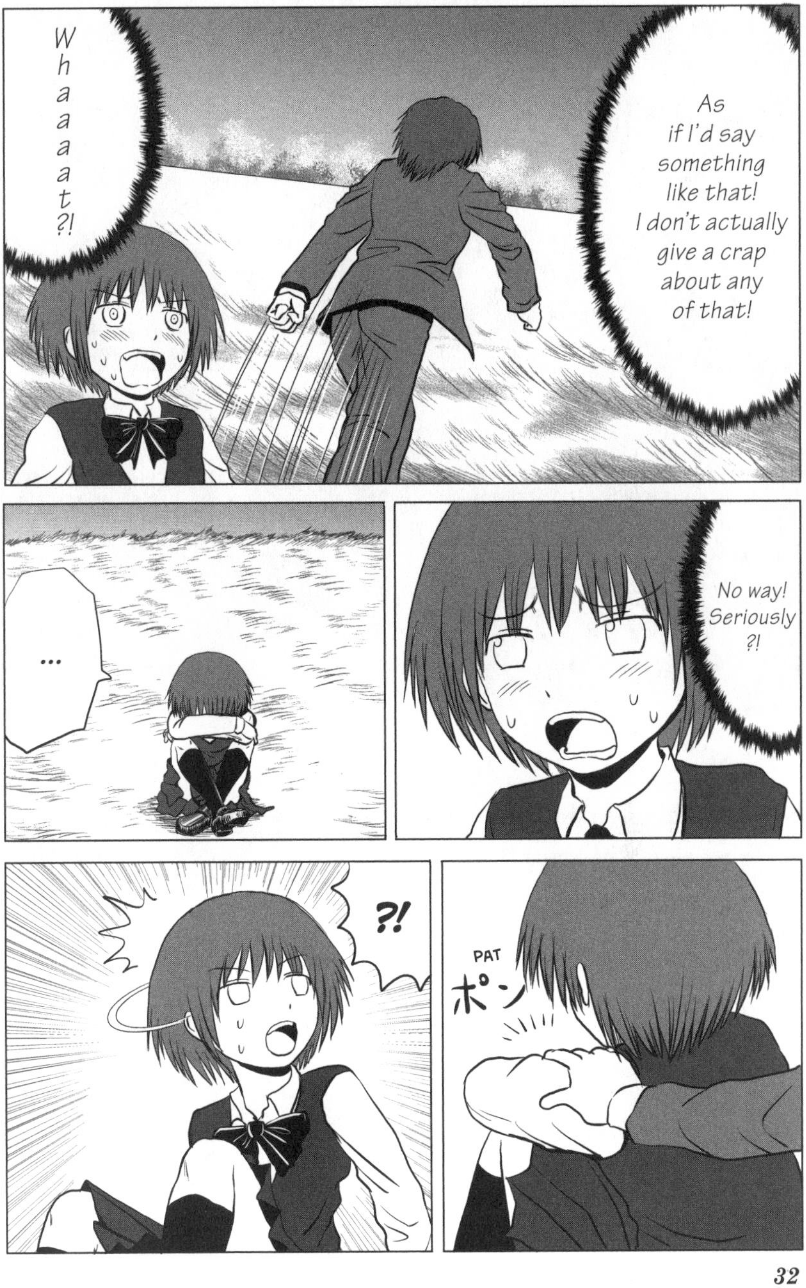
As if I'd say something like that! I don't actually give a crap about any of that!
Whaaaaat?!
No way! Seriously?!
...
PAT
ポン
?!

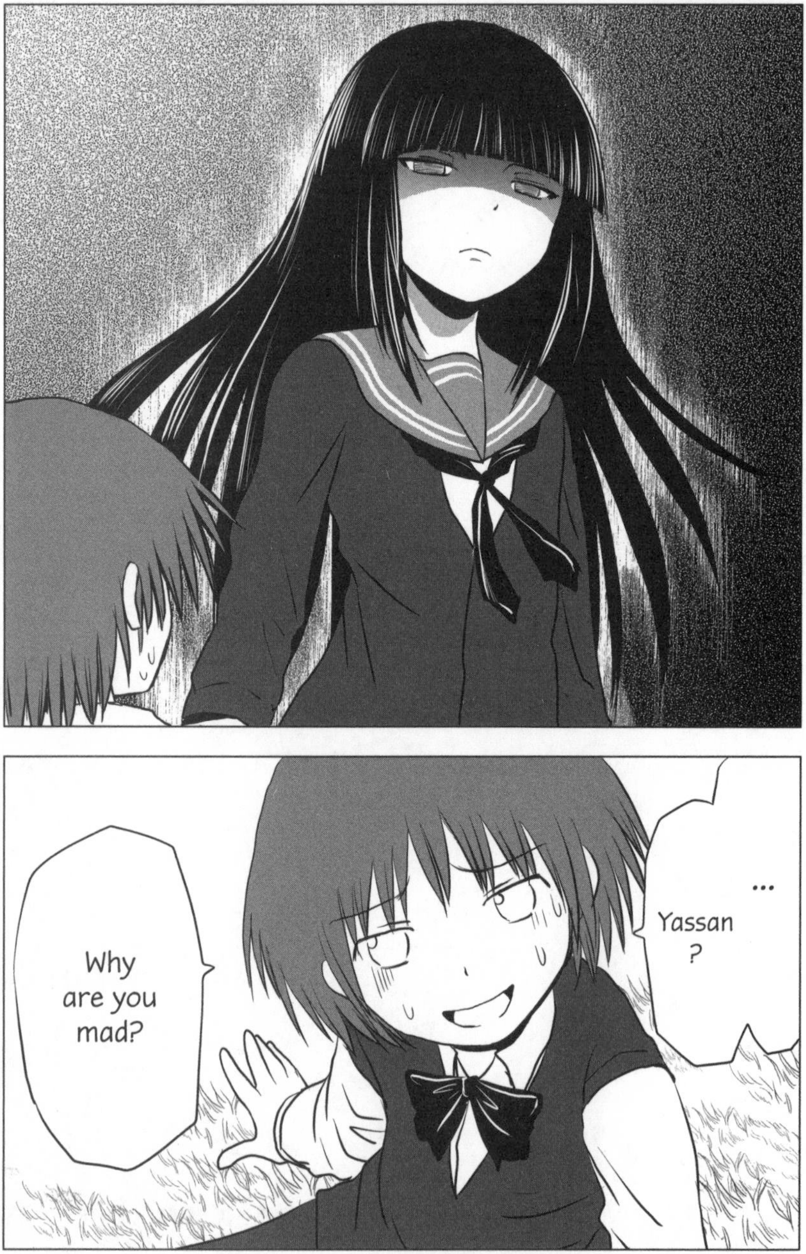
...Yassan?
Why are you mad?

the

daily

lives

of

5 high school boys

chapter 72:
high school boys and conflict

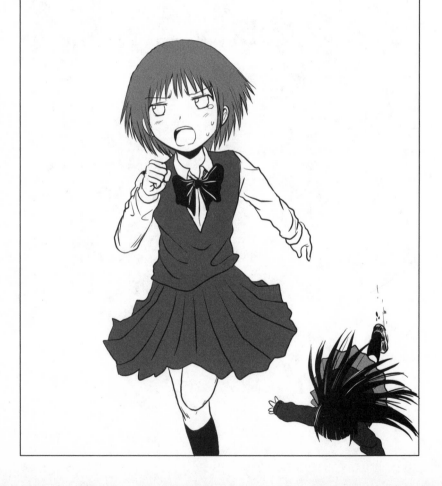

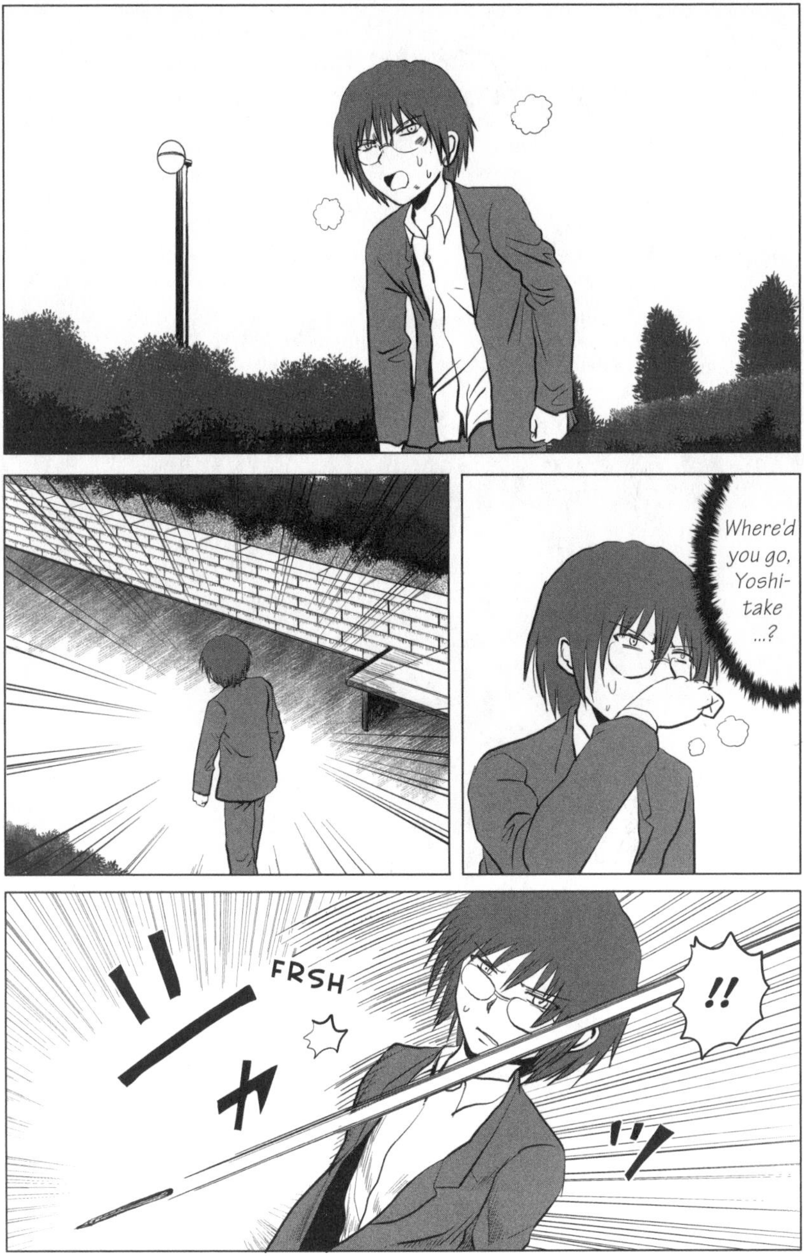
Where'd you go, Yoshi-take ...?
!!
FRSH

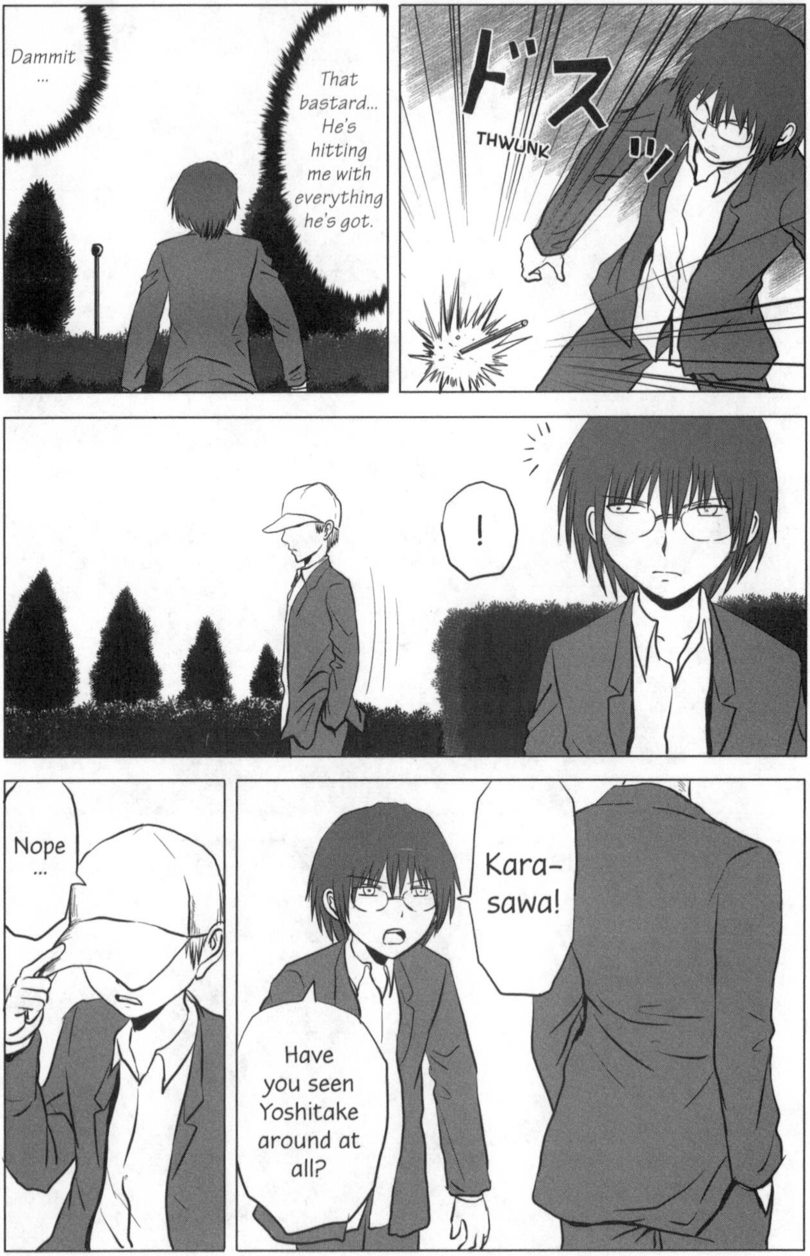
ドス
ッ
THWUNK
Dammit ...
That bastard... He's hitting me with everything he's got.
!
Kara-sawa!
Have you seen Yoshitake around at all?
Nope ...

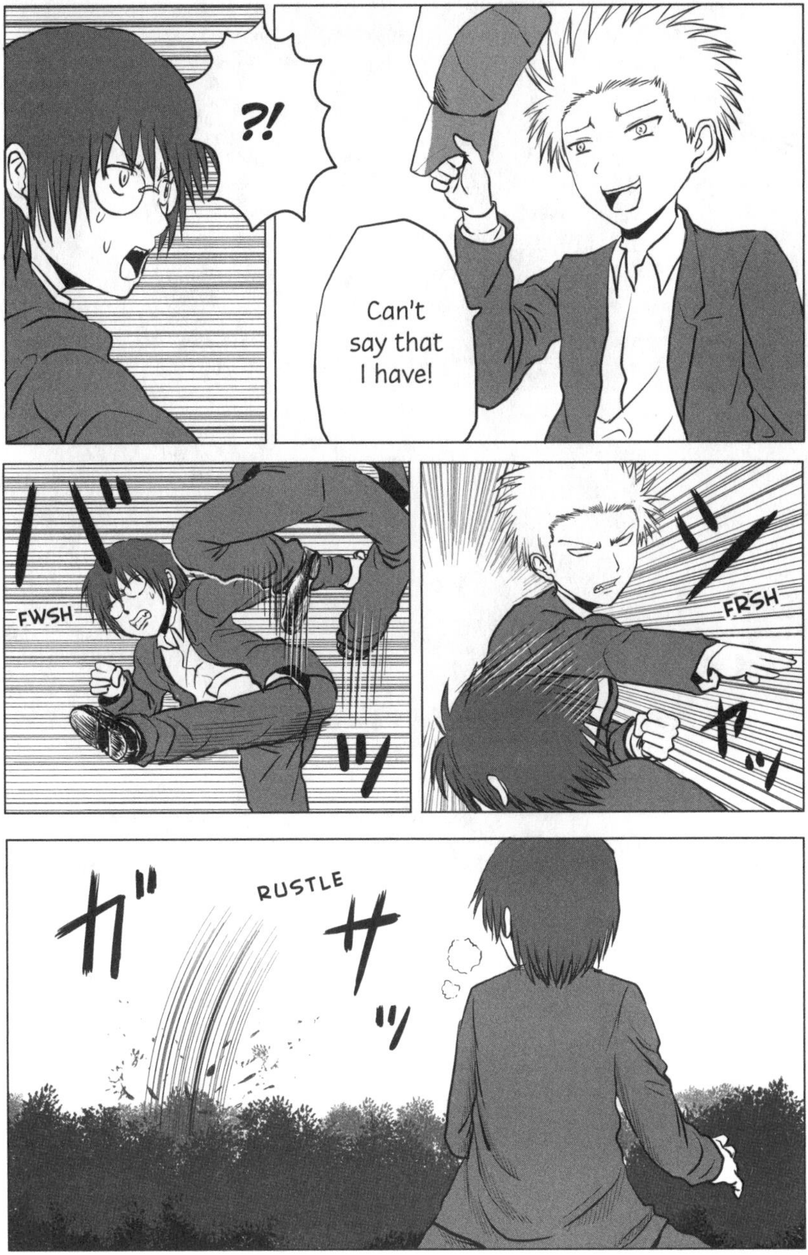
Can't say that I have!
?!
FRSH
シャッ
FWSH
バッ
RUSTLE
ガサッ

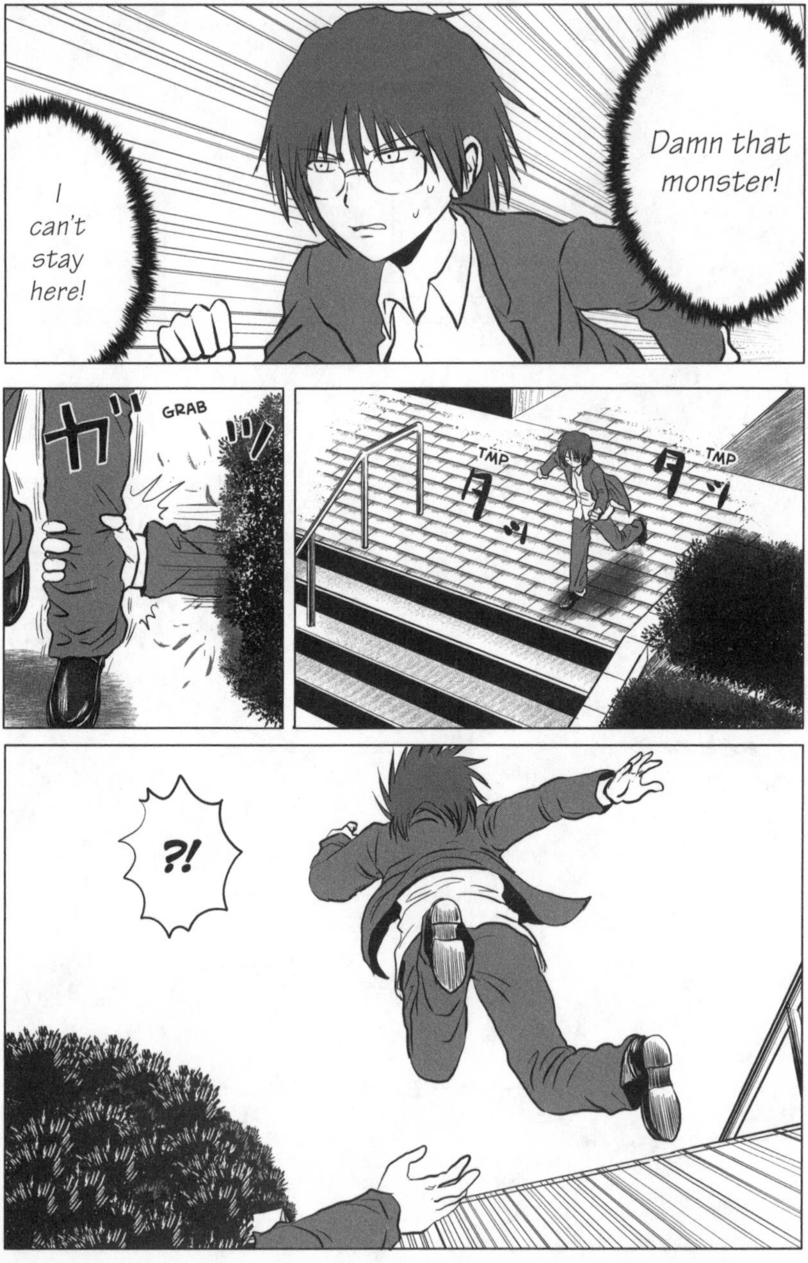

Damn that monster!
I can't stay here!
TMP
タッ
TMP
タッ
ガッ
GRAB
?!

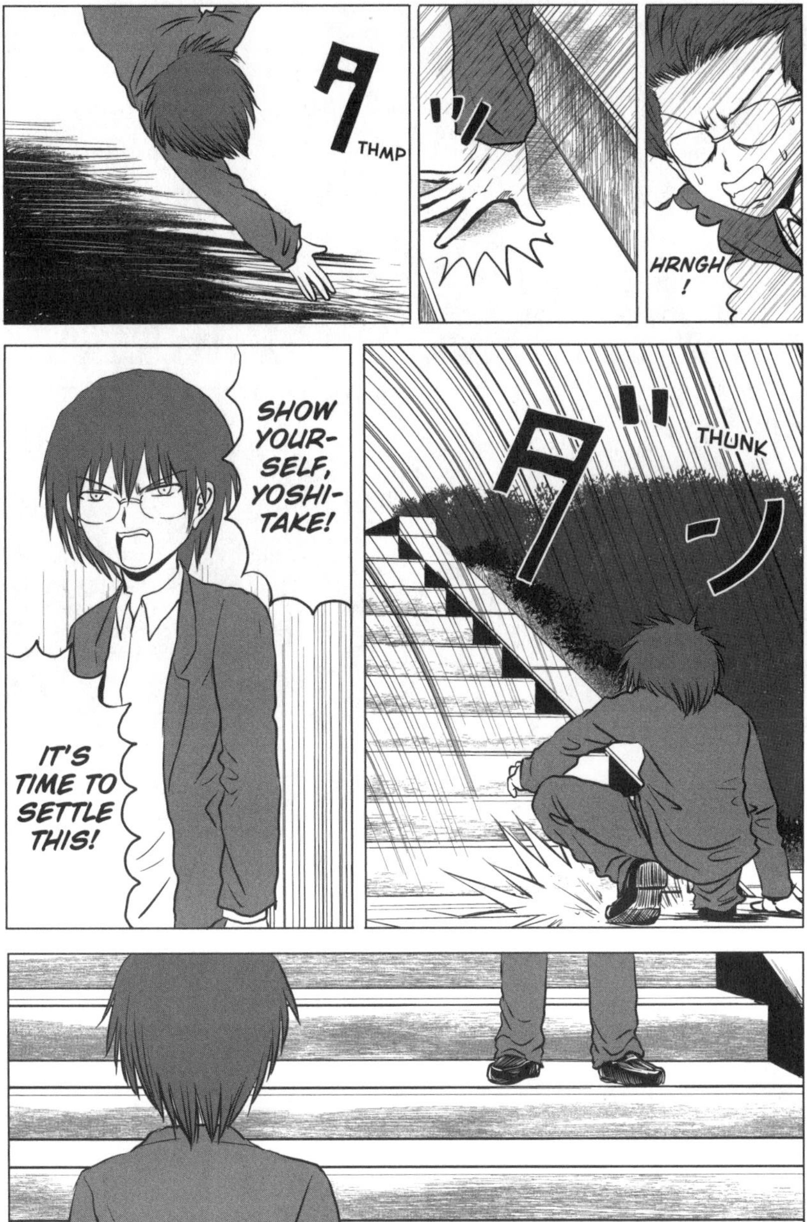
HRNGH!
THMP
THUNK
SHOW YOUR-SELF, YOSHI-TAKE!
IT'S TIME TO SETTLE THIS!

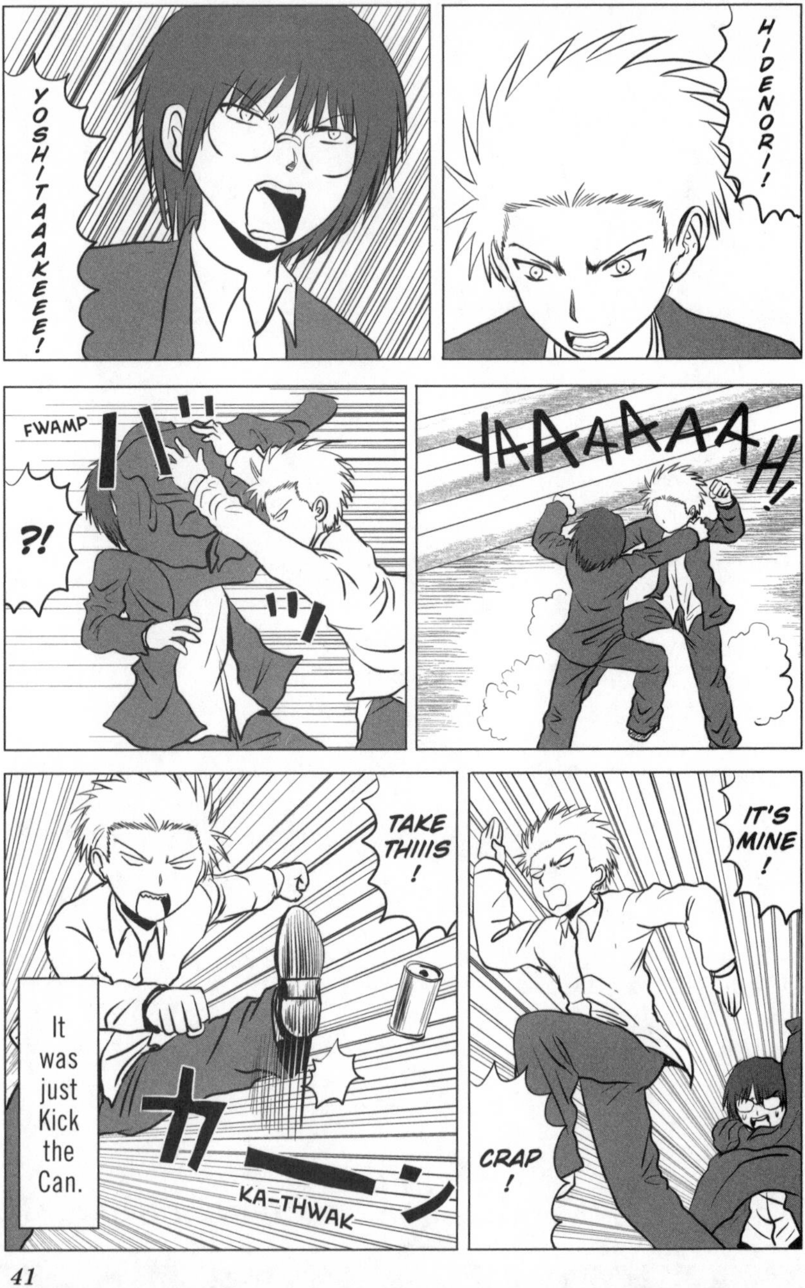
HIDENORI!
YOSHITAAAAKEEEE!
YAAAAAAAH!
FWAMP
?!
IT'S MINE!
CRAP!
TAKE THIIIS!
It was just Kick the Can.
KA-THWAK

the

daily

lives

of

5 high school boys

chapter 73:
high school boys and kick the can

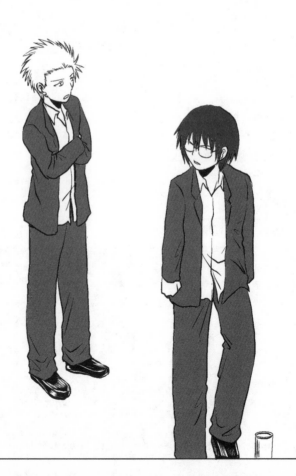

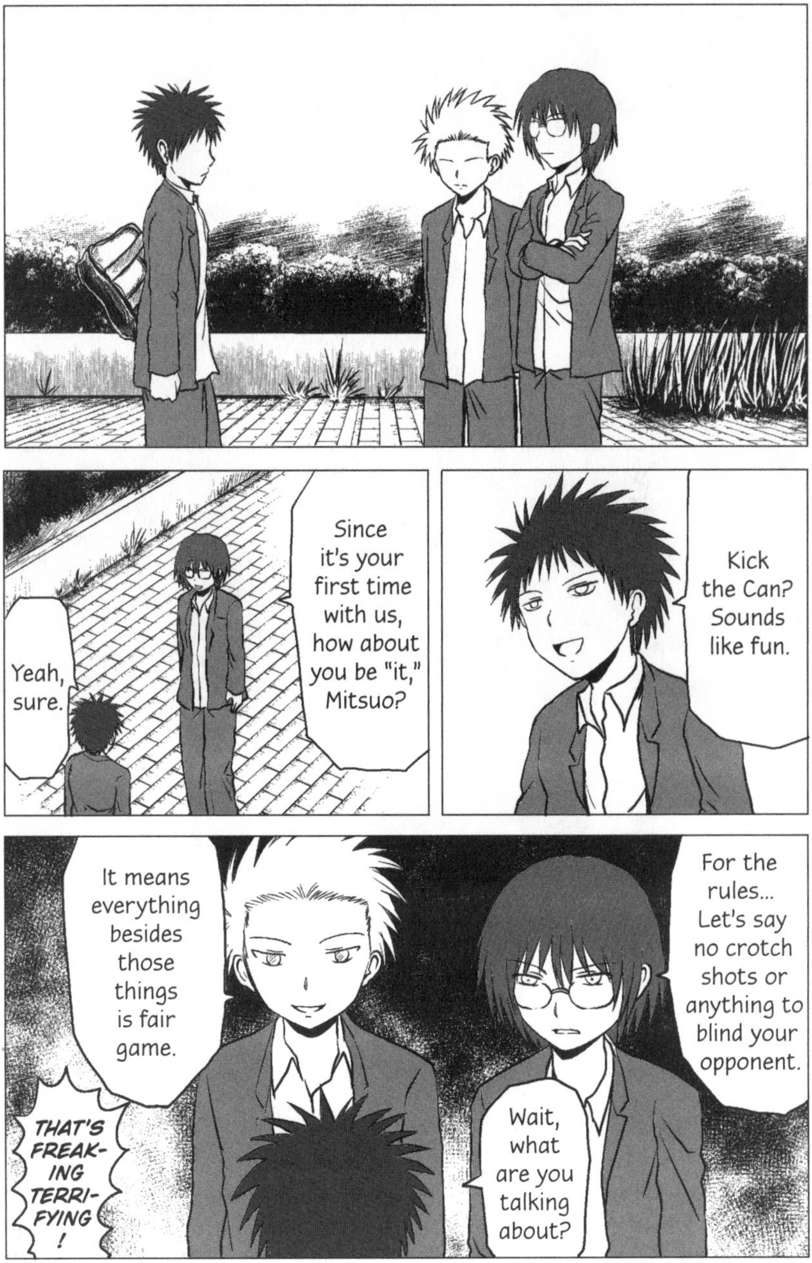
Kick the Can? Sounds like fun.
Since it's your first time with us, how about you be "it," Mitsuo?
Yeah, sure.
For the rules... Let's say no crotch shots or anything to blind your opponent.
It means everything besides those things is fair game.
Wait, what are you talking about?
THAT'S FREAKING TERRIFYING!

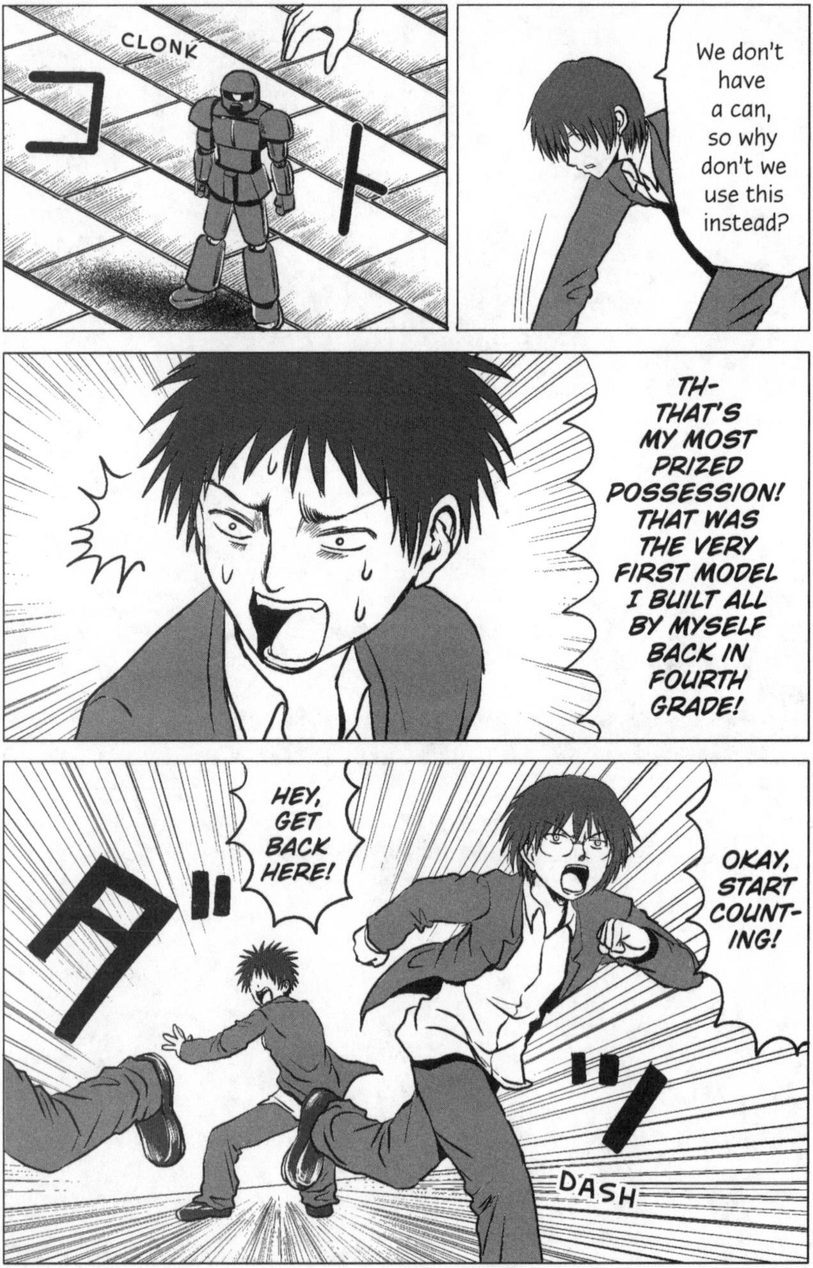
We don't have a can, so why don't we use this instead?
CLONK
コト
TH- THAT'S MY MOST PRIZED POSSESSION! THAT WAS THE VERY FIRST MODEL I BUILT ALL BY MYSELF BACK IN FOURTH GRADE!
OKAY, START COUNTING!
HEY, GET BACK HERE!
DASH

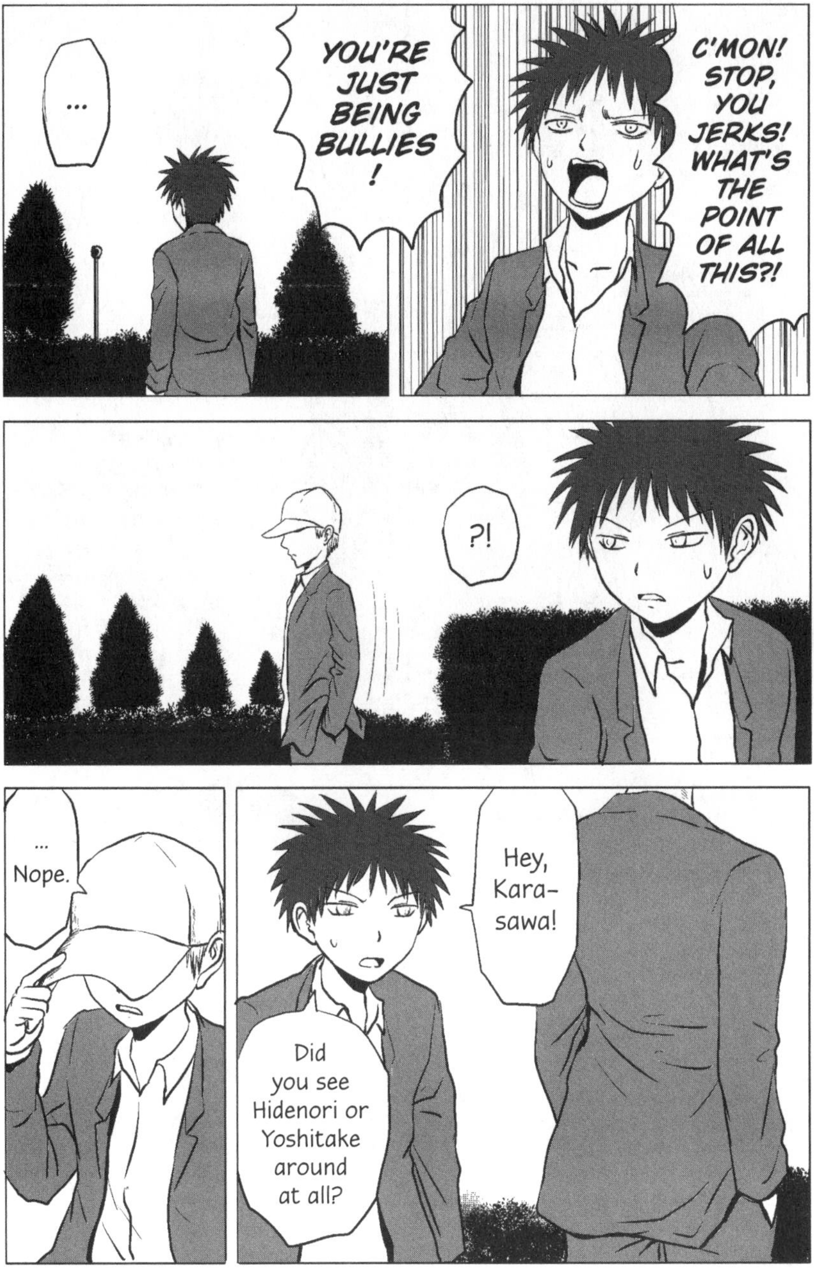
C'MON! STOP, YOU JERKS! WHAT'S THE POINT OF ALL THIS?!
YOU'RE JUST BEING BULLIES!
...
?!
Hey, Kara-sawa!
Did you see Hidenori or Yoshitake around at all?
... Nope.

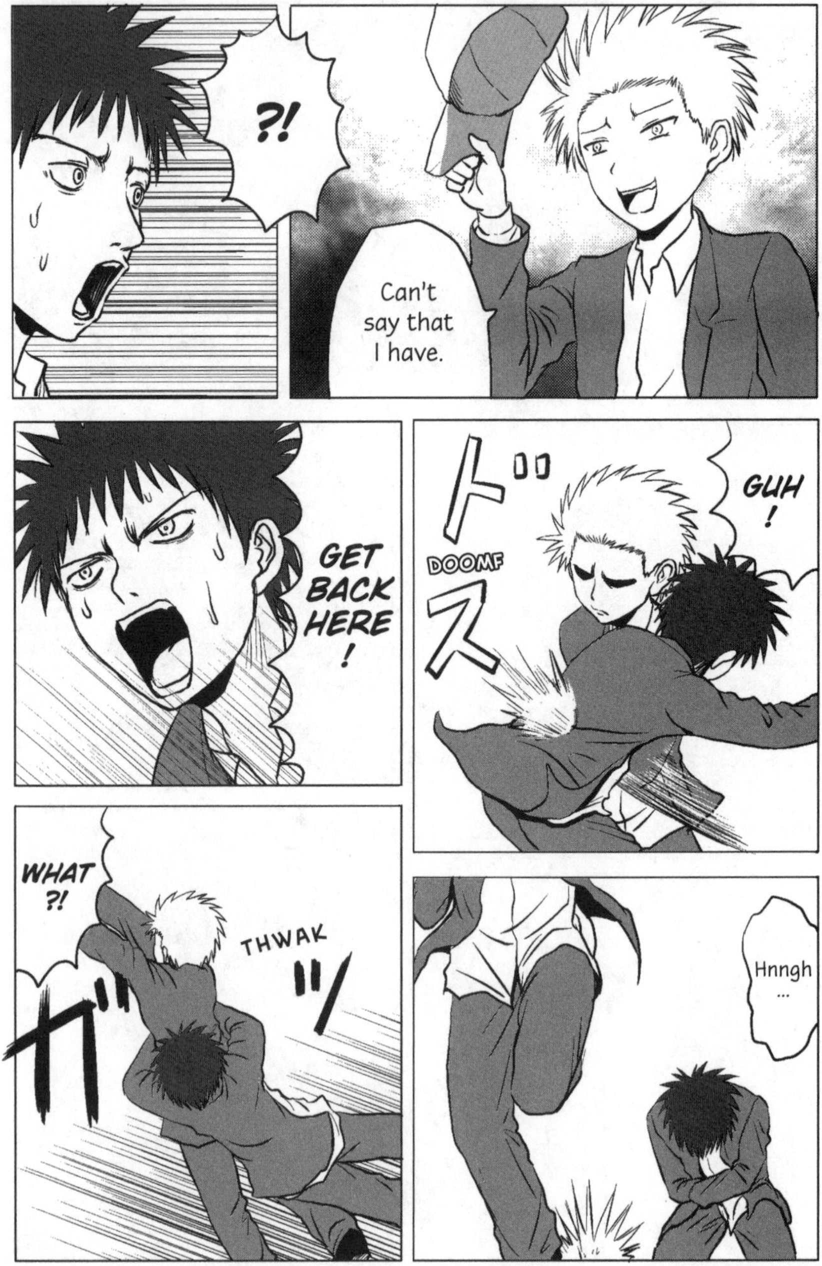
Can't say that I have.
?!
GUH!
ドス
DOOMF
GET BACK HERE!
Hnngh...
WHAT?!
THWAK
ガッ

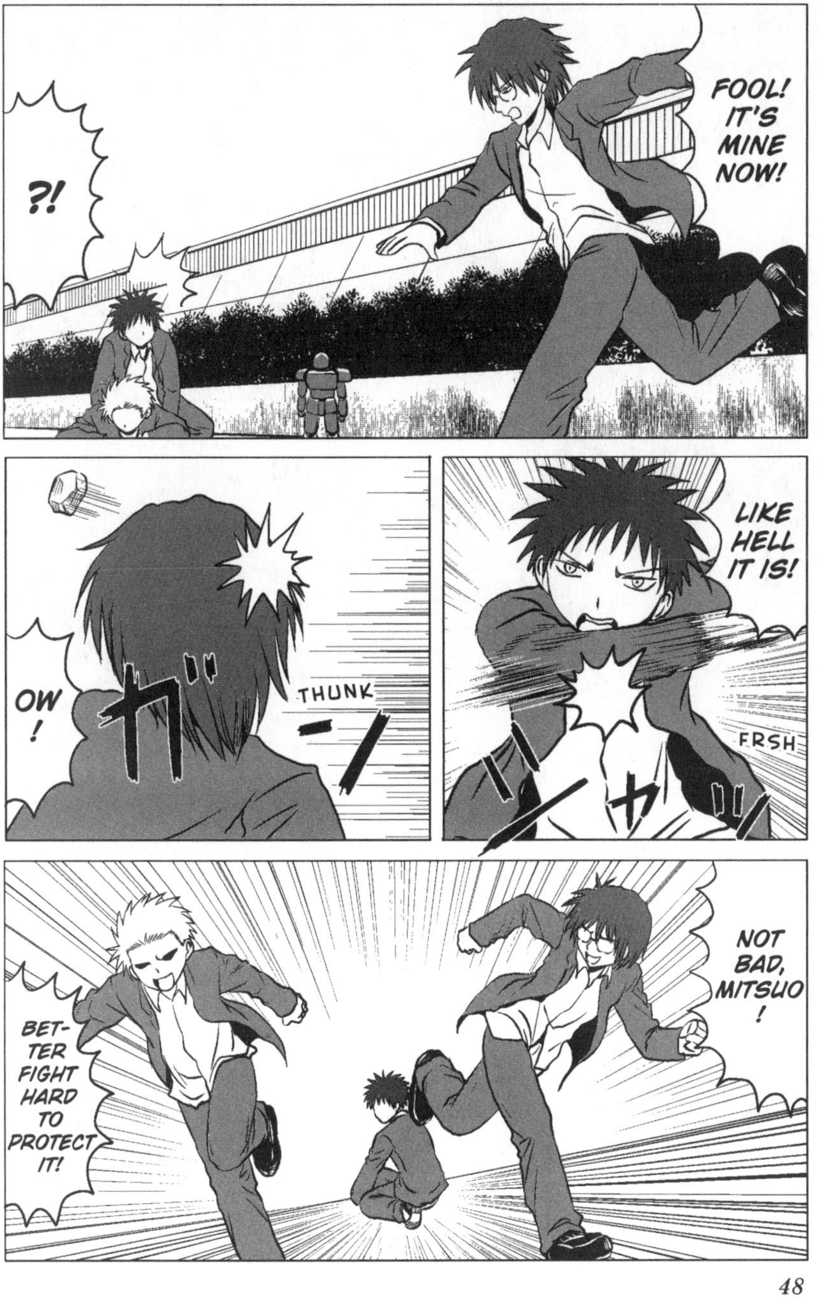
FOOL! IT'S MINE NOW!
?!
LIKE HELL IT IS!
FRSH
THUNK
OW!
NOT BAD, MITSUO!
BET-TER FIGHT HARD TO PROTECT IT!

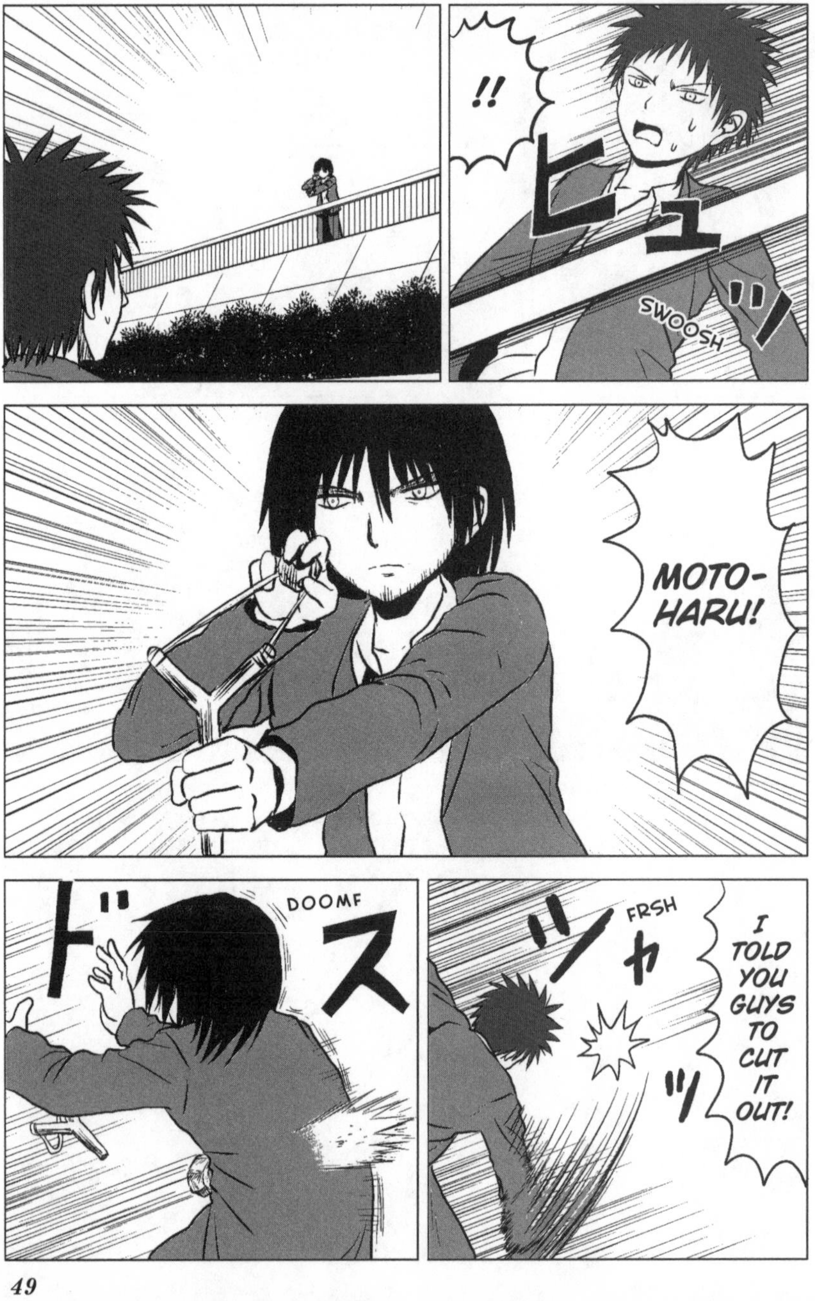
!!
ヒュッ
SWOOSH
MOTO-HARU!
シャッ
FRSH
I TOLD YOU GUYS TO CUT IT OUT!
ドス
DOOMF

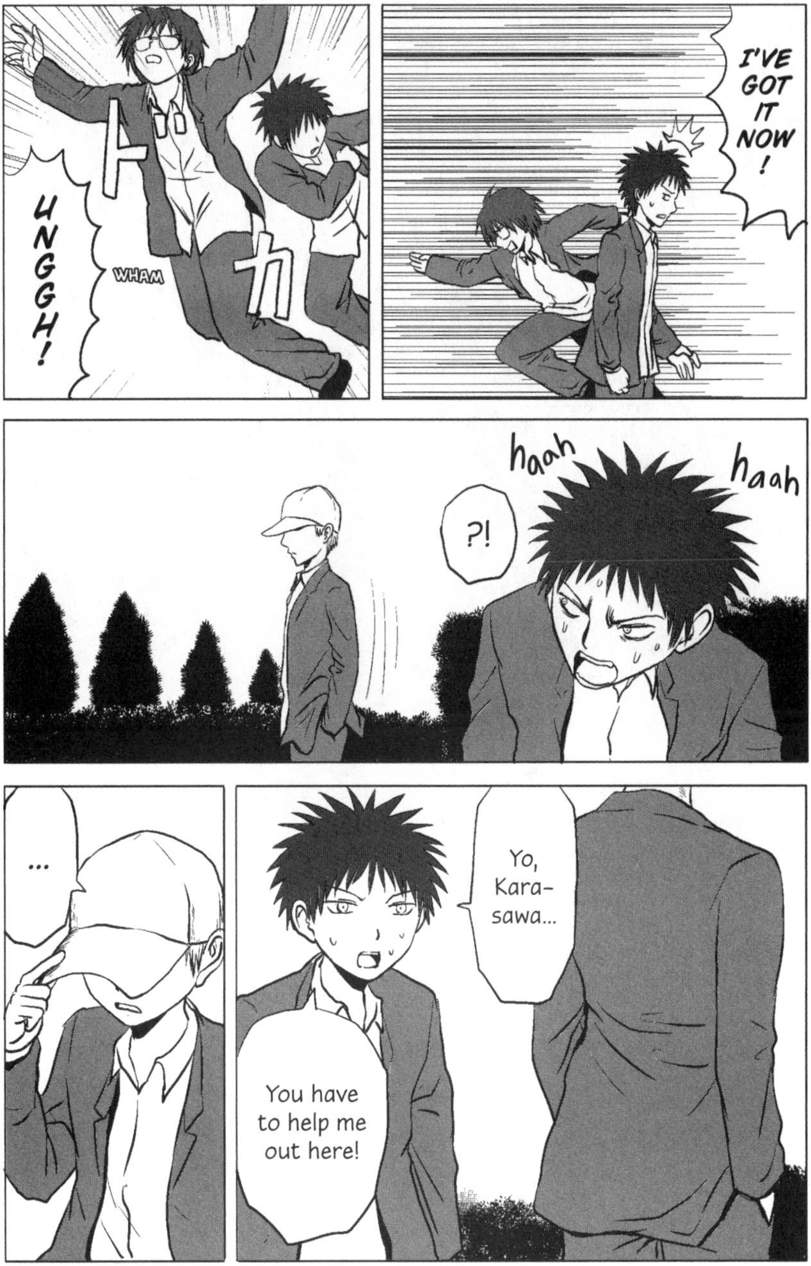
I'VE GOT IT NOW!
UNGGGH!
WHAM
ドカ
haah
haah
?!
Yo, Kara-sawa...
You have to help me out here!
...

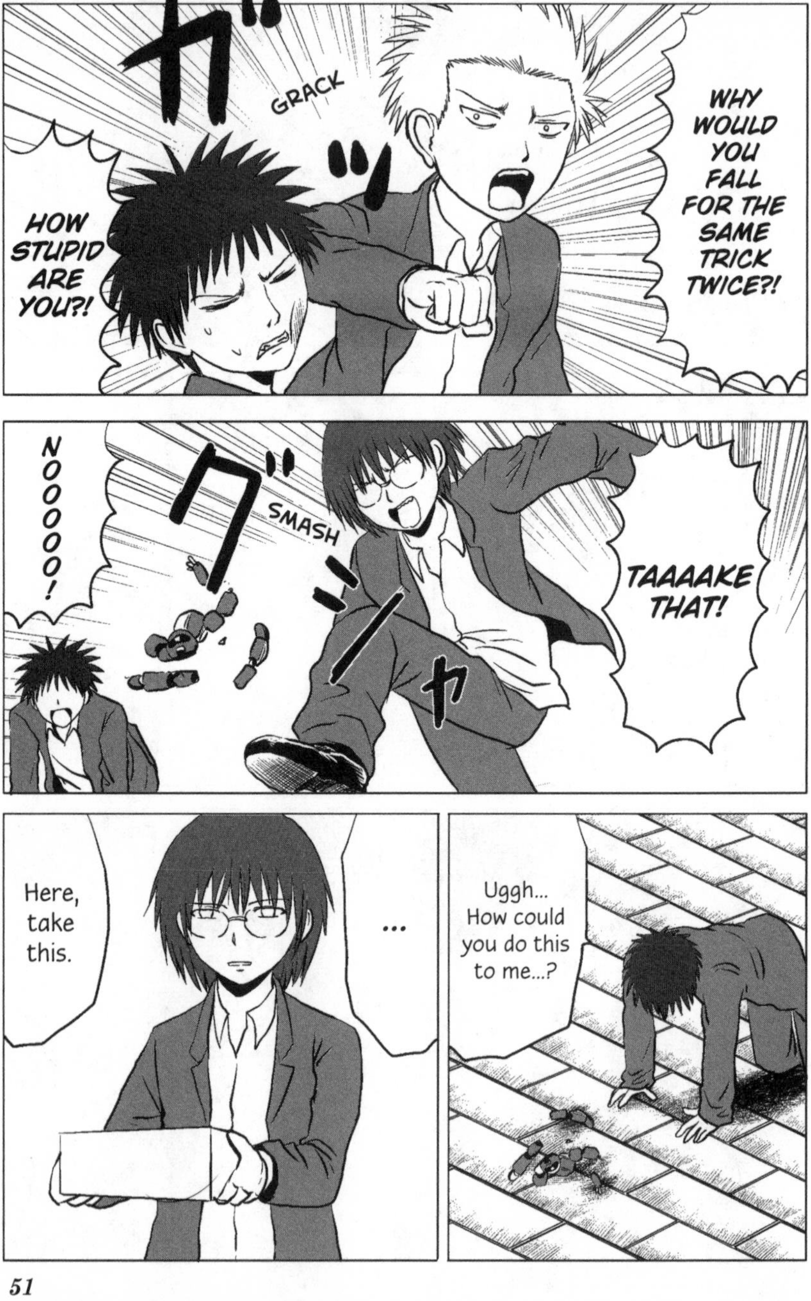
WHY WOULD YOU FALL FOR THE SAME TRICK TWICE?!
ガッ
GRACK
HOW STUPID ARE YOU?!
TAAAAKE THAT!
グシャ
SMASH
NOOOOOO!
Uggh... How could you do this to me...?
...
Here, take this.

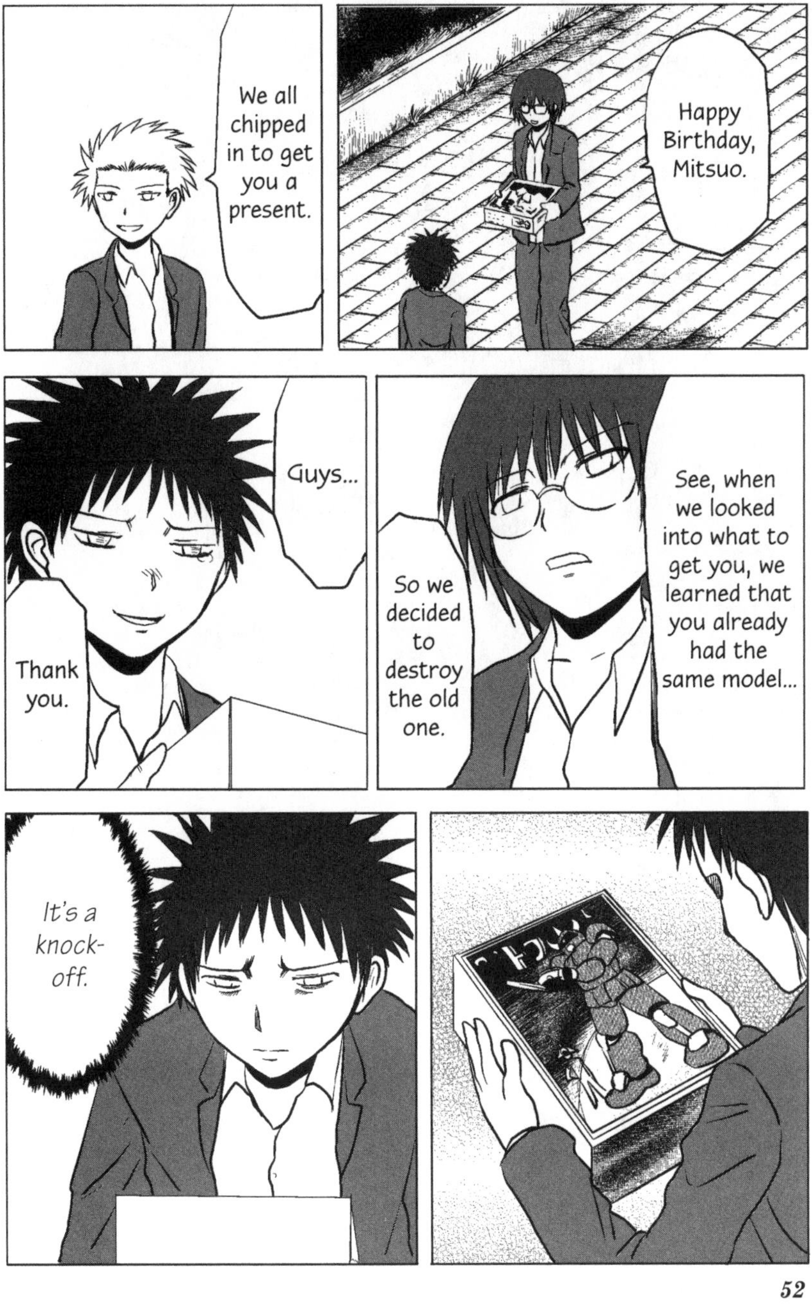
Happy Birthday, Mitsuo.
We all chipped in to get you a present.
See, when we looked into what to get you, we learned that you already had the same model...
So we decided to destroy the old one.
Guys...
Thank you.
It's a knock-off.

chapter 74:
high school boys and chatting

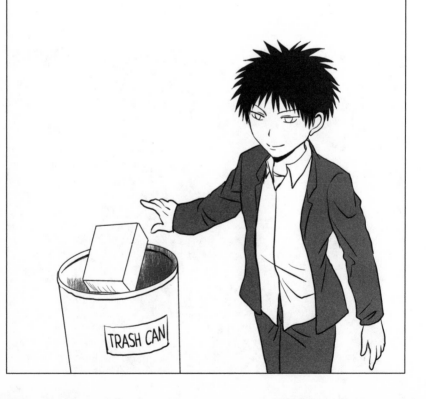

TRASH CAN

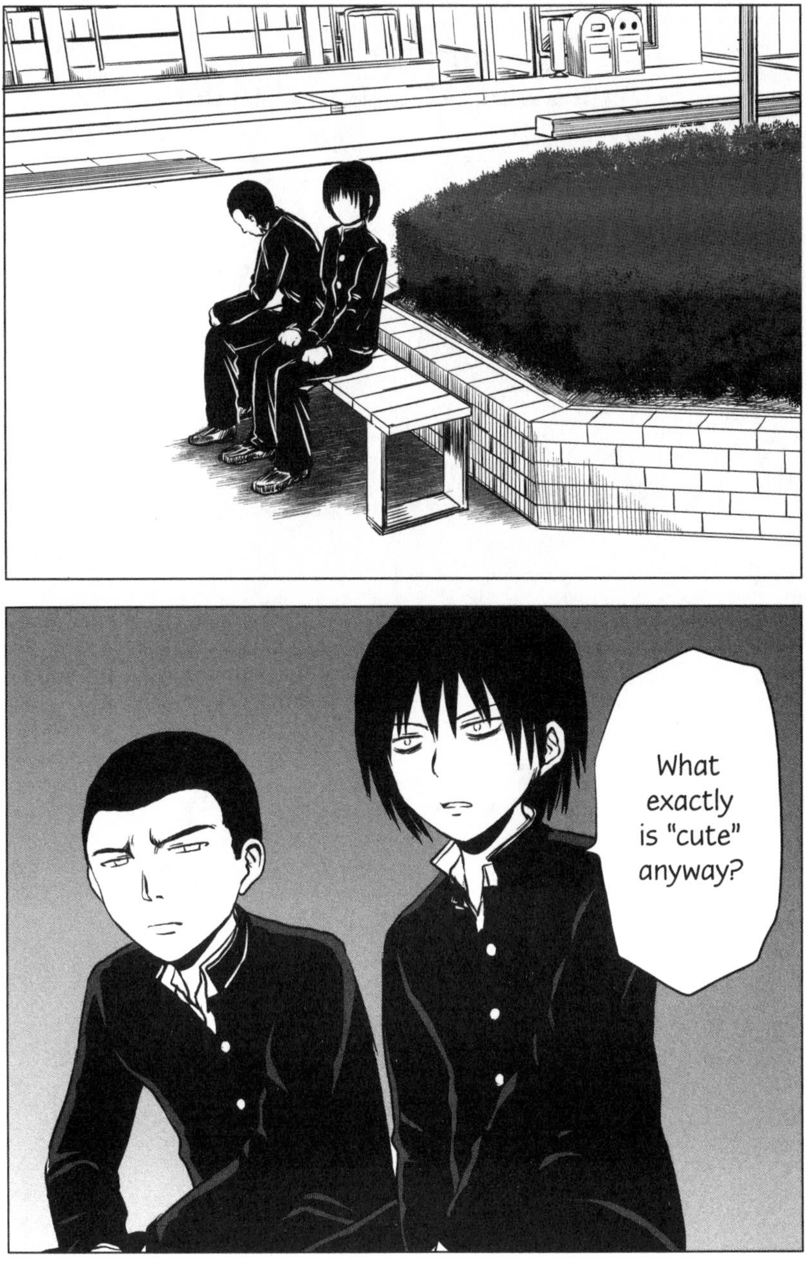
What exactly is "cute" anyway?

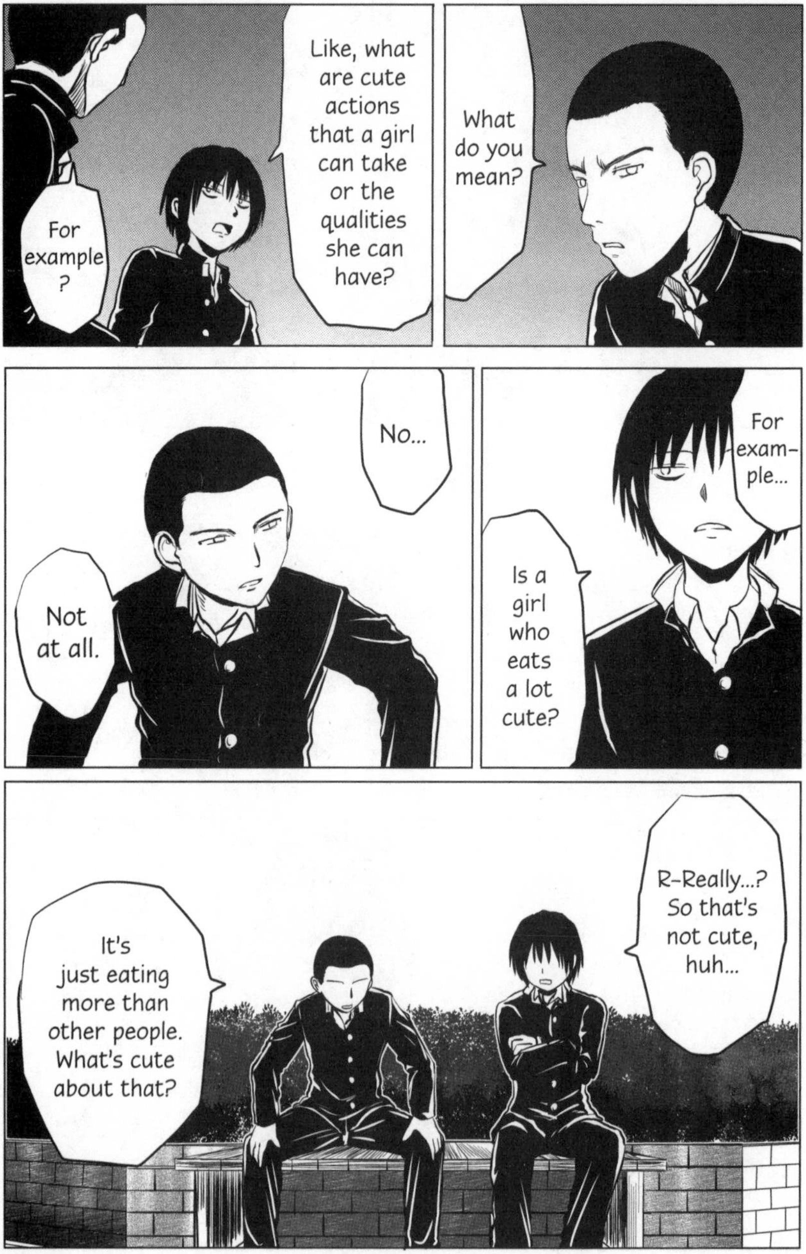
What do you mean?
Like, what are cute actions that a girl can take or the qualities she can have?
For example?
For example...
Is a girl who eats a lot cute?
No...
Not at all.
R-Really...? So that's not cute, huh...
It's just eating more than other people. What's cute about that?

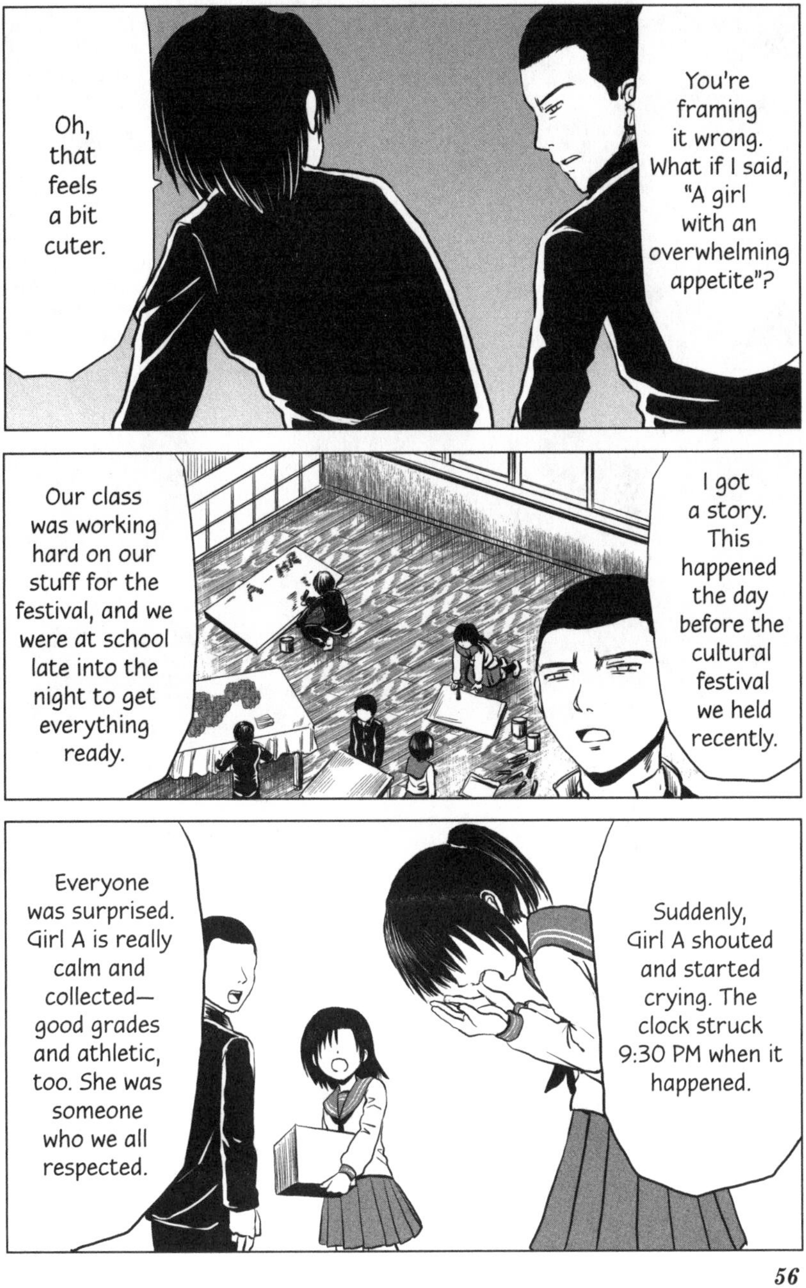
You're framing it wrong. What if I said, "A girl with an overwhelming appetite"?
Oh, that feels a bit cuter.
I got a story. This happened the day before the cultural festival we held recently.
Our class was working hard on our stuff for the festival, and we were at school late into the night to get everything ready.
Suddenly, Girl A shouted and started crying. The clock struck 9:30 PM when it happened.
Everyone was surprised. Girl A is really calm and collected—good grades and athletic, too. She was someone who we all respected.

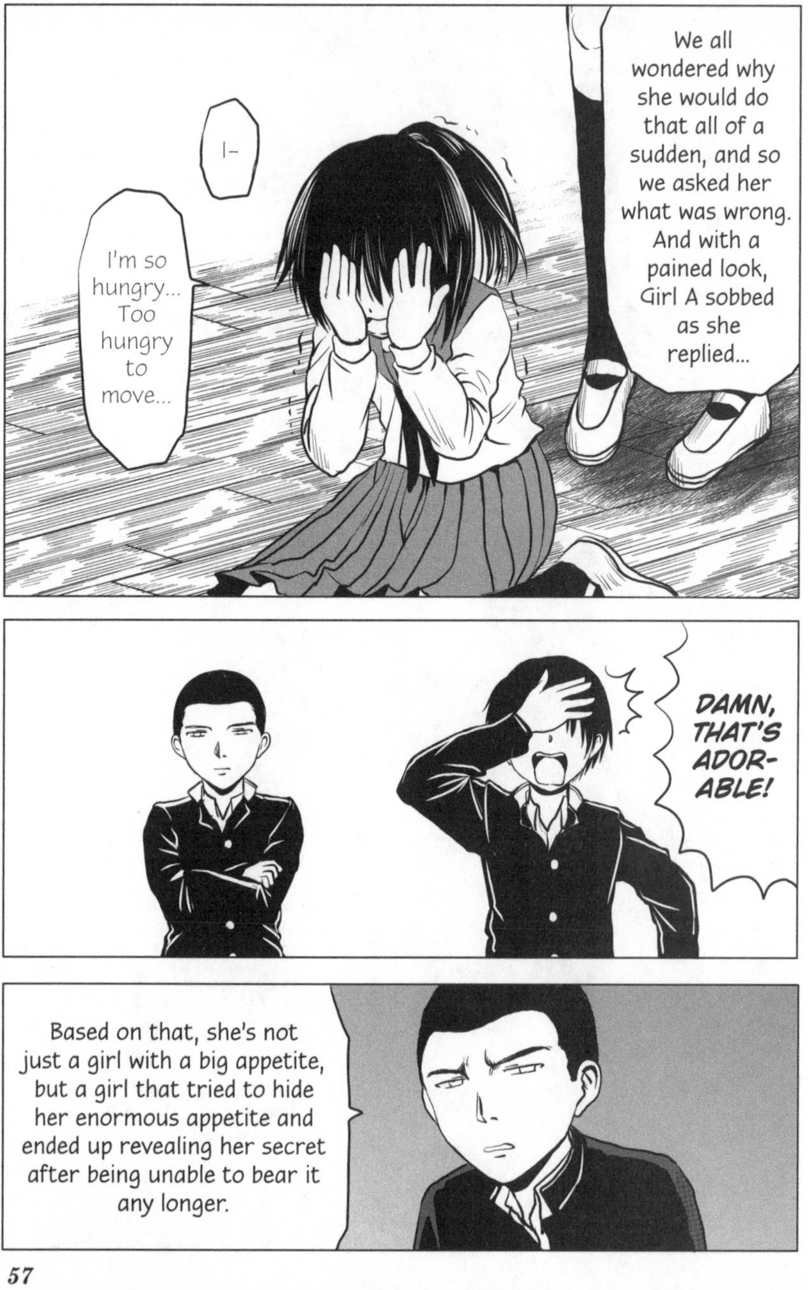
We all wondered why she would do that all of a sudden, and so we asked her what was wrong. And with a pained look, Girl A sobbed as she replied...
I–
I'm so hungry... Too hungry to move...
DAMN, THAT'S ADOR-ABLE!
Based on that, she's not just a girl with a big appetite, but a girl that tried to hide her enormous appetite and ended up revealing her secret after being unable to bear it any longer.

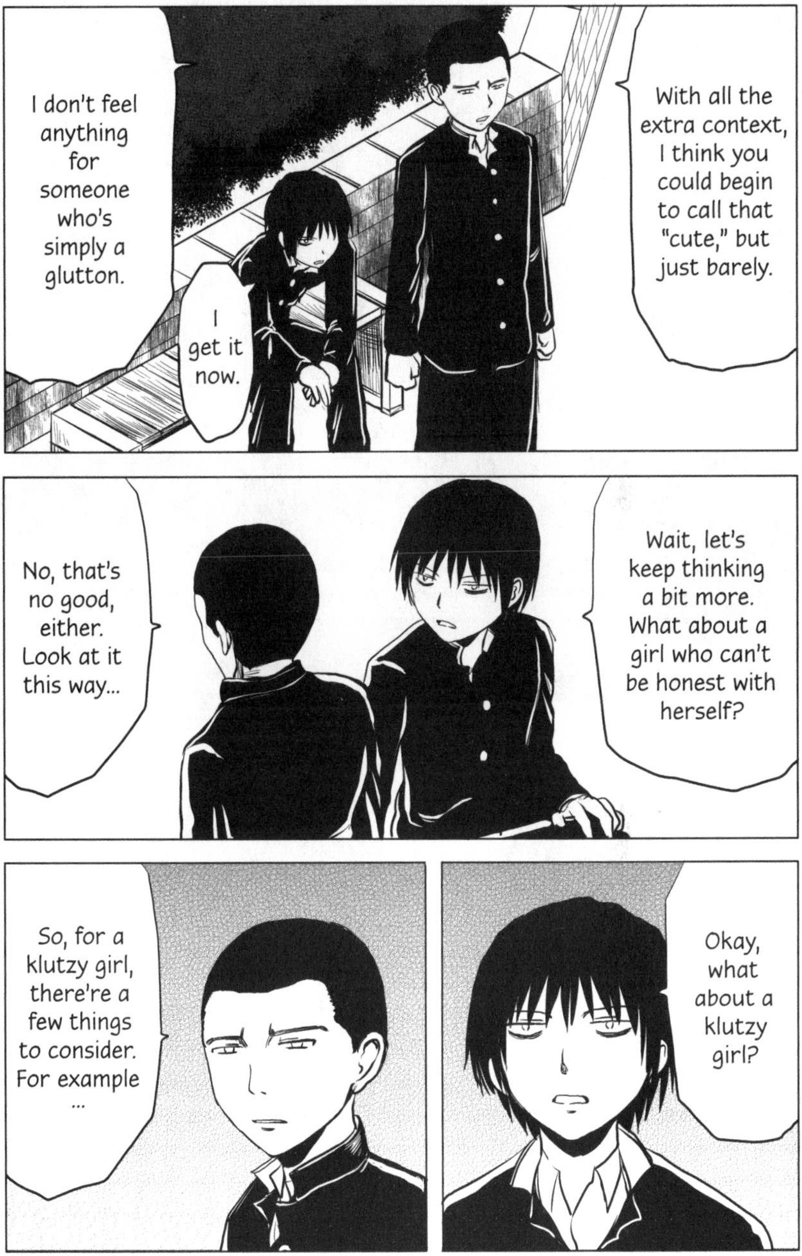
With all the extra context, I think you could begin to call that "cute," but just barely.
I get it now.
I don't feel anything for someone who's simply a glutton.
Wait, let's keep thinking a bit more. What about a girl who can't be honest with herself?
No, that's no good, either. Look at it this way...
Okay, what about a klutzy girl?
So, for a klutzy girl, there're a few things to consider. For example ...

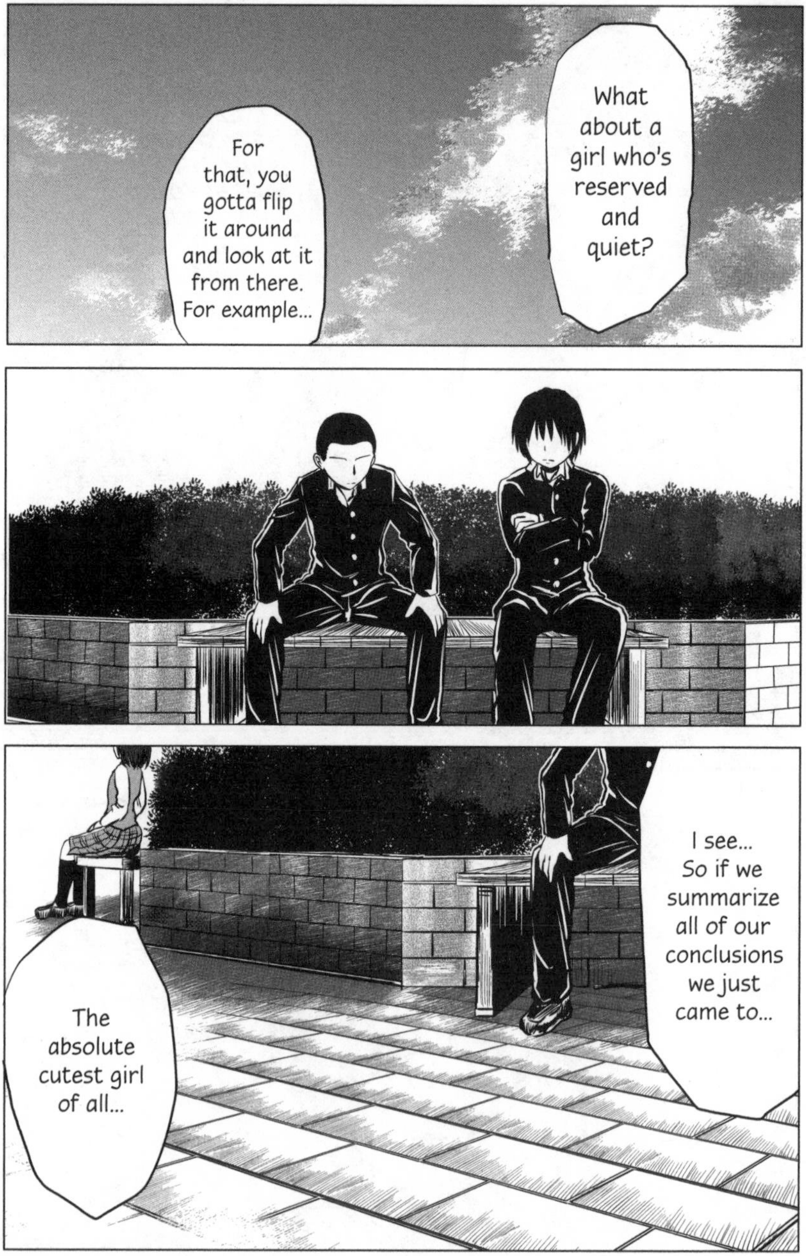
What about a girl who's reserved and quiet?
For that, you gotta flip it around and look at it from there. For example...
I see... So if we summarize all of our conclusions we just came to...
The absolute cutest girl of all...

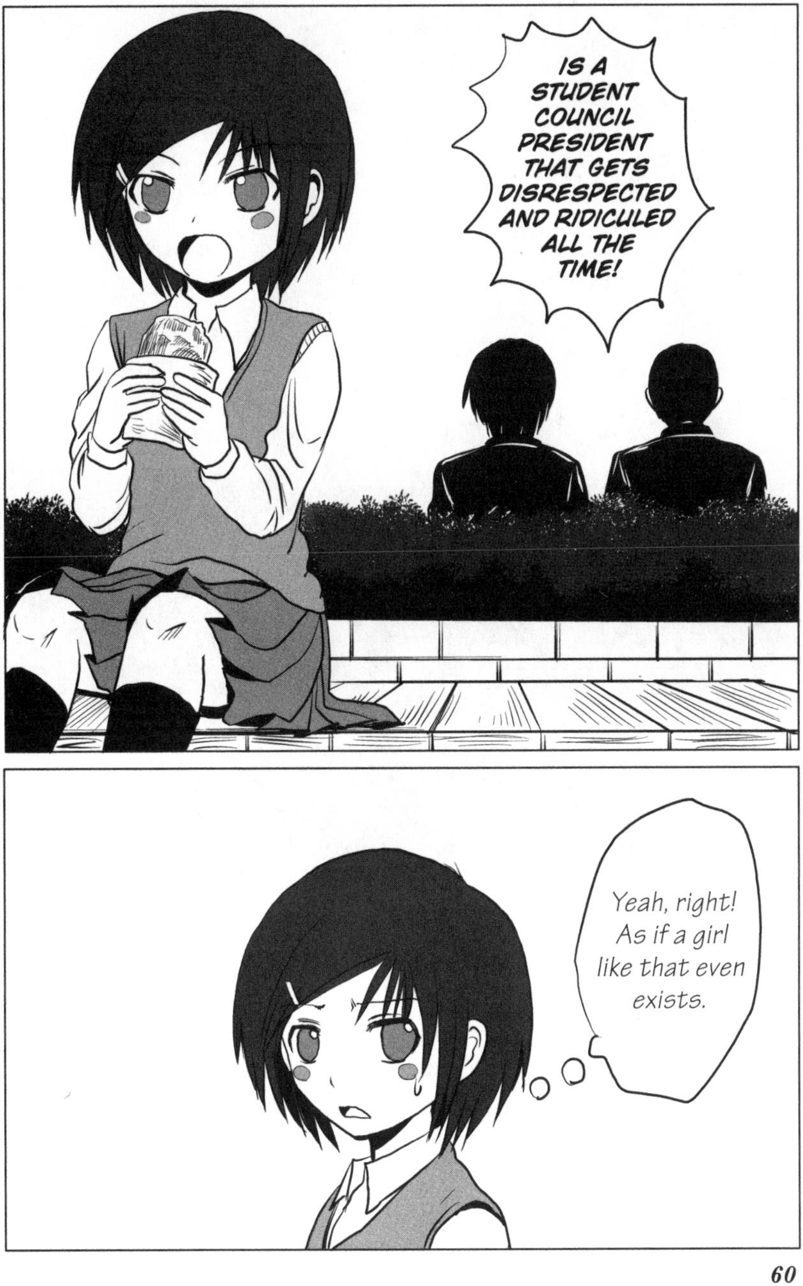
IS A STUDENT COUNCIL PRESIDENT THAT GETS DISRESPECTED AND RIDICULED ALL THE TIME!
Yeah, right! As if a girl like that even exists.

chapter 75:
high school boys and love letters

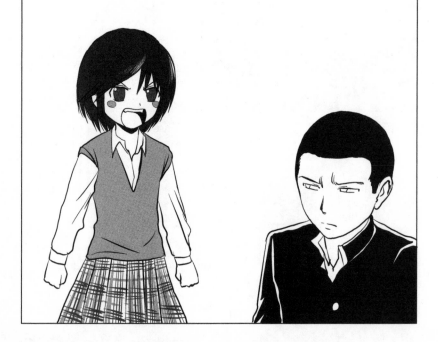

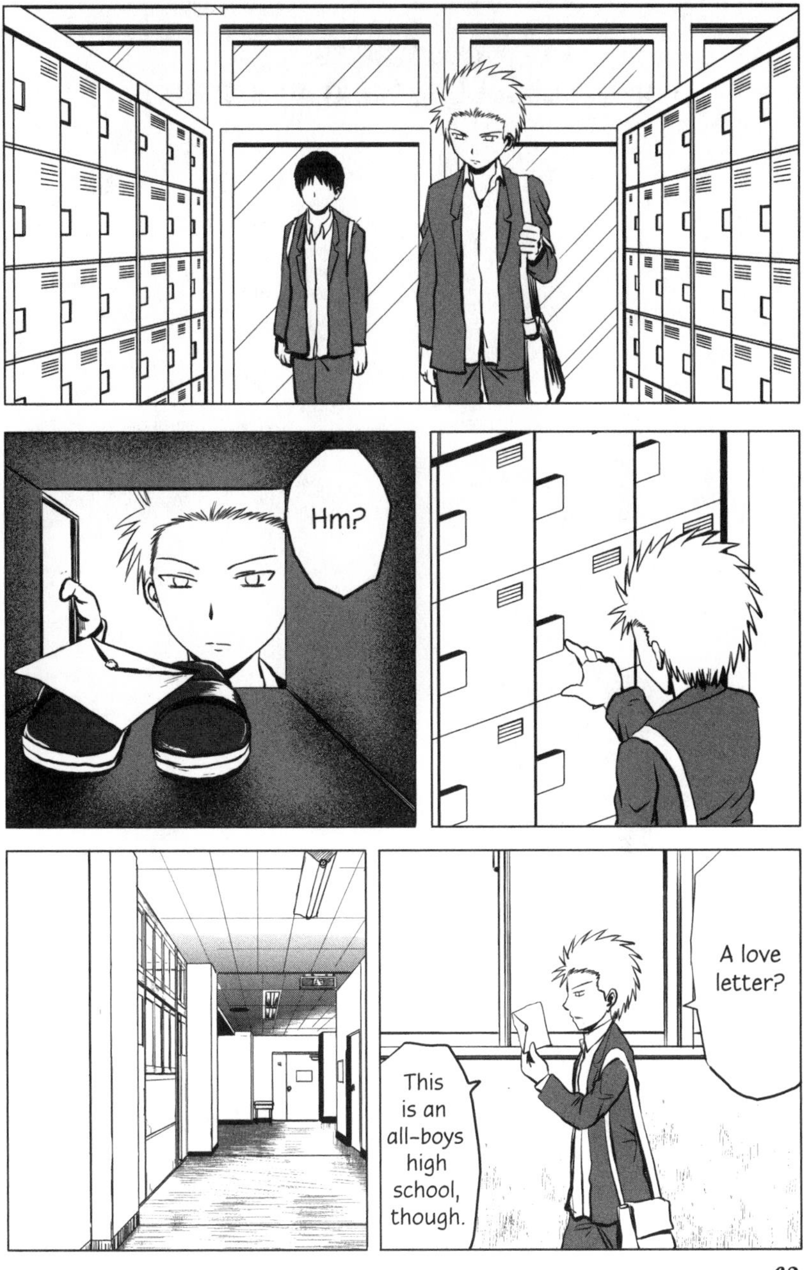
Hm?
A love letter?
This is an all-boys high school, though.

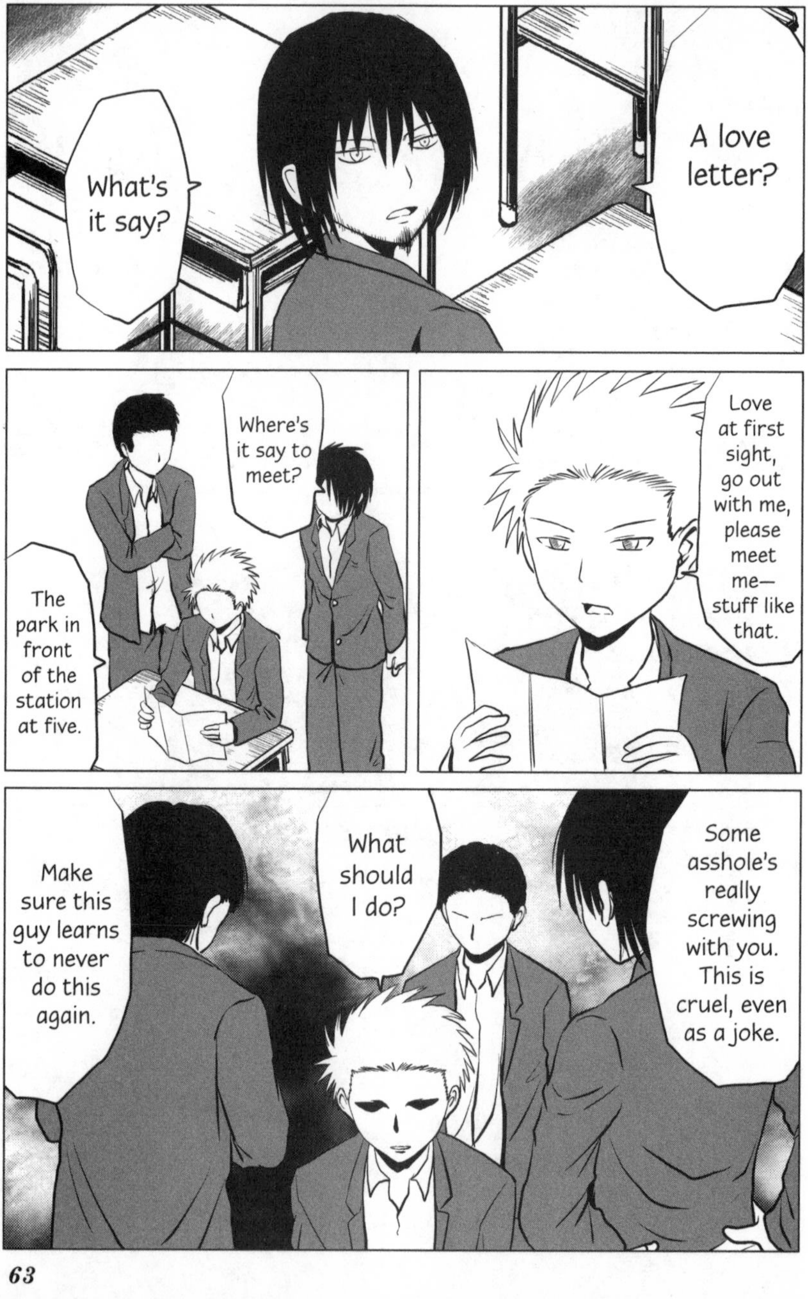
A love letter?
What's it say?
Love at first sight, go out with me, please meet me—stuff like that.
Where's it say to meet?
The park in front of the station at five.
Some asshole's really screwing with you. This is cruel, even as a joke.
What should I do?
Make sure this guy learns to never do this again.

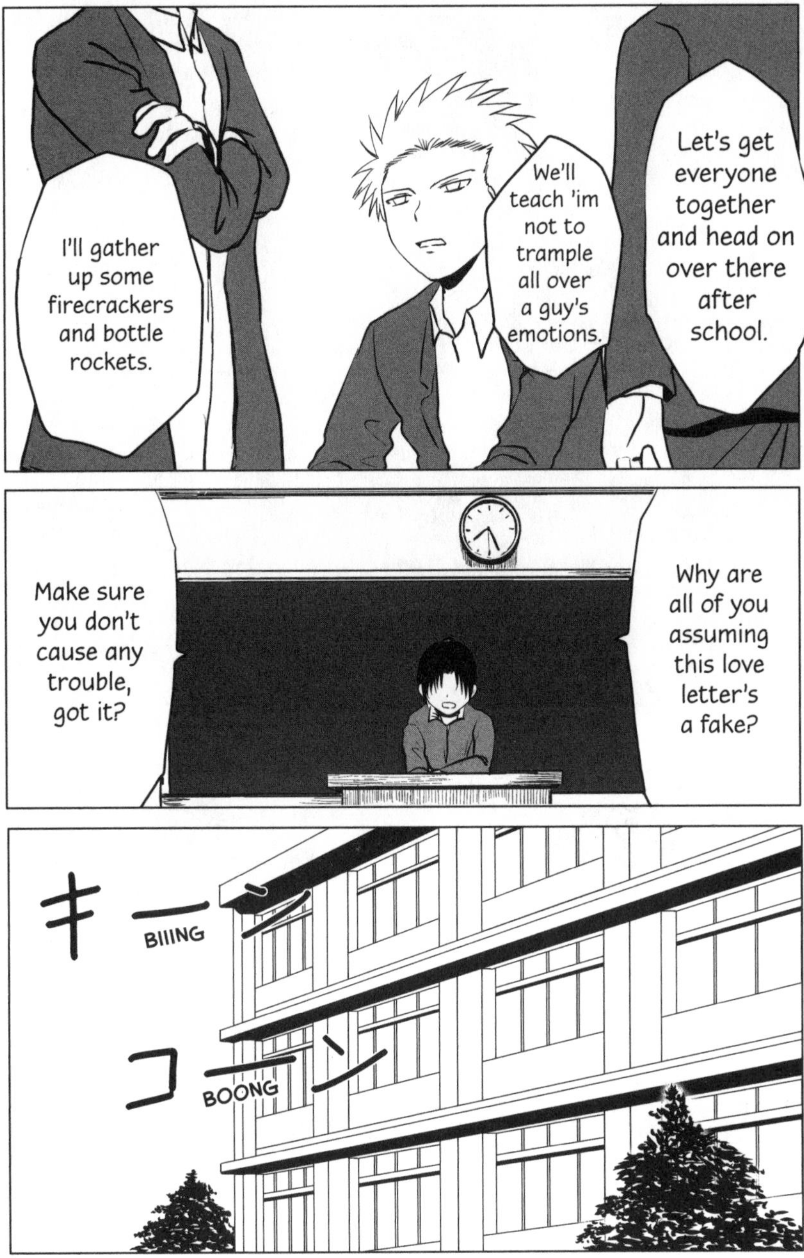
Let's get everyone together and head on over there after school.
We'll teach 'im not to trample all over a guy's emotions.
I'll gather up some firecrackers and bottle rockets.
Why are all of you assuming this love letter's a fake?
Make sure you don't cause any trouble, got it?
キーン
BIIING
コーン
BOONG

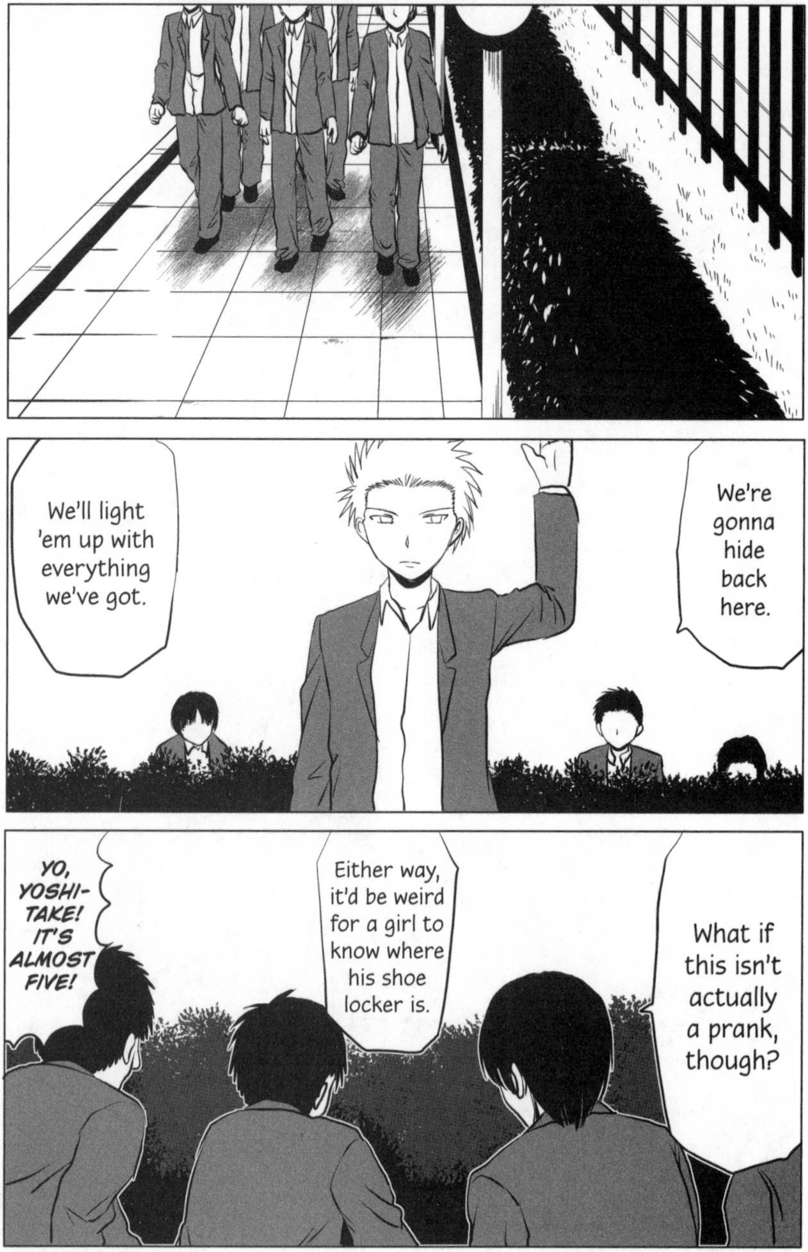
We're gonna hide back here.
We'll light 'em up with everything we've got.
What if this isn't actually a prank, though?
Either way, it'd be weird for a girl to know where his shoe locker is.
YO, YOSHI-TAKE! IT'S ALMOST FIVE!

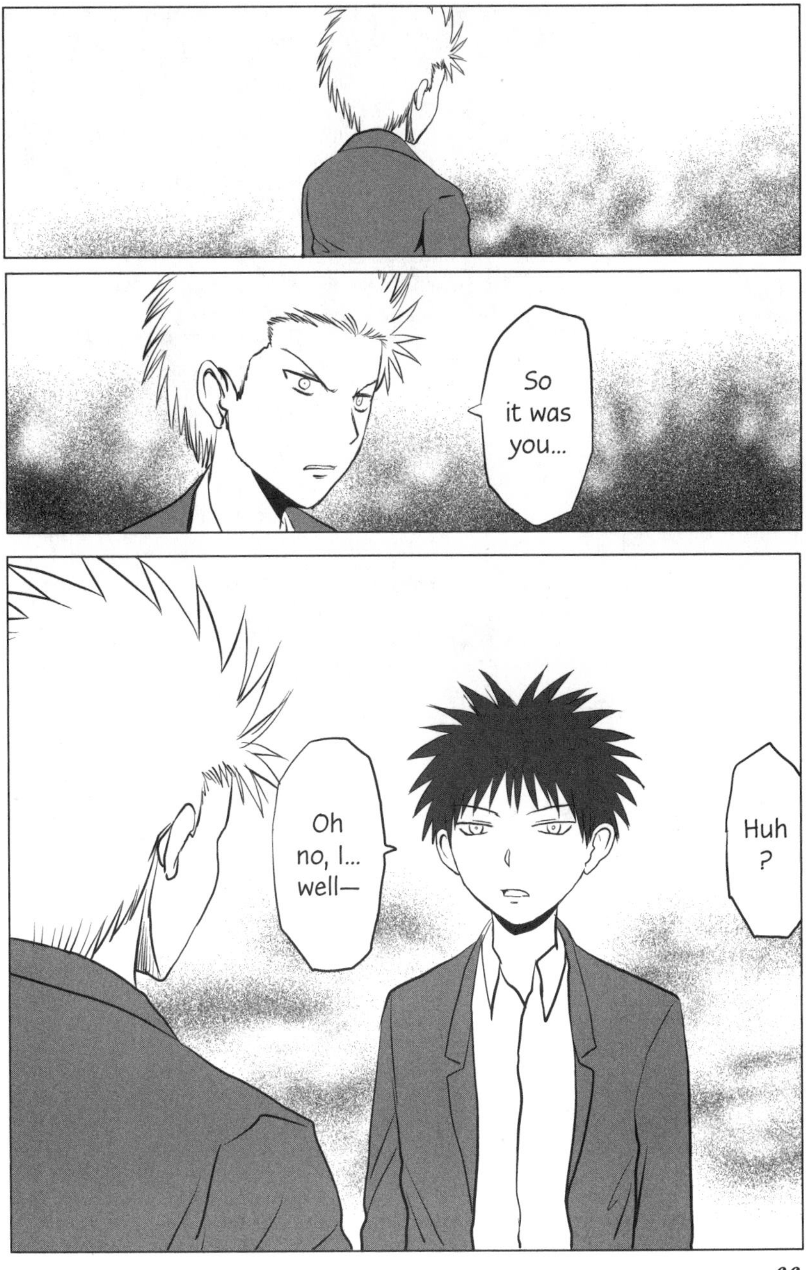
So it was you...
Huh?
Oh no, I... well—

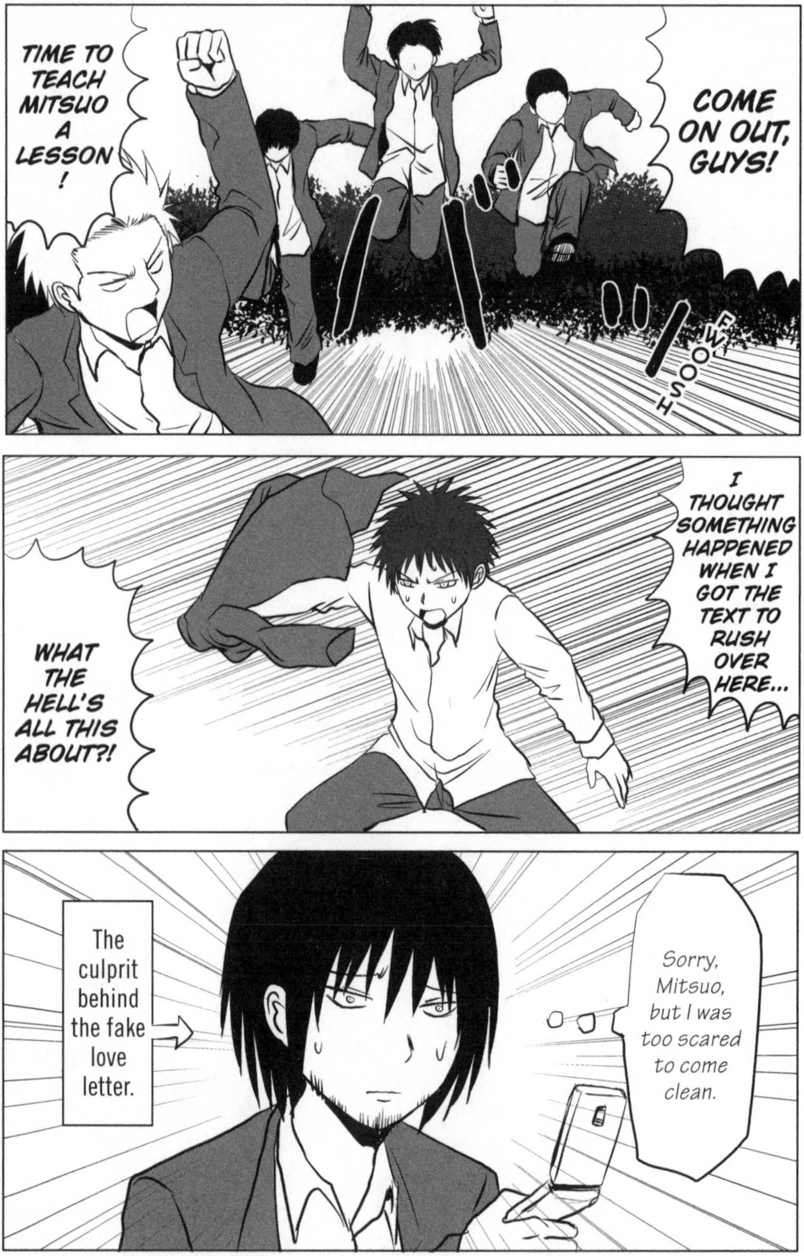
COME ON OUT, GUYS!
TIME TO TEACH MITSUO A LESSON!
FWOOSH
I THOUGHT SOMETHING HAPPENED WHEN I GOT THE TEXT TO RUSH OVER HERE...
WHAT THE HELL'S ALL THIS ABOUT?!
Sorry, Mitsuo, but I was too scared to come clean.
The culprit behind the fake love letter.

the

daily

lives

of

5 high school boys

chapter 76:
high school boys and distance

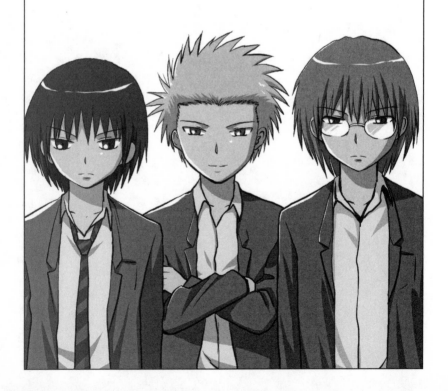

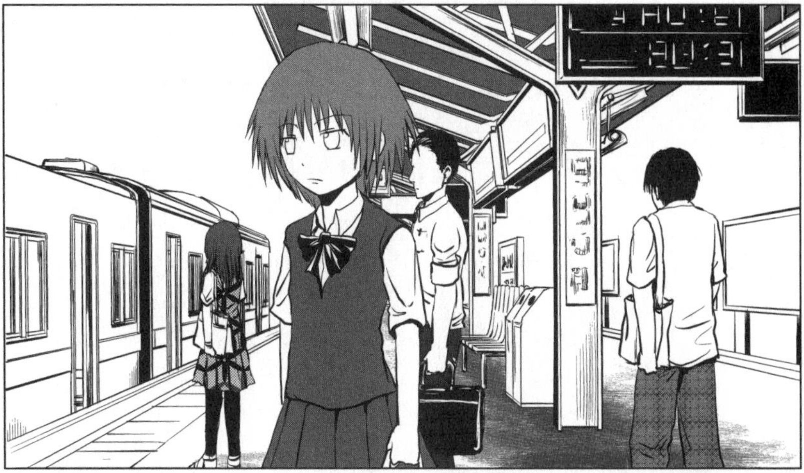

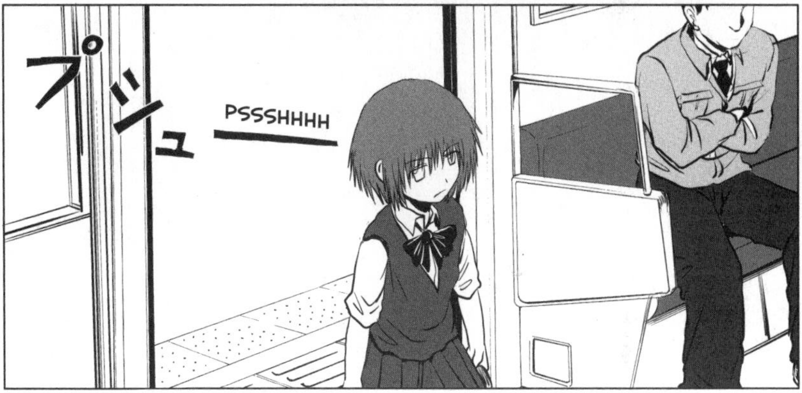
プシュー
PSSSHHHH

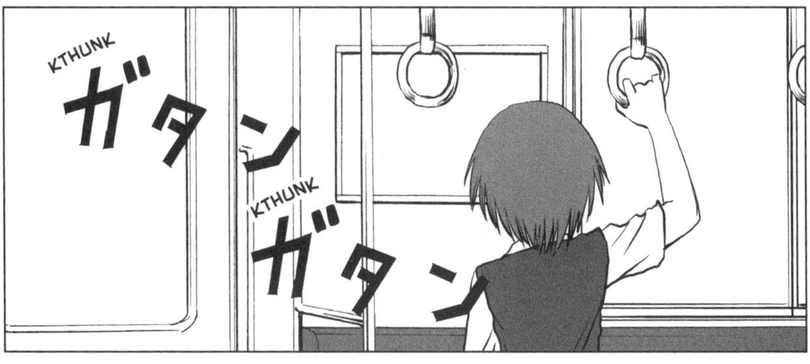
KTHUNK
ガタン
KTHUNK
ガタン

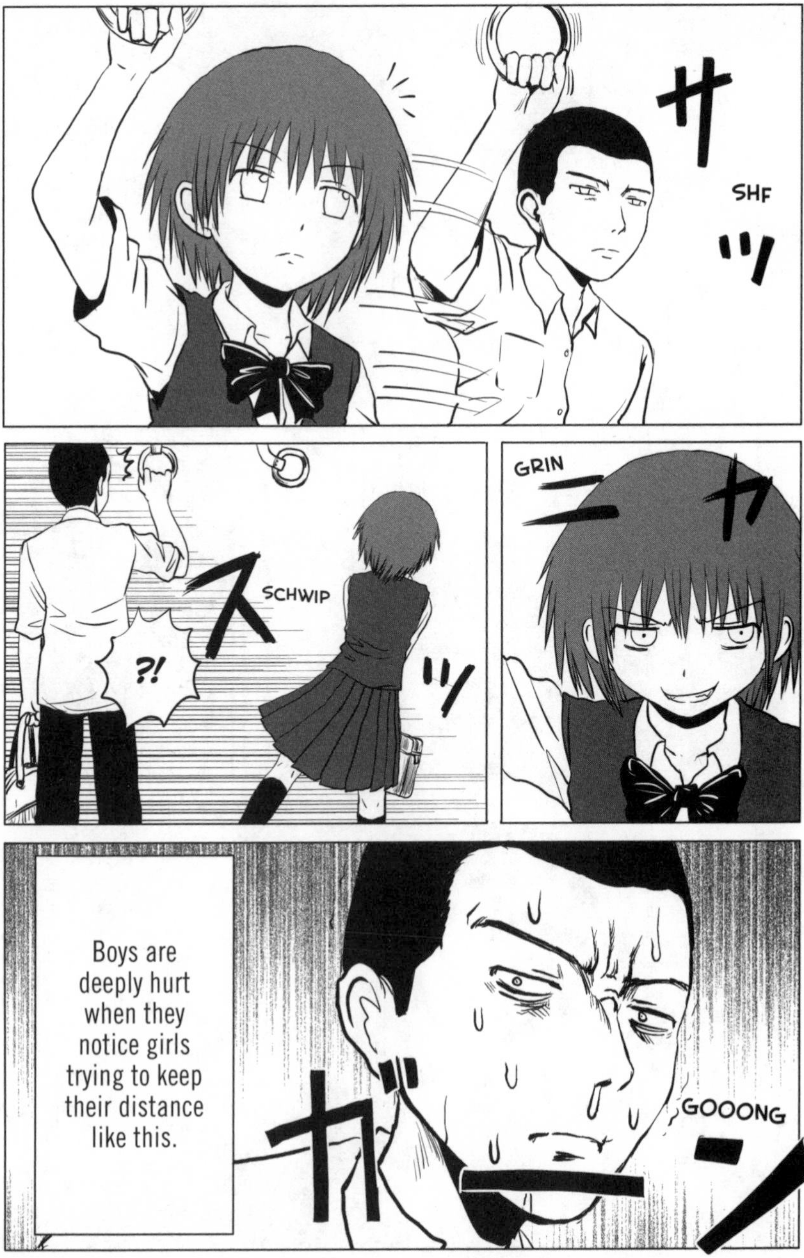
サッ
SHF
GRIN
ニヤ
スッ
SCHWIP
?!
Boys are deeply hurt when they notice girls trying to keep their distance like this.
ガーン
GOOONG

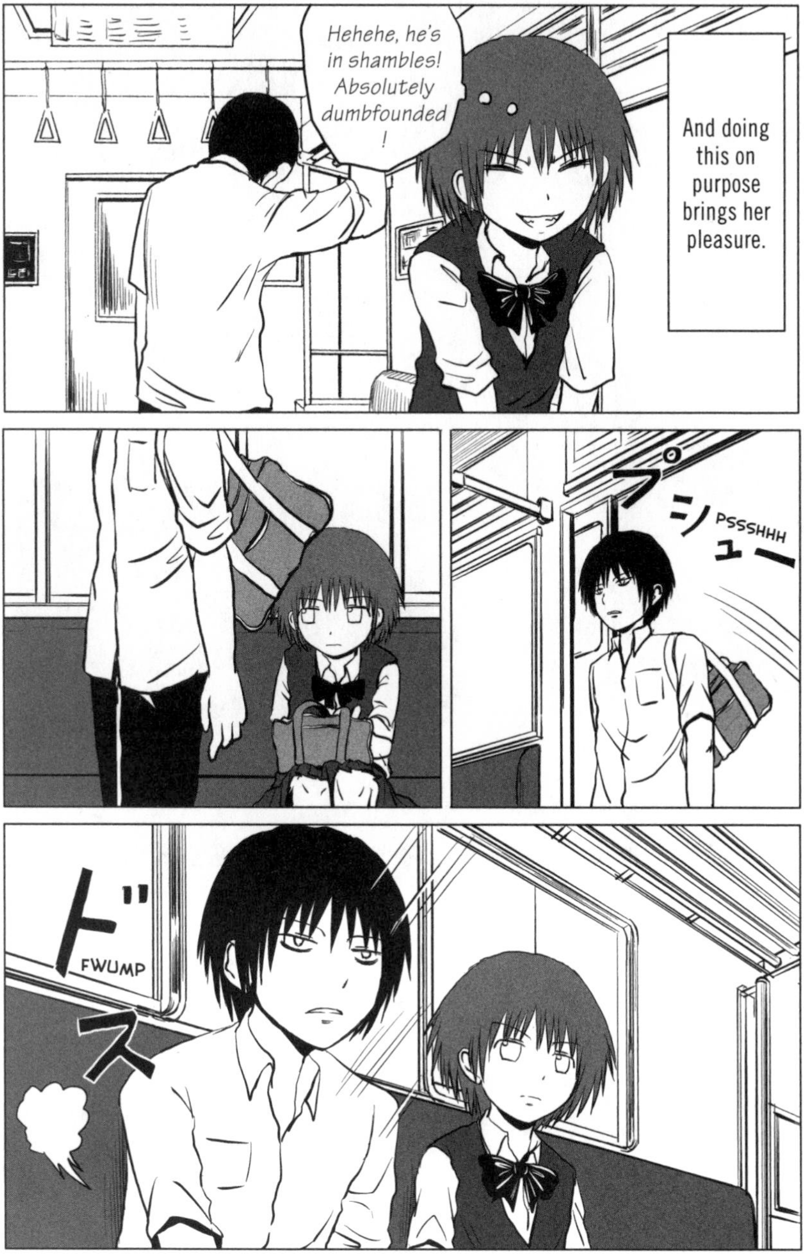
And doing this on purpose brings her pleasure.
Hehehe, he's in shambles! Absolutely dumbfounded!
プシュー
PSSSHHH
ドス
FWUMP

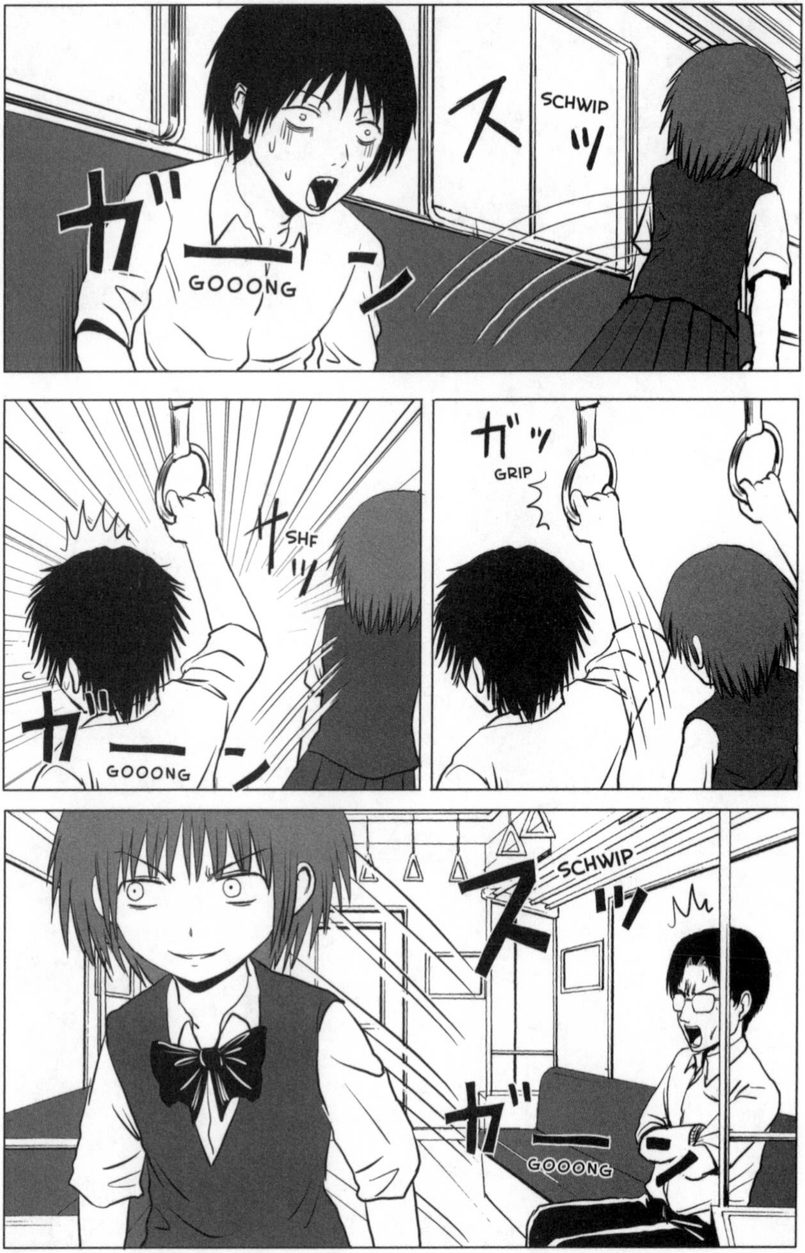
スッ
SCHWIP
ガーーン
GOOONG
ガッ
GRIP
サッ
SHF
ガーーン
GOOONG
ズッ
SCHWIP
ガーーン
GOOONG

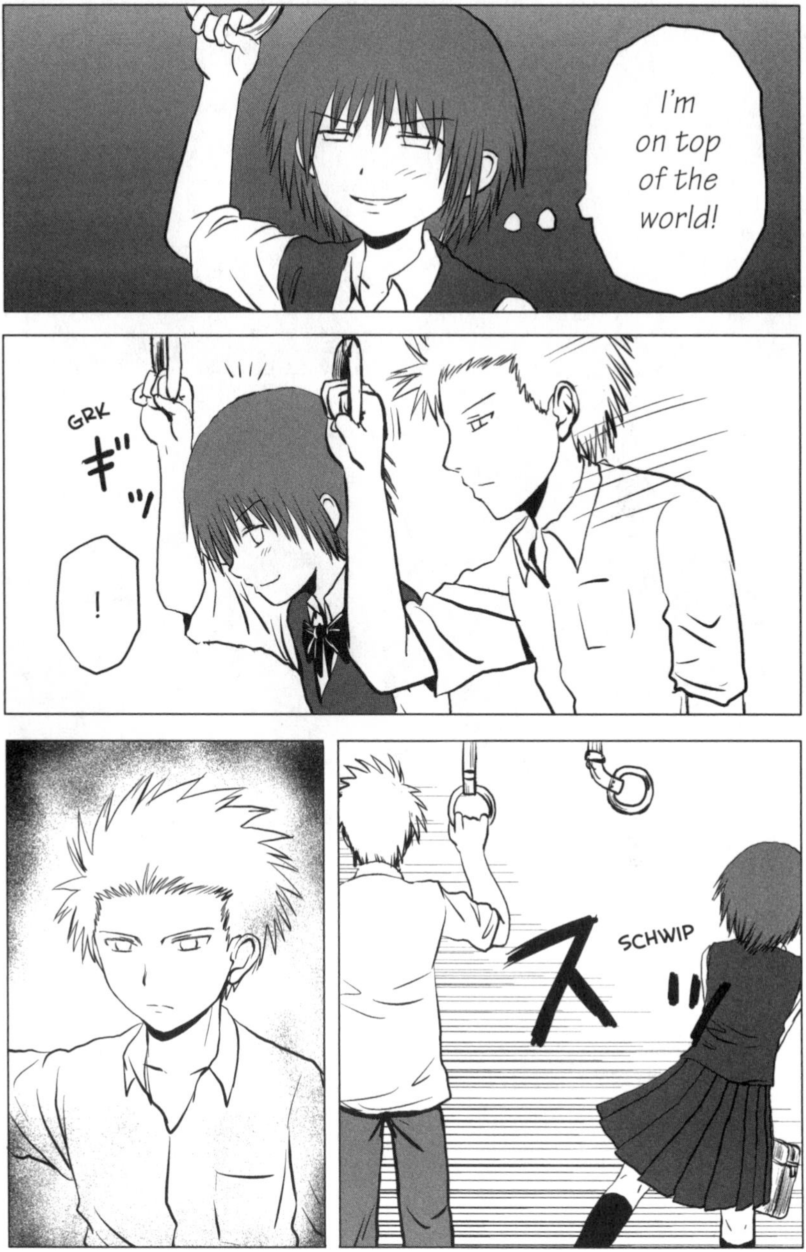

I'm on top of the world!
GRK
ギッ
!
SCHWIP
スッ

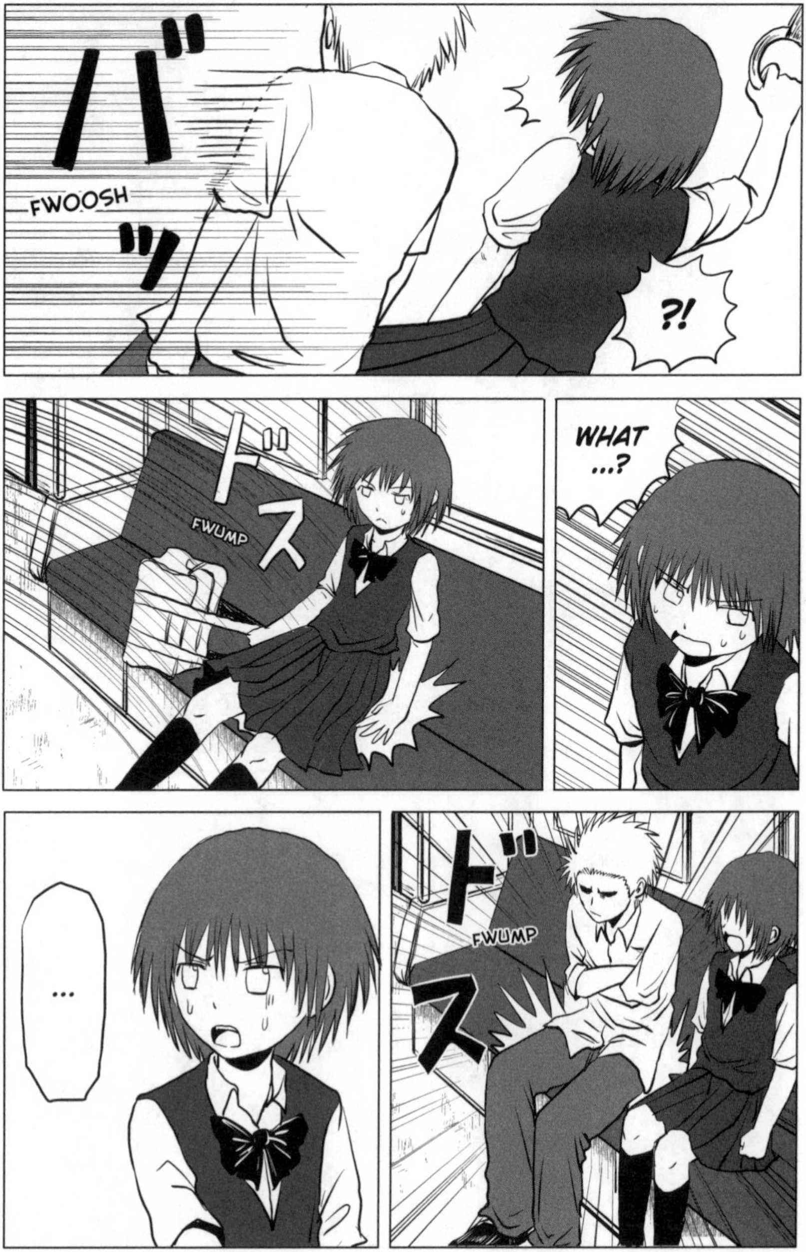
バッ
FWOOSH
?!
WHAT ...?
ドス
FWUMP
ドス
FWUMP
...

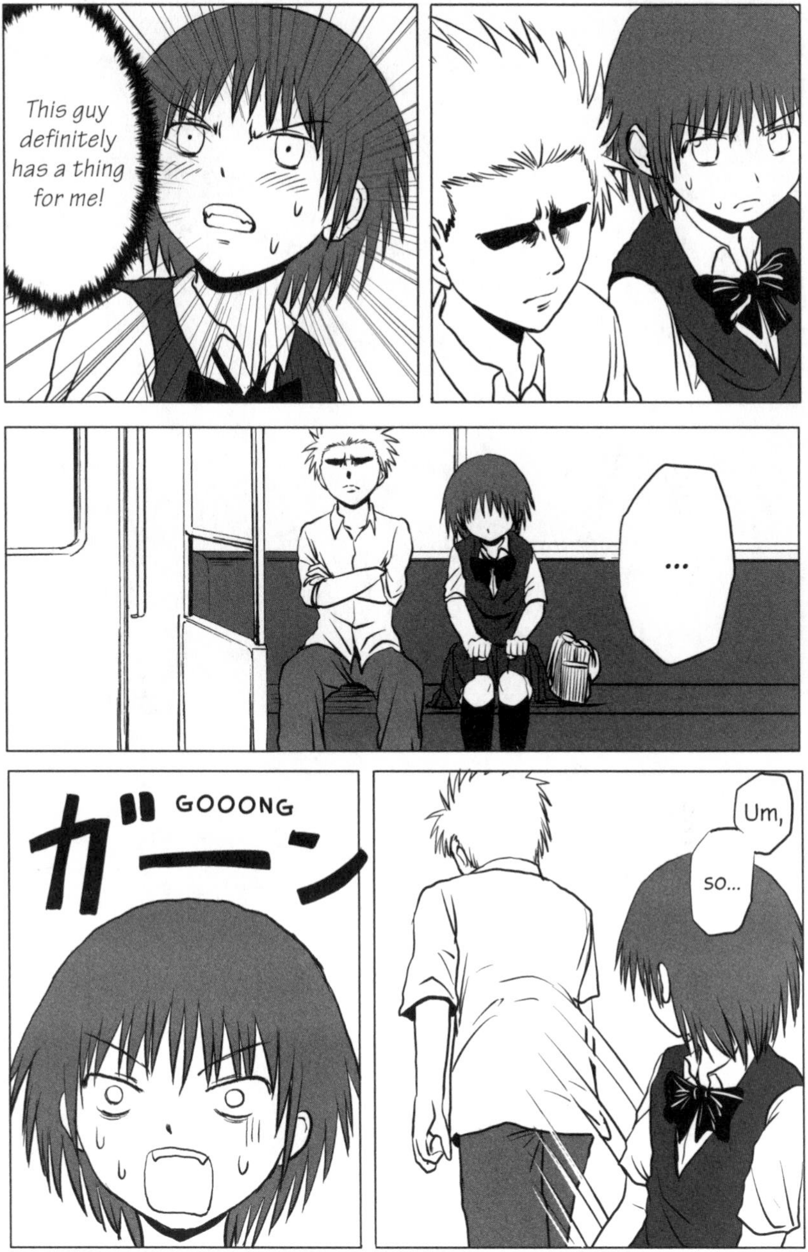
This guy definitely has a thing for me!
...
Um,
so...
GOOONG
ガーン

chapter 77:
high school boys and chemistry club

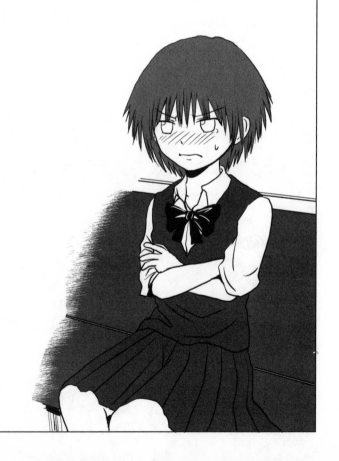

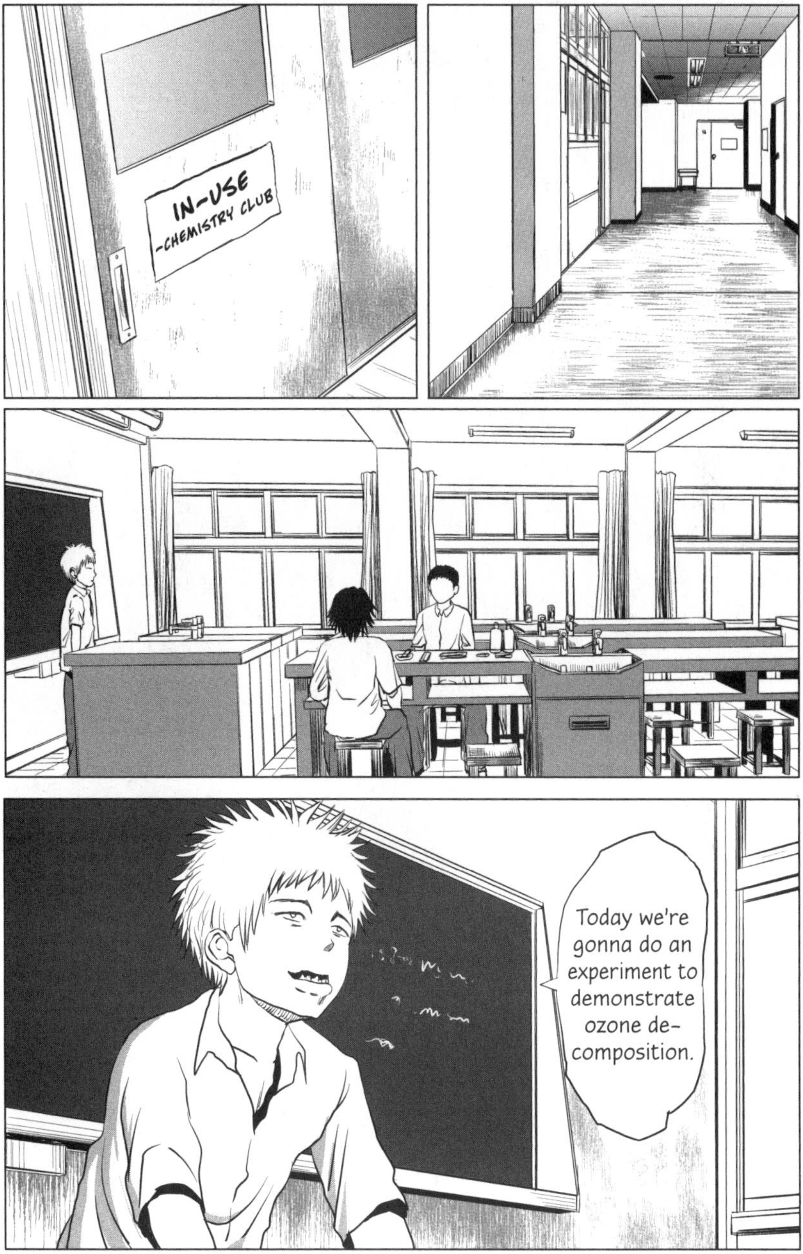
IN-USE
-CHEMISTRY CLUB
Today we're gonna do an experiment to demonstrate ozone de-composition.

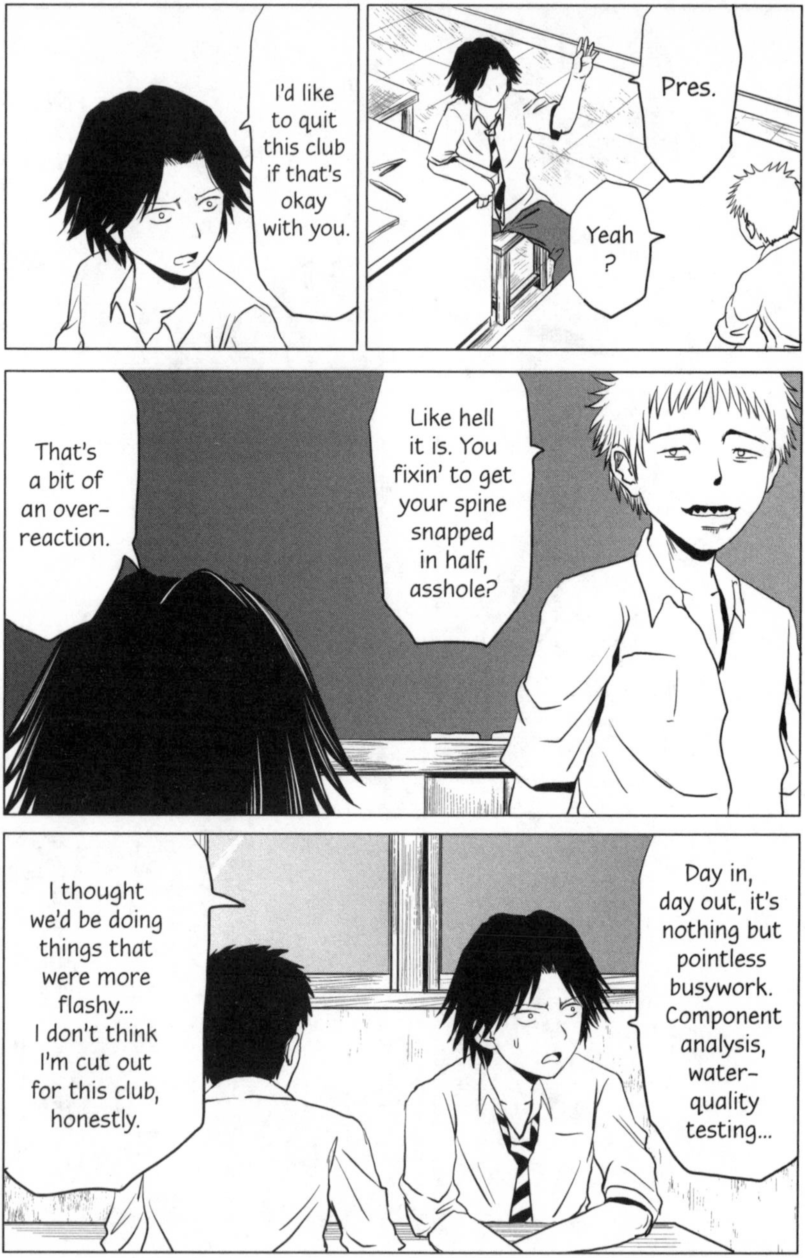
Pres.
Yeah?
I'd like to quit this club if that's okay with you.
Like hell it is. You fixin' to get your spine snapped in half, asshole?
That's a bit of an over-reaction.
Day in, day out, it's nothing but pointless busywork. Component analysis, water-quality testing...
I thought we'd be doing things that were more flashy... I don't think I'm cut out for this club, honestly.

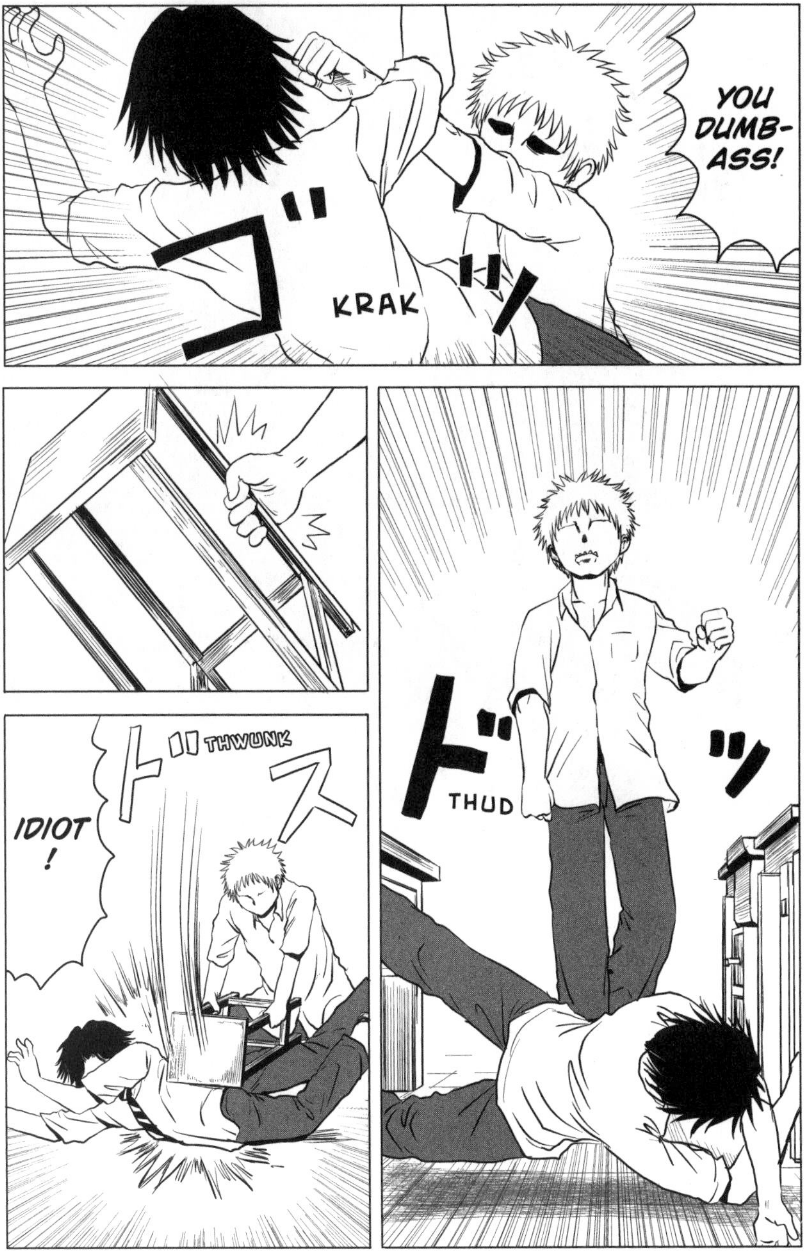
YOU DUMB-ASS!
ゴッ
KRAK
ドッ
THUD
ドス
THWUNK
IDIOT!

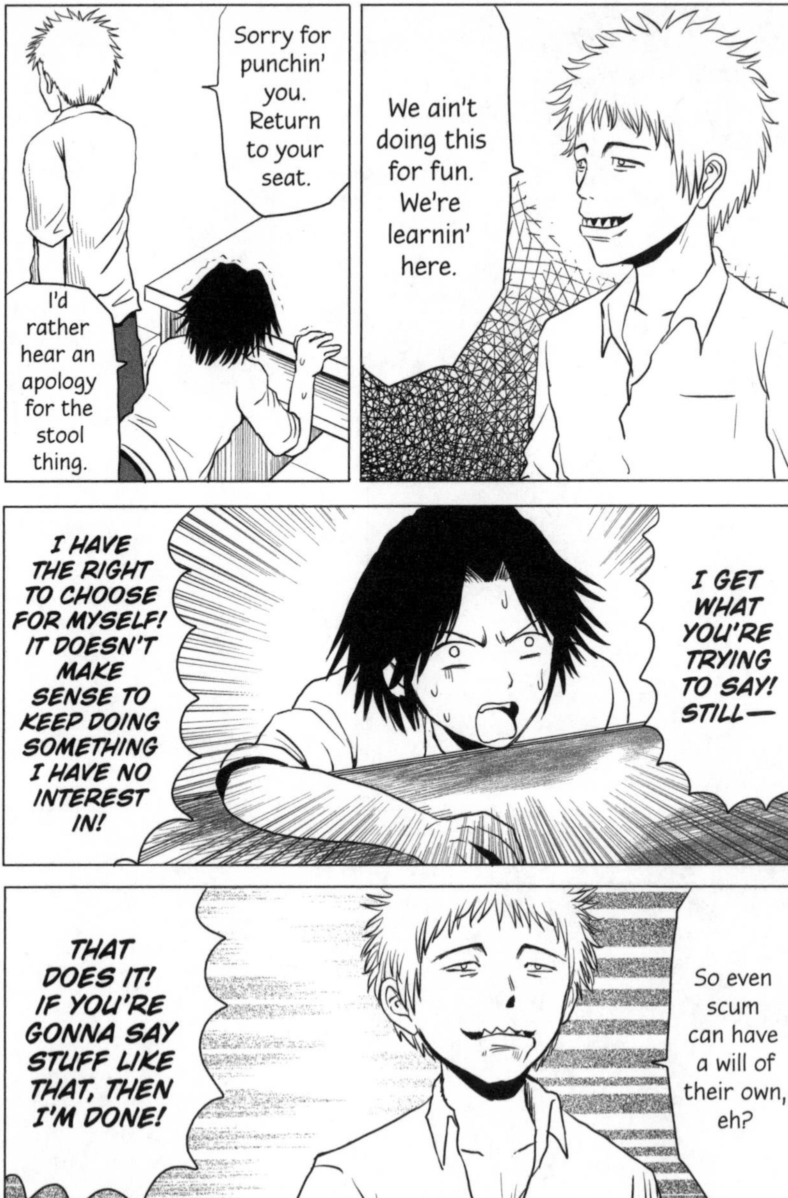
We ain't doing this for fun. We're learnin' here.
Sorry for punchin' you. Return to your seat.
I'd rather hear an apology for the stool thing.
I GET WHAT YOU'RE TRYING TO SAY! STILL—
I HAVE THE RIGHT TO CHOOSE FOR MYSELF! IT DOESN'T MAKE SENSE TO KEEP DOING SOMETHING I HAVE NO INTEREST IN!
So even scum can have a will of their own, eh?
THAT DOES IT! IF YOU'RE GONNA SAY STUFF LIKE THAT, THEN I'M DONE!

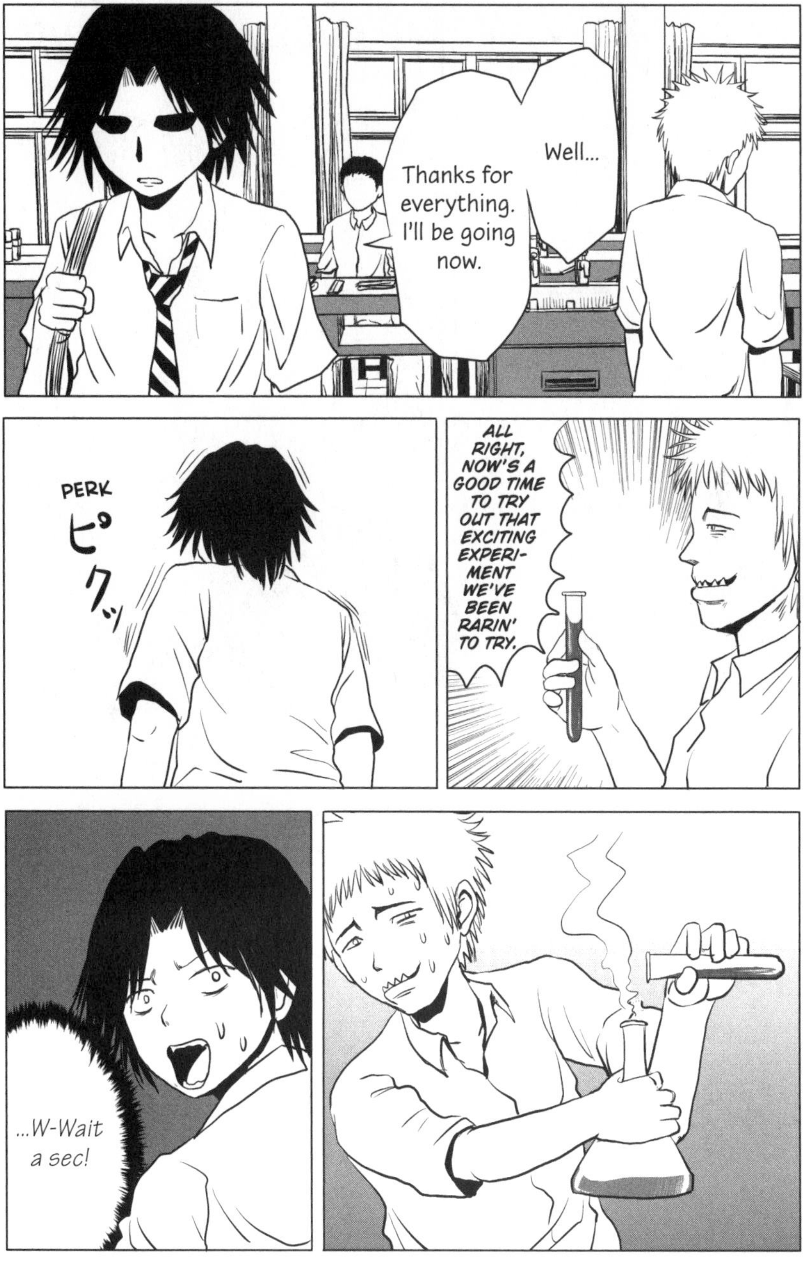
Well...
Thanks for everything. I'll be going now.
ALL RIGHT, NOW'S A GOOD TIME TO TRY OUT THAT EXCITING EXPERIMENT WE'VE BEEN RARIN' TO TRY.
PERK
ピクッ
...W-Wait a sec!

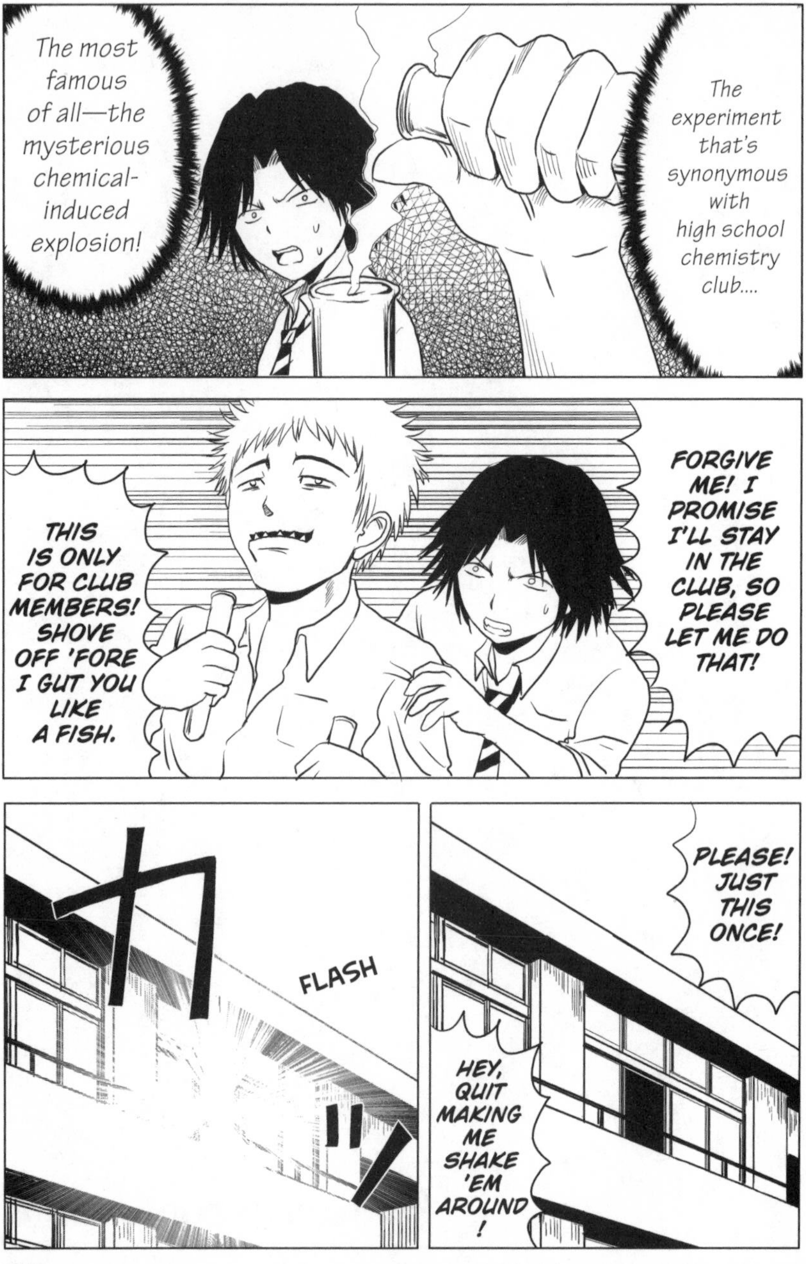
The experiment that's synonymous with high school chemistry club....
The most famous of all—the mysterious chemical-induced explosion!
FORGIVE ME! I PROMISE I'LL STAY IN THE CLUB, SO PLEASE LET ME DO THAT!
THIS IS ONLY FOR CLUB MEMBERS! SHOVE OFF 'FORE I GUT YOU LIKE A FISH.
PLEASE! JUST THIS ONCE!
HEY, QUIT MAKING ME SHAKE 'EM AROUND!
FLASH

the

daily

lives

of

5 high school boys

chapter 78:
high school boys and film club

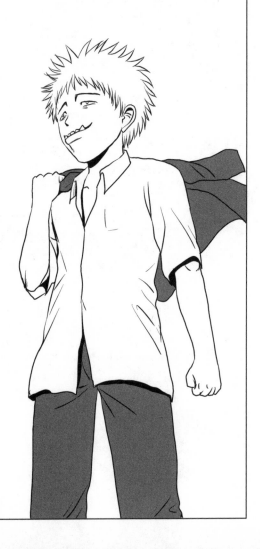

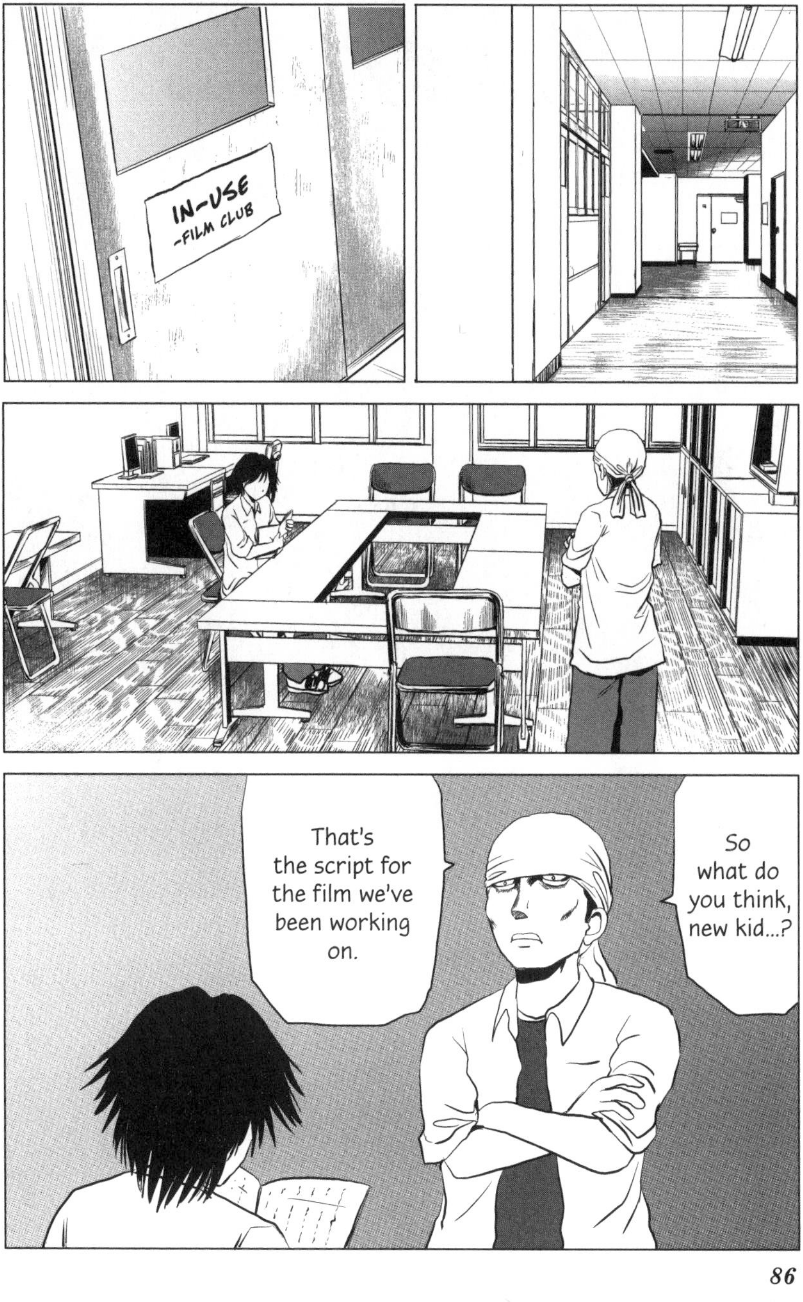
IN-USE
-FILM CLUB
So what do you think, new kid...?
That's the script for the film we've been working on.

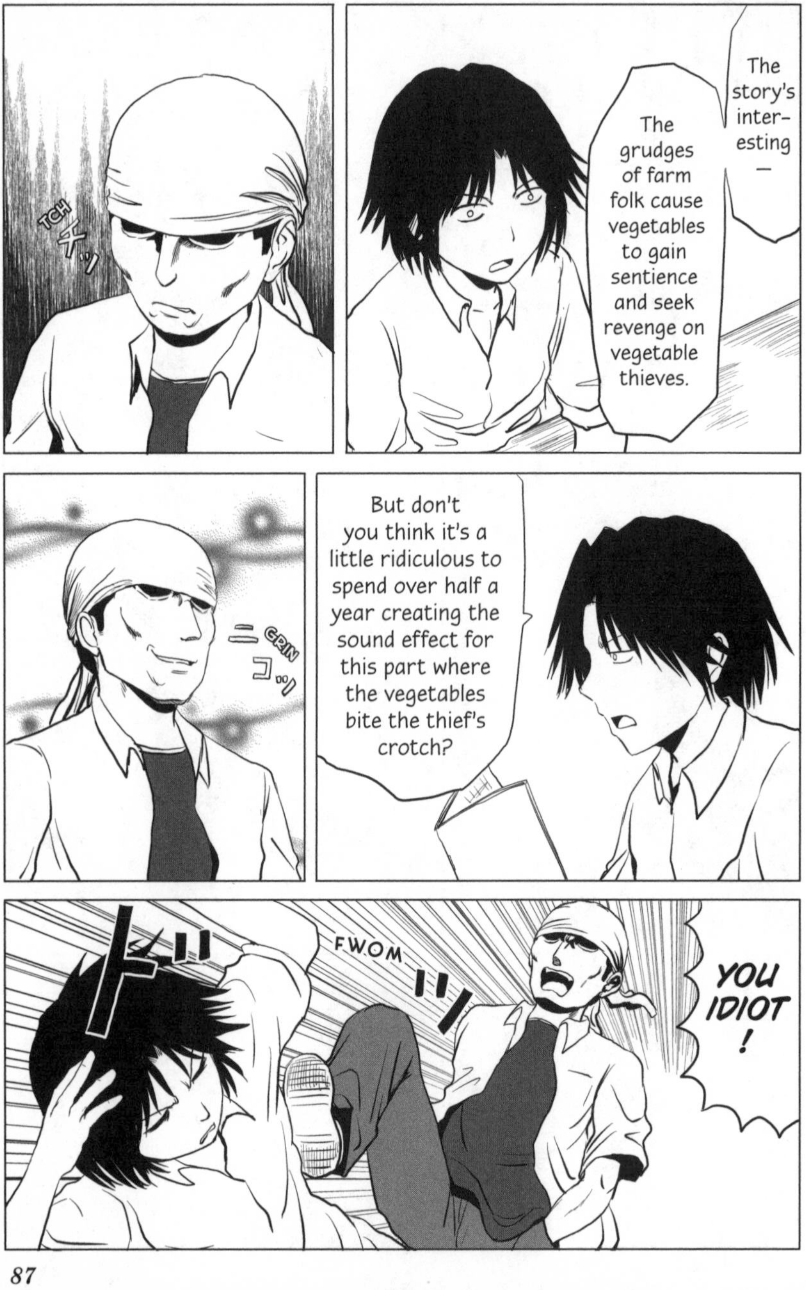
The story's inter-esting —
The grudges of farm folk cause vegetables to gain sentience and seek revenge on vegetable thieves.
TCH
チッ
But don't you think it's a little ridiculous to spend over half a year creating the sound effect for this part where the vegetables bite the thief's crotch?
GRIN
ニコッ
YOU IDIOT!
FWOM
ドッ

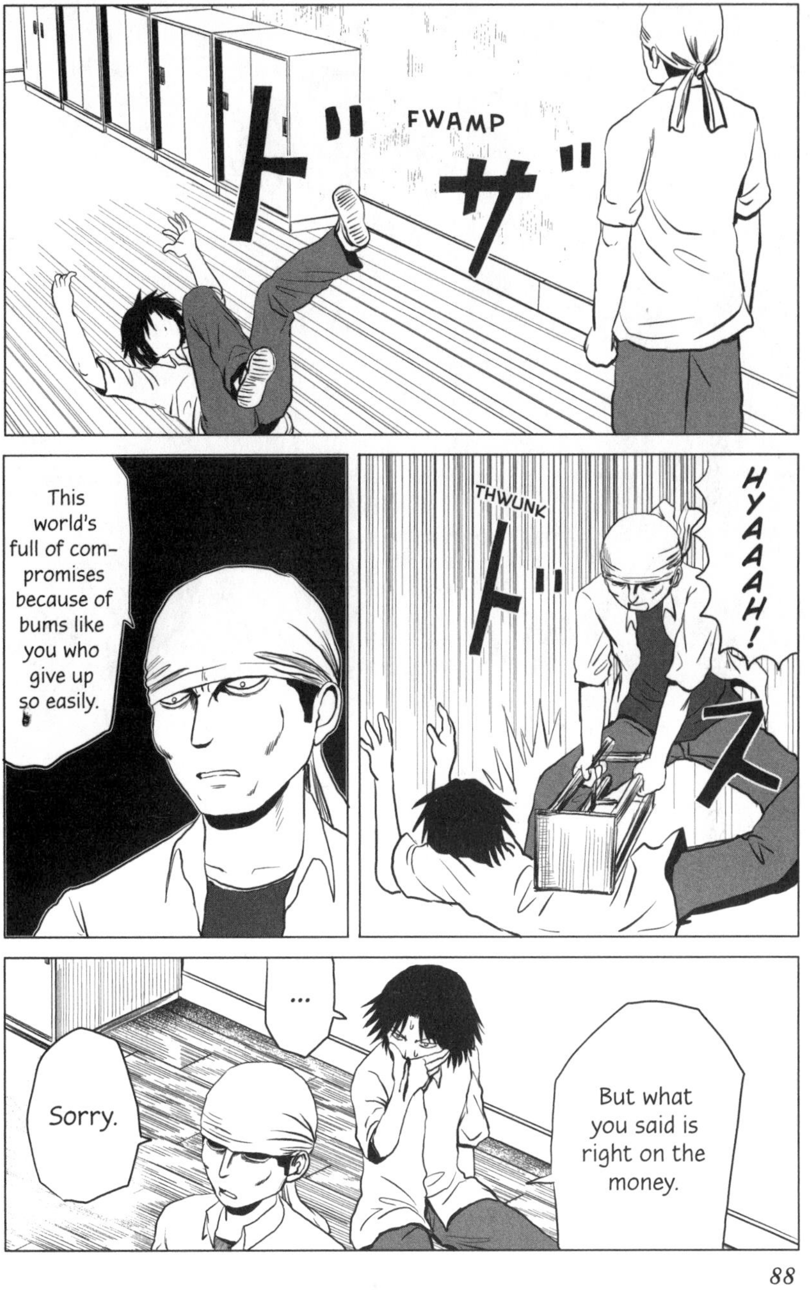
ド
ザ
FWAMP
HYAAAAH!
THWUNK
ド
ス
This world's full of com-promises because of bums like you who give up so easily.
...
But what you said is right on the money.
Sorry.

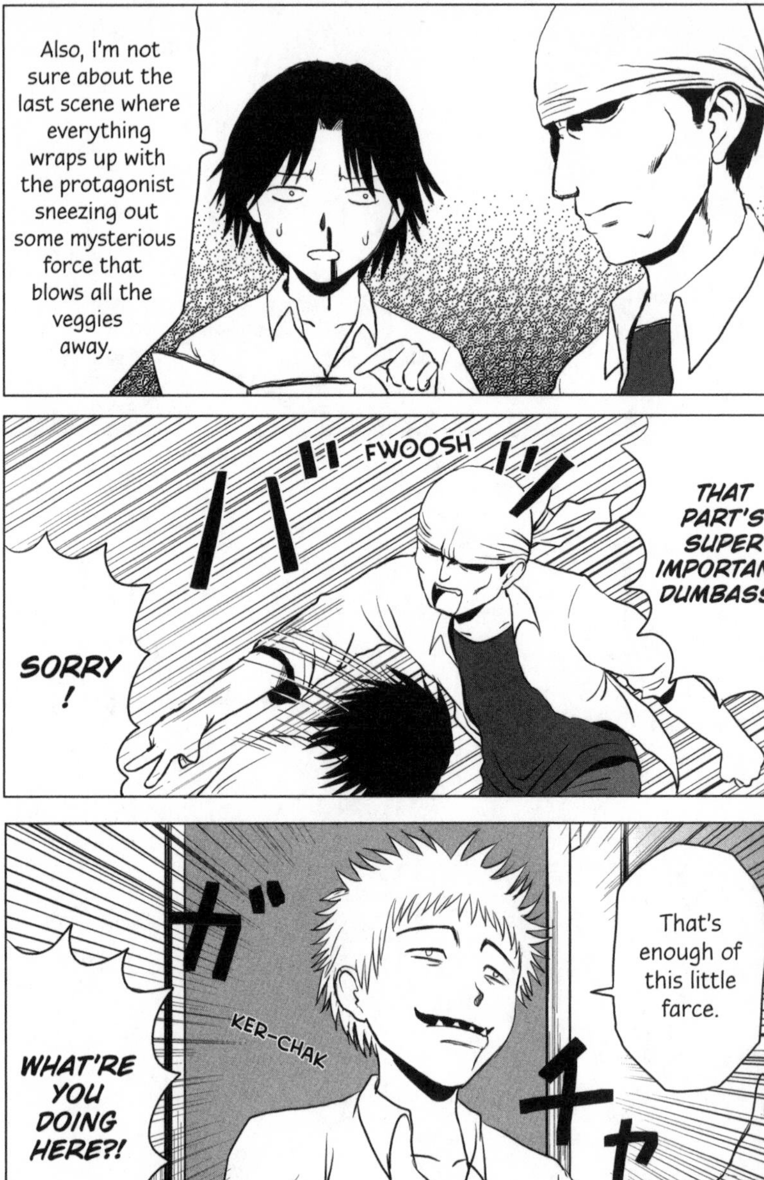

Also, I'm not sure about the last scene where everything wraps up with the protagonist sneezing out some mysterious force that blows all the veggies away.
バ
FWOOSH
ッ
THAT PART'S SUPER IMPORTANT, DUMBASS!
SORRY!
That's enough of this little farce.
イャ
ガ
KER-CHAK
WHAT'RE YOU DOING HERE?!

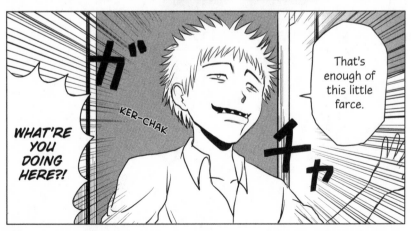

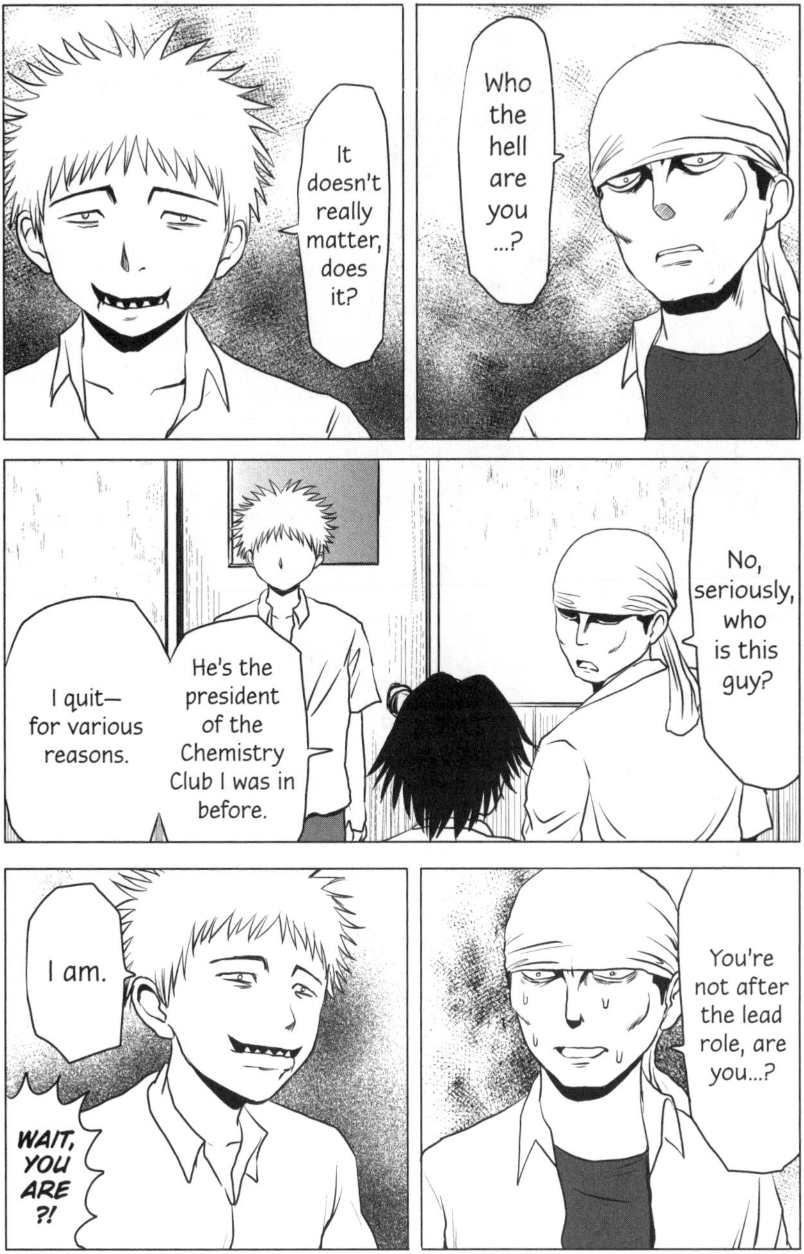
Who the hell are you ...?
It doesn't really matter, does it?
No, seriously, who is this guy?
He's the president of the Chemistry Club I was in before.
I quit— for various reasons.
You're not after the lead role, are you...?
I am.
WAIT, YOU ARE ?!

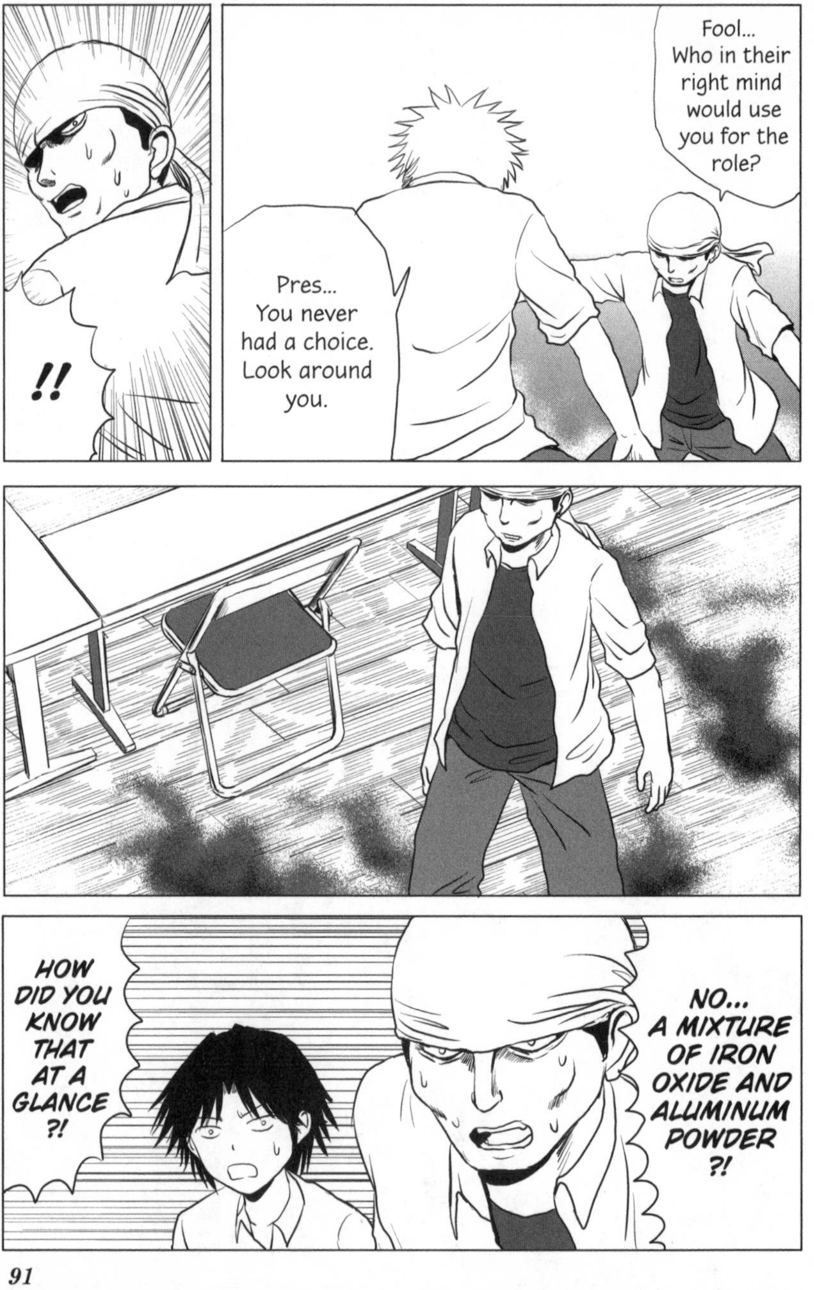
Fool... Who in their right mind would use you for the role?
Pres... You never had a choice. Look around you.
!!
NO... A MIXTURE OF IRON OXIDE AND ALUMINUM POWDER ?!
HOW DID YOU KNOW THAT AT A GLANCE ?!

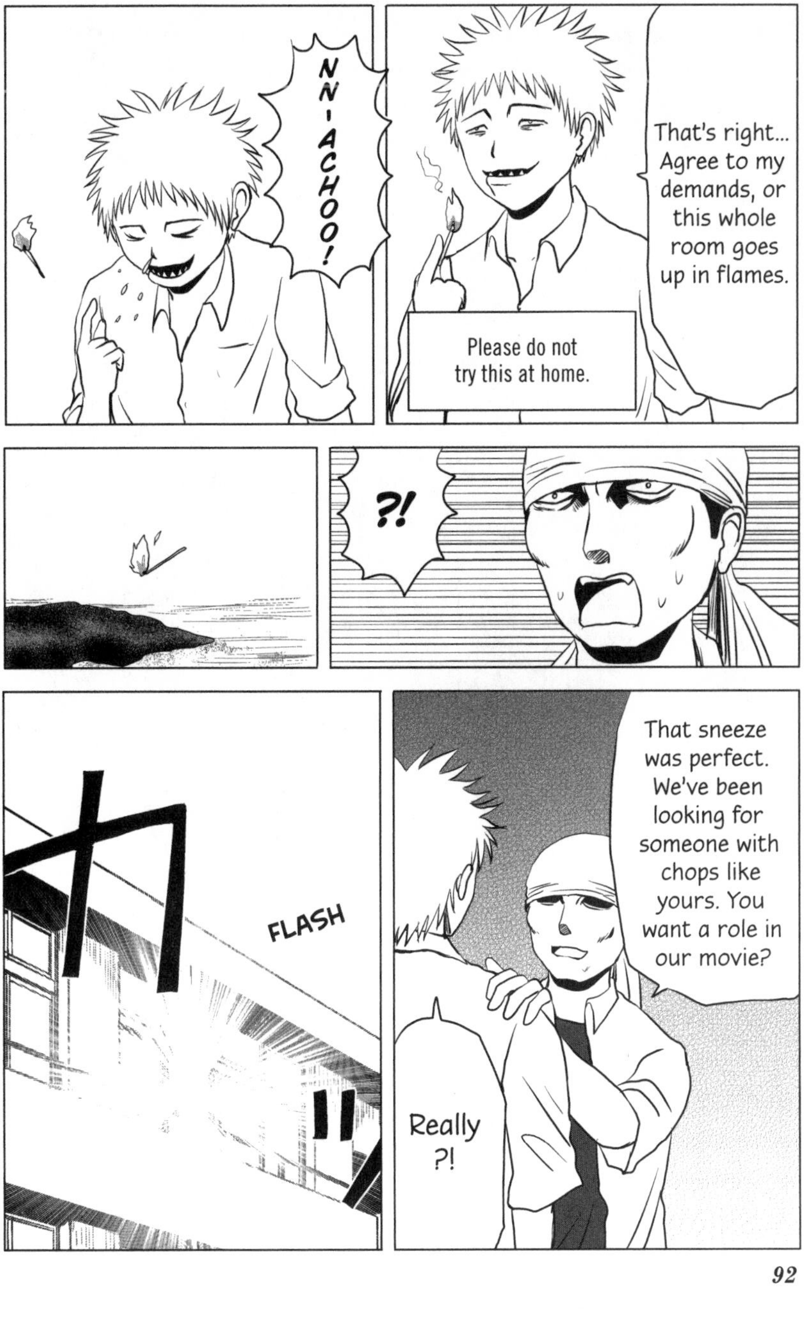
That's right... Agree to my demands, or this whole room goes up in flames.
Please do not try this at home.
NN-ACHOO!
?!
That sneeze was perfect. We've been looking for someone with chops like yours. You want a role in our movie?
Really ?!
FLASH

chapter 79:
high school boys and computer club

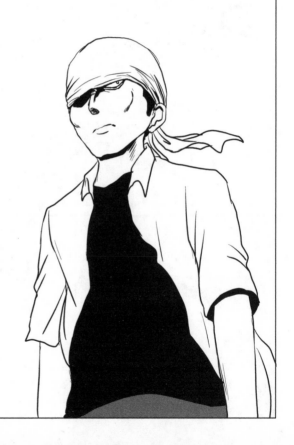

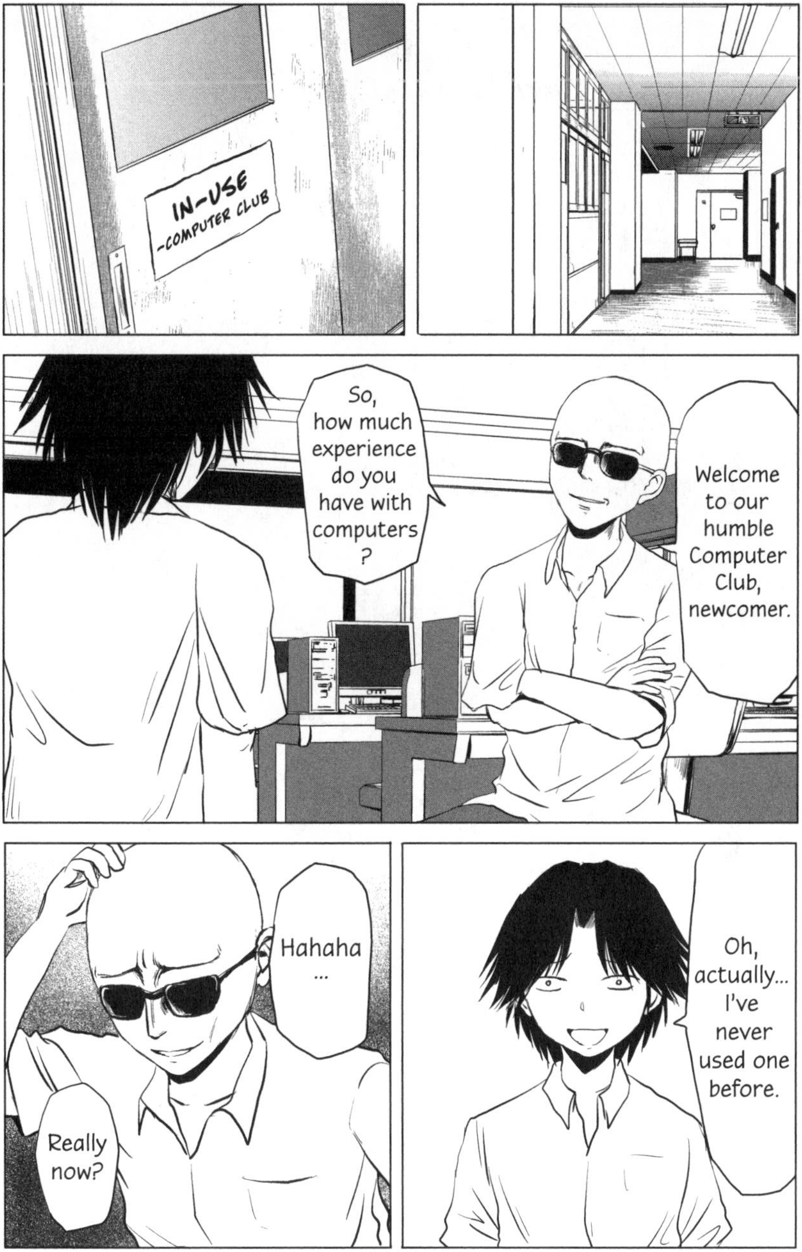
IN-USE
-COMPUTER CLUB
Welcome to our humble Computer Club, newcomer.
So, how much experience do you have with computers?
Oh, actually... I've never used one before.
Hahaha ...
Really now?

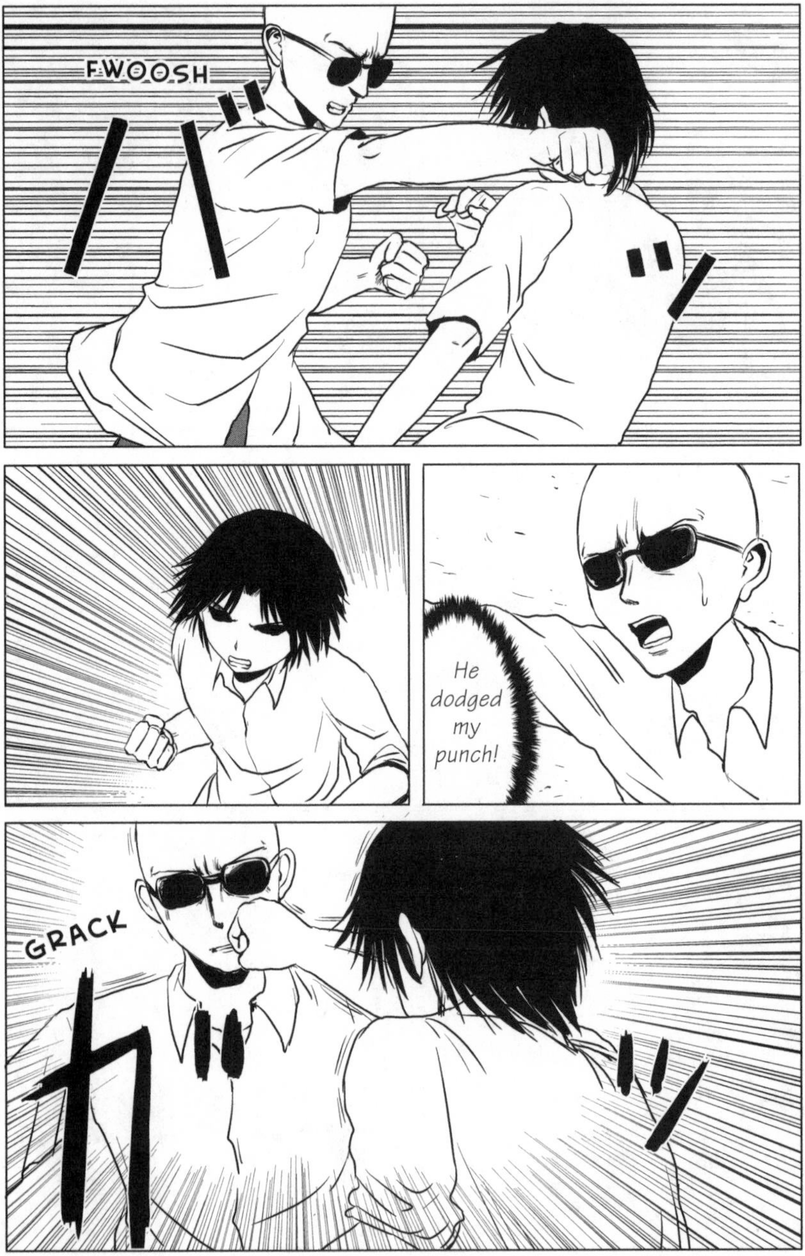
FWOOSH
He dodged my punch!
GRACK

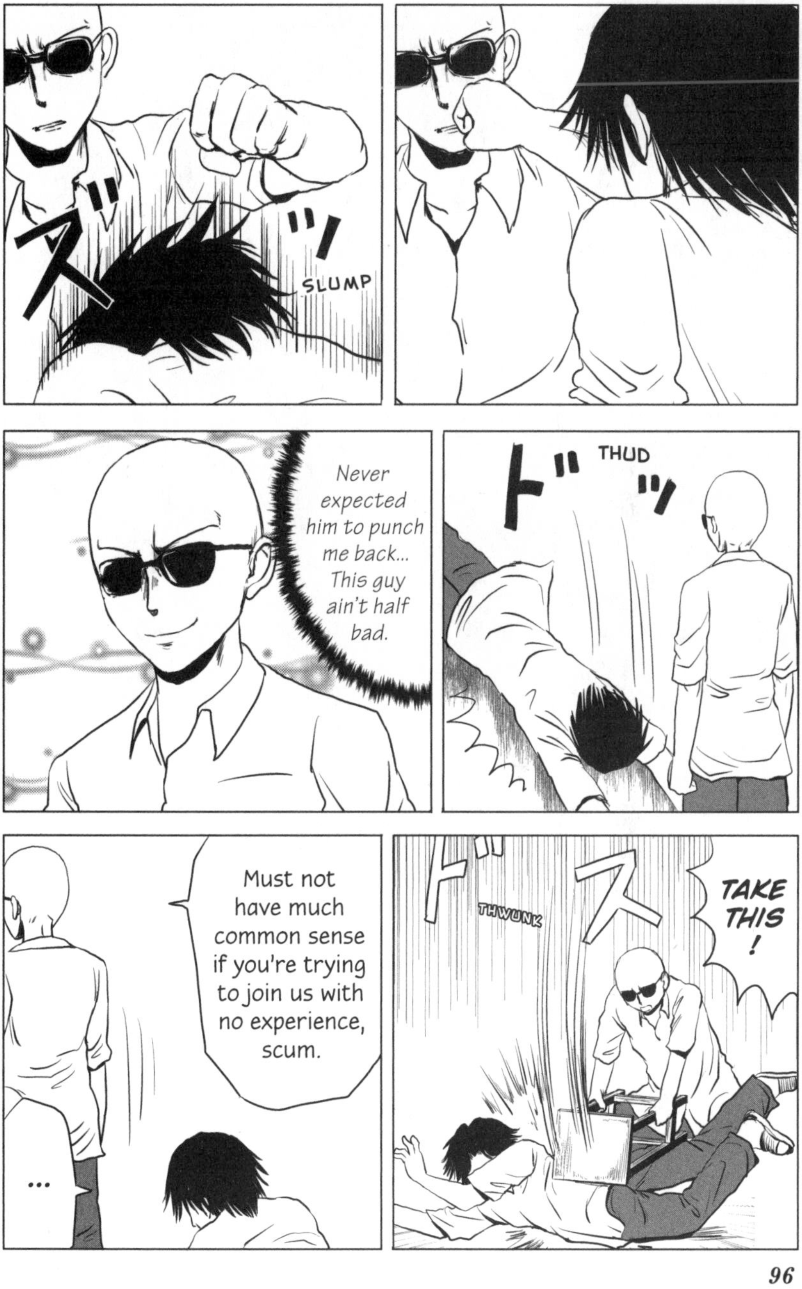
ズッ
SLUMP
ドッ
THUD
Never expected him to punch me back... This guy ain't half bad.
ドス
THWUNK
TAKE THIS!
Must not have much common sense if you're trying to join us with no experience, scum.
...

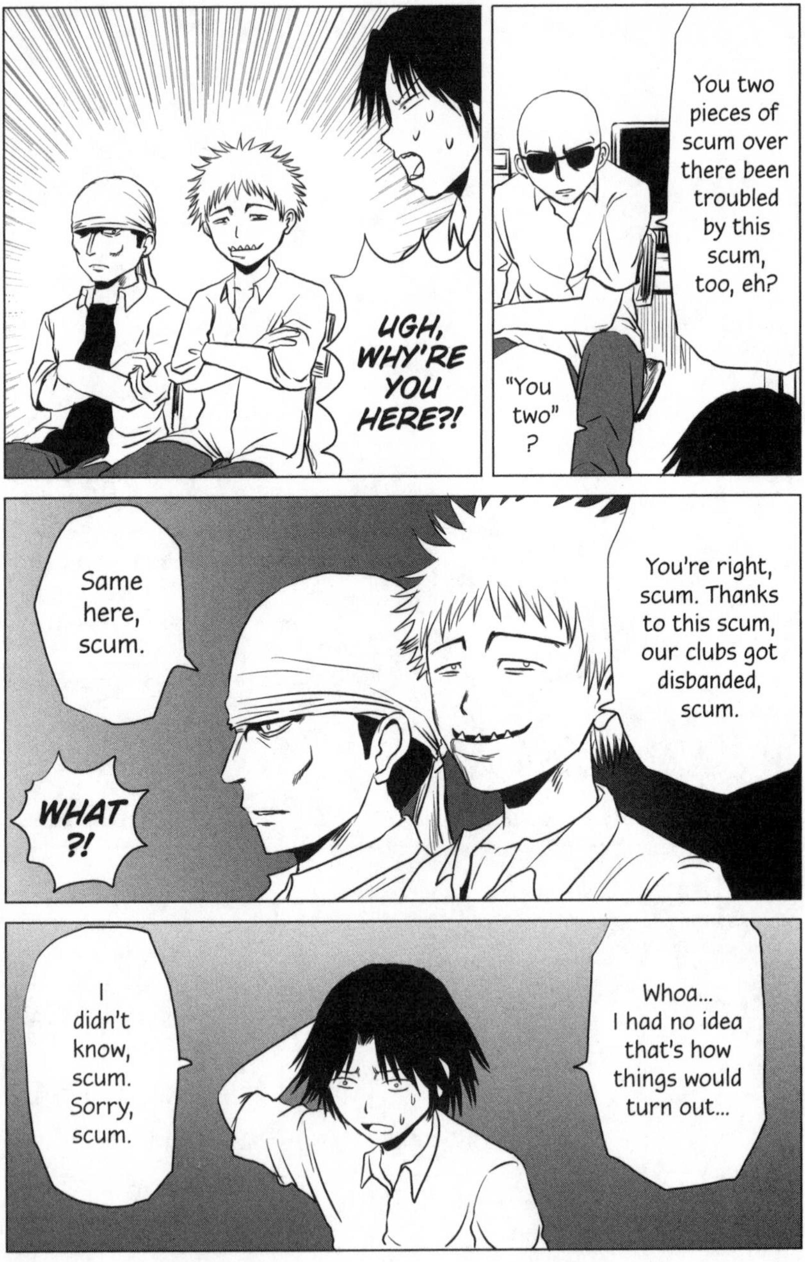
You two pieces of scum over there been troubled by this scum, too, eh?
"You two"?
UGH, WHY'RE YOU HERE?!
You're right, scum. Thanks to this scum, our clubs got disbanded, scum.
Same here, scum.
WHAT?!
Whoa... I had no idea that's how things would turn out...
I didn't know, scum. Sorry, scum.

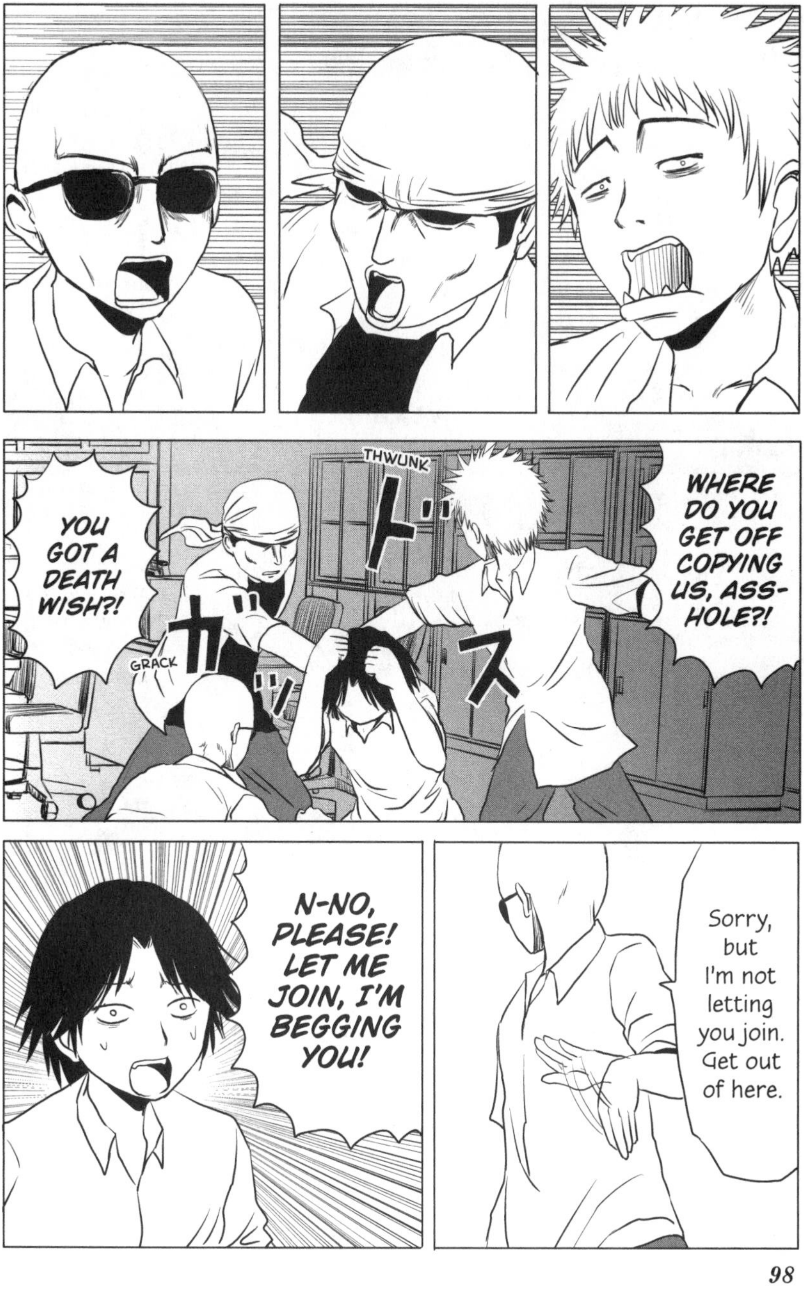
WHERE DO YOU GET OFF COPYING US, ASS-HOLE?!
THWUNK
ドス
YOU GOT A DEATH WISH?!
ガッ
GRACK
Sorry, but I'm not letting you join. Get out of here.
N-NO, PLEASE! LET ME JOIN, I'M BEGGING YOU!

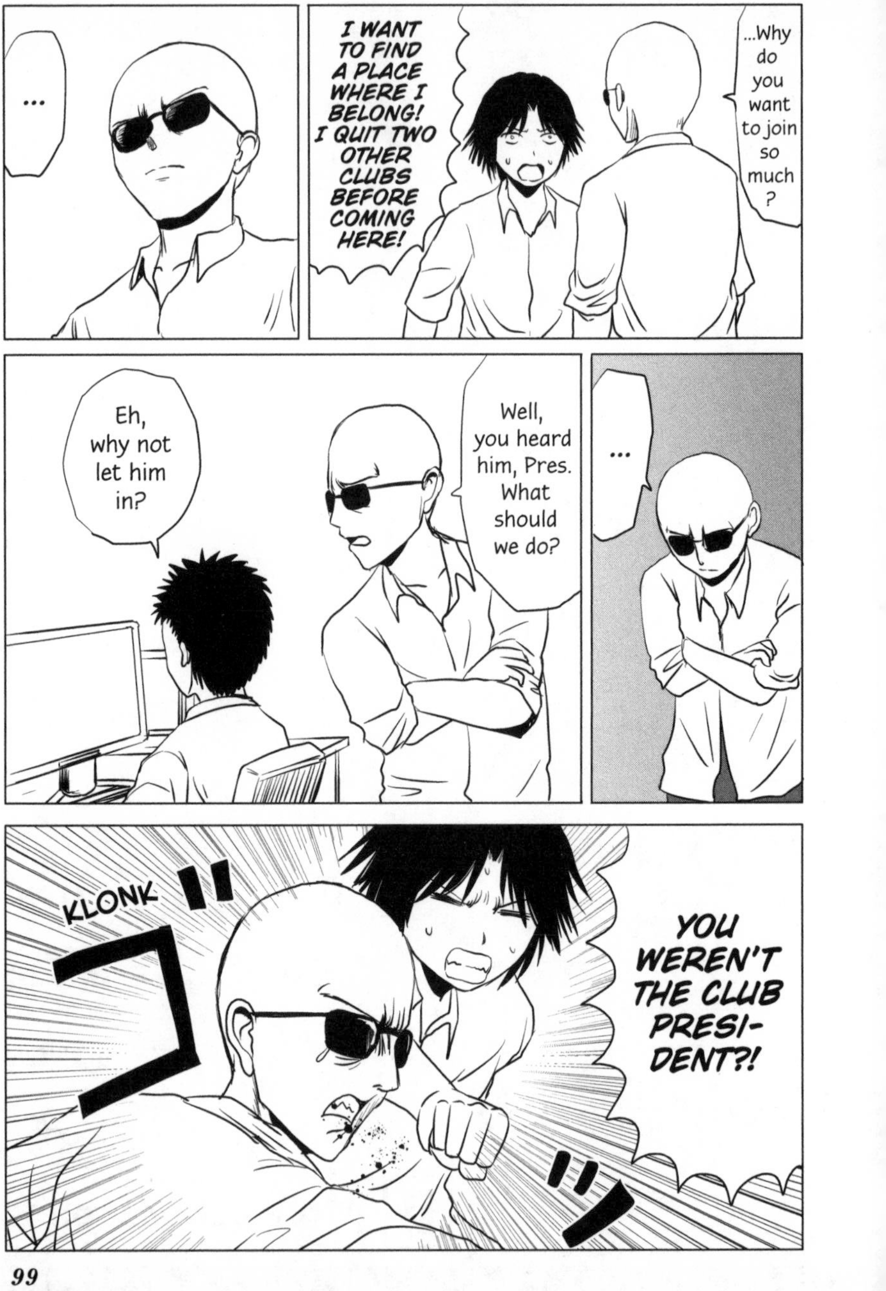
...Why do you want to join so much?
I WANT TO FIND A PLACE WHERE I BELONG! I QUIT TWO OTHER CLUBS BEFORE COMING HERE!
...
...
Well, you heard him, Pres. What should we do?
Eh, why not let him in?
YOU WEREN'T THE CLUB PRESI-DENT?!
KLONK

the

daily

lives

of

5 high school boys

chapter 80:
high school boys and arts and crafts club

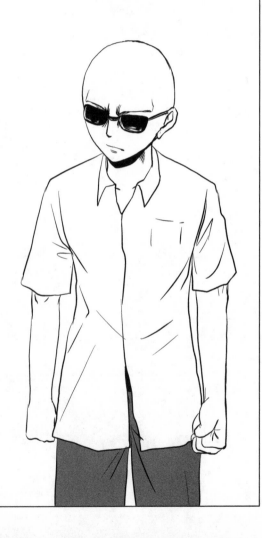

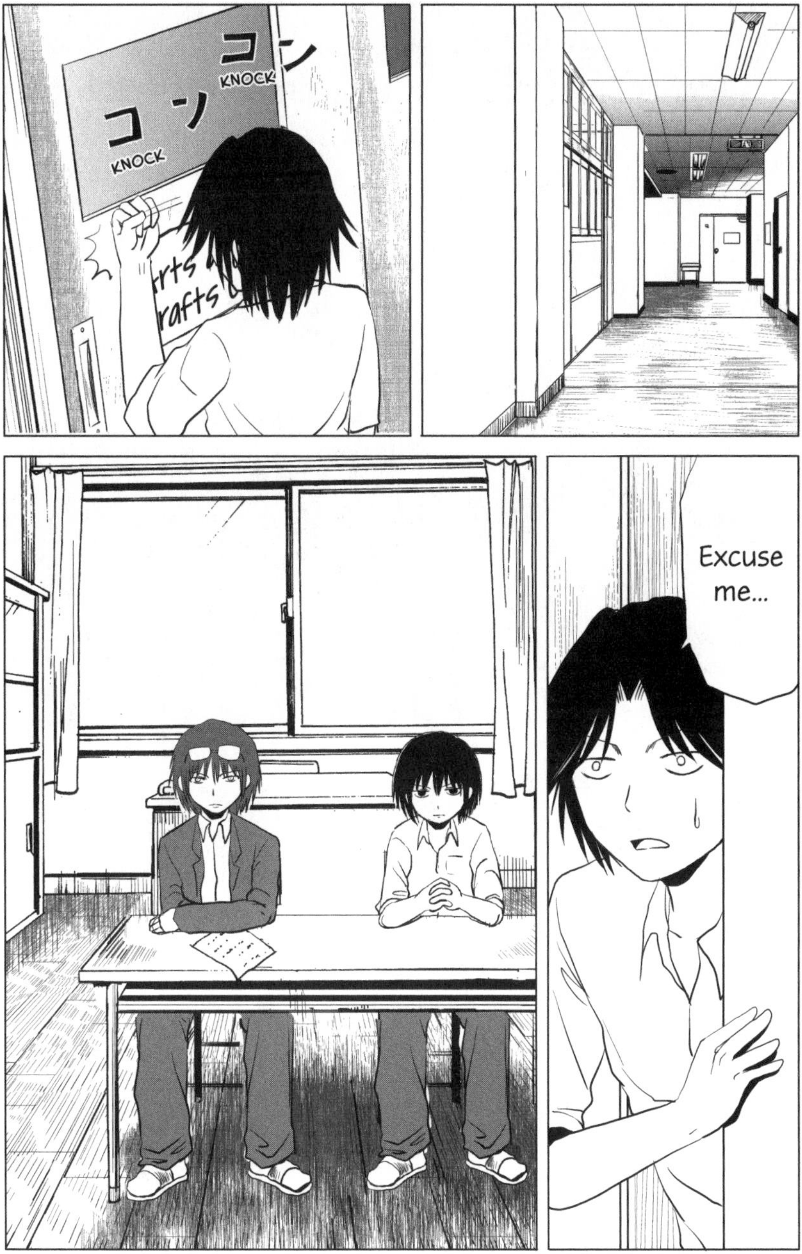
コン
KNOCK
コン
KNOCK
Excuse me...

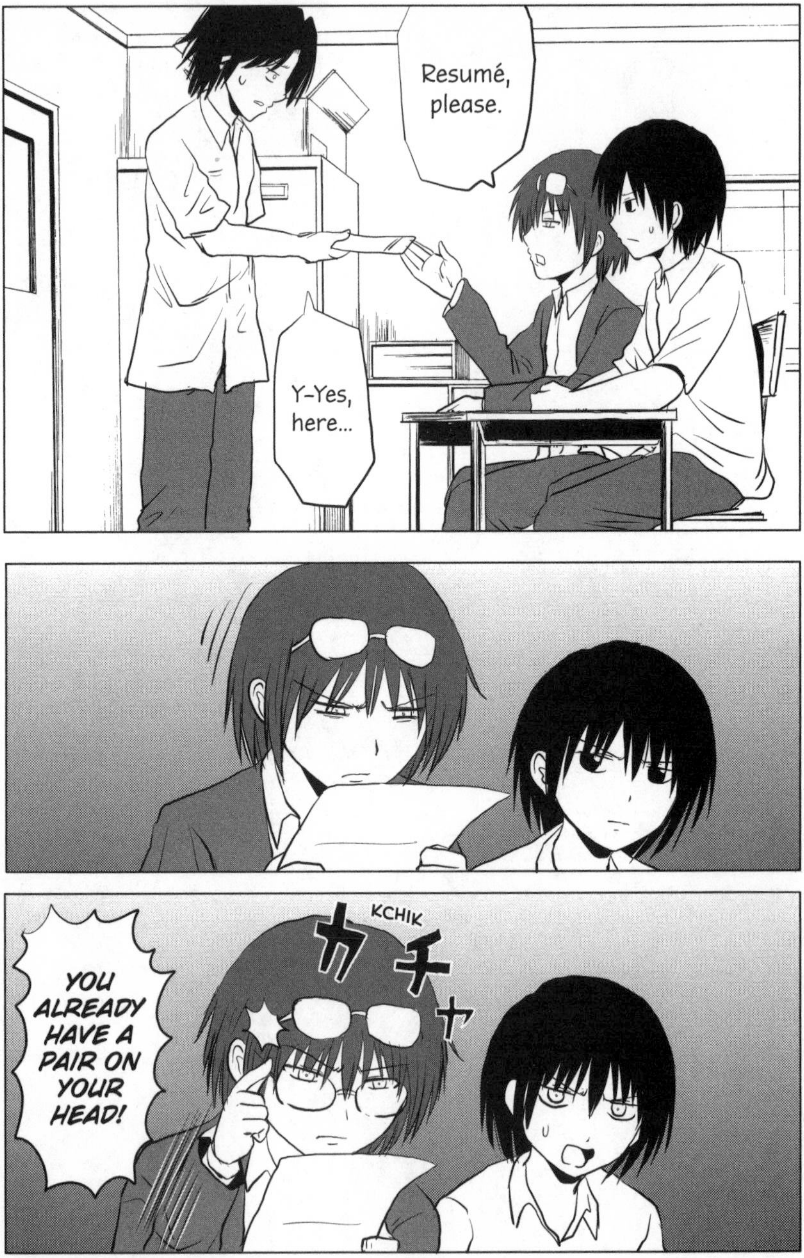
Resumé, please.
Y-Yes, here...
カチャ
KCHIK
YOU ALREADY HAVE A PAIR ON YOUR HEAD!

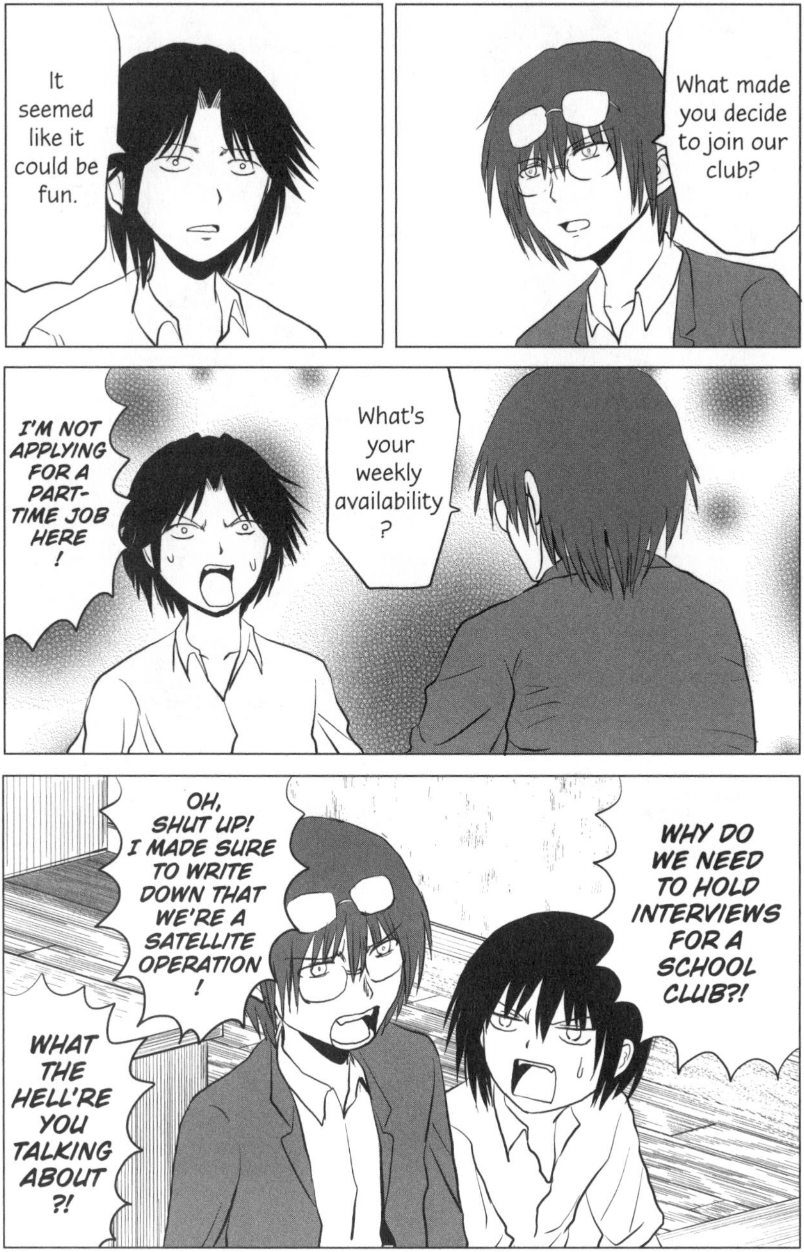
What made you decide to join our club?
It seemed like it could be fun.
What's your weekly availability?
I'M NOT APPLYING FOR A PART-TIME JOB HERE!
WHY DO WE NEED TO HOLD INTERVIEWS FOR A SCHOOL CLUB?!
OH, SHUT UP! I MADE SURE TO WRITE DOWN THAT WE'RE A SATELLITE OPERATION!
WHAT THE HELL'RE YOU TALKING ABOUT?!

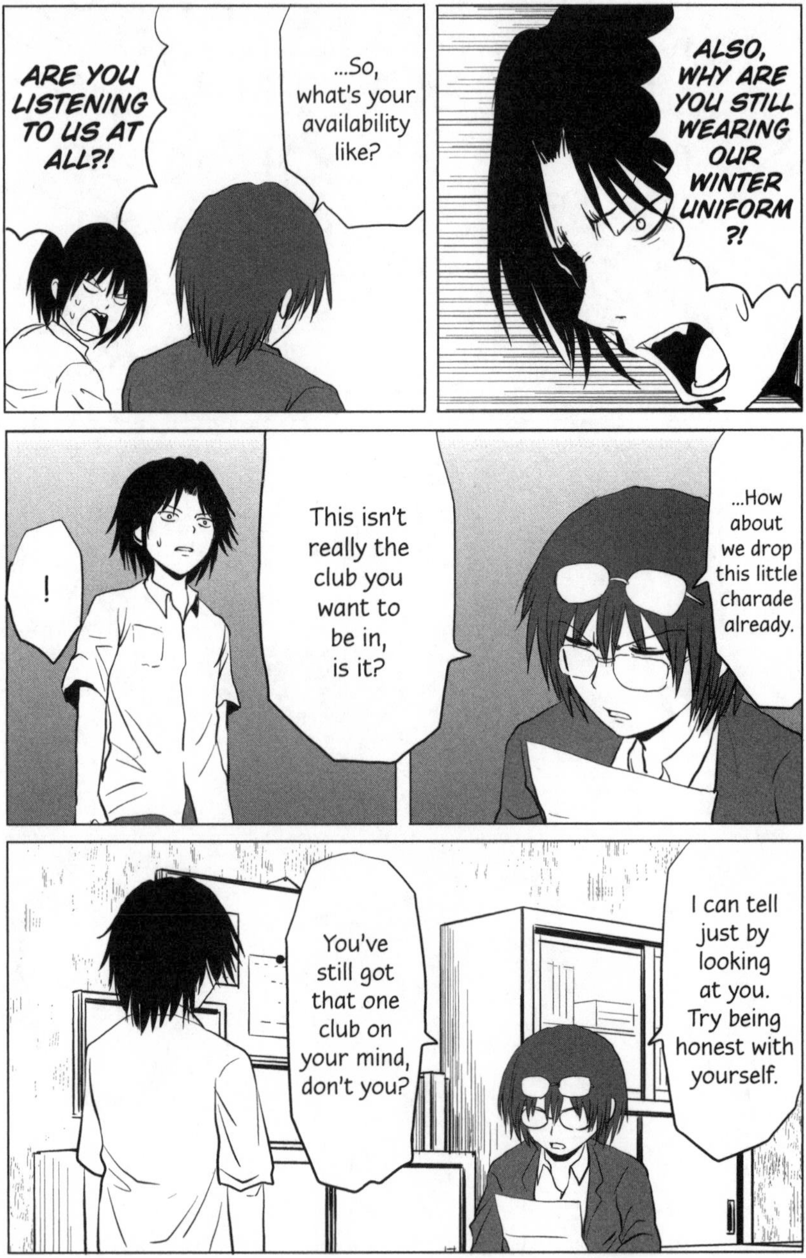
ALSO, WHY ARE YOU STILL WEARING OUR WINTER UNIFORM ?!
...So, what's your availability like?
ARE YOU LISTENING TO US AT ALL?!
...How about we drop this little charade already.
This isn't really the club you want to be in, is it?
!
I can tell just by looking at you. Try being honest with yourself.
You've still got that one club on your mind, don't you?

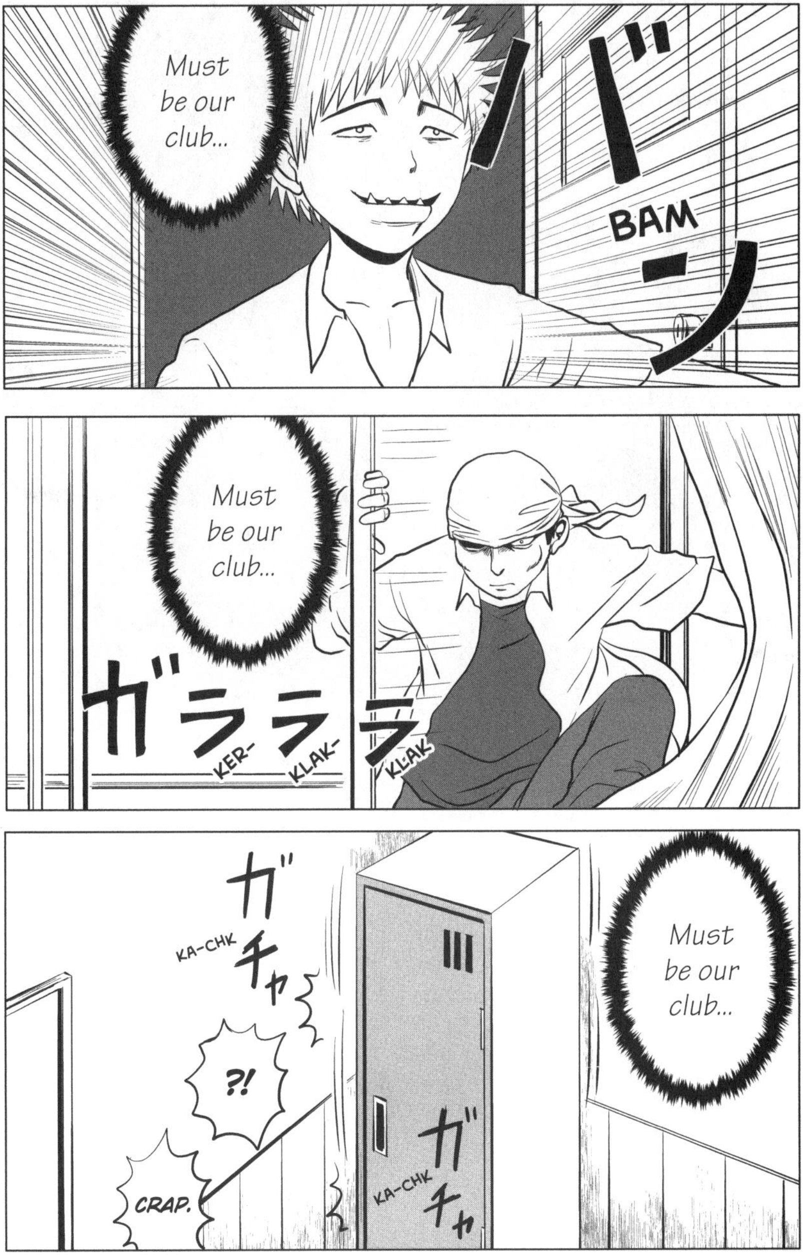
バーン
BAM
Must be our club...
Must be our club...
ガラララ
KER-KLAK-KLAK
Must be our club...
ガチャ
KA-CHK
?!
ガチャ
KA-CHK
CRAP.

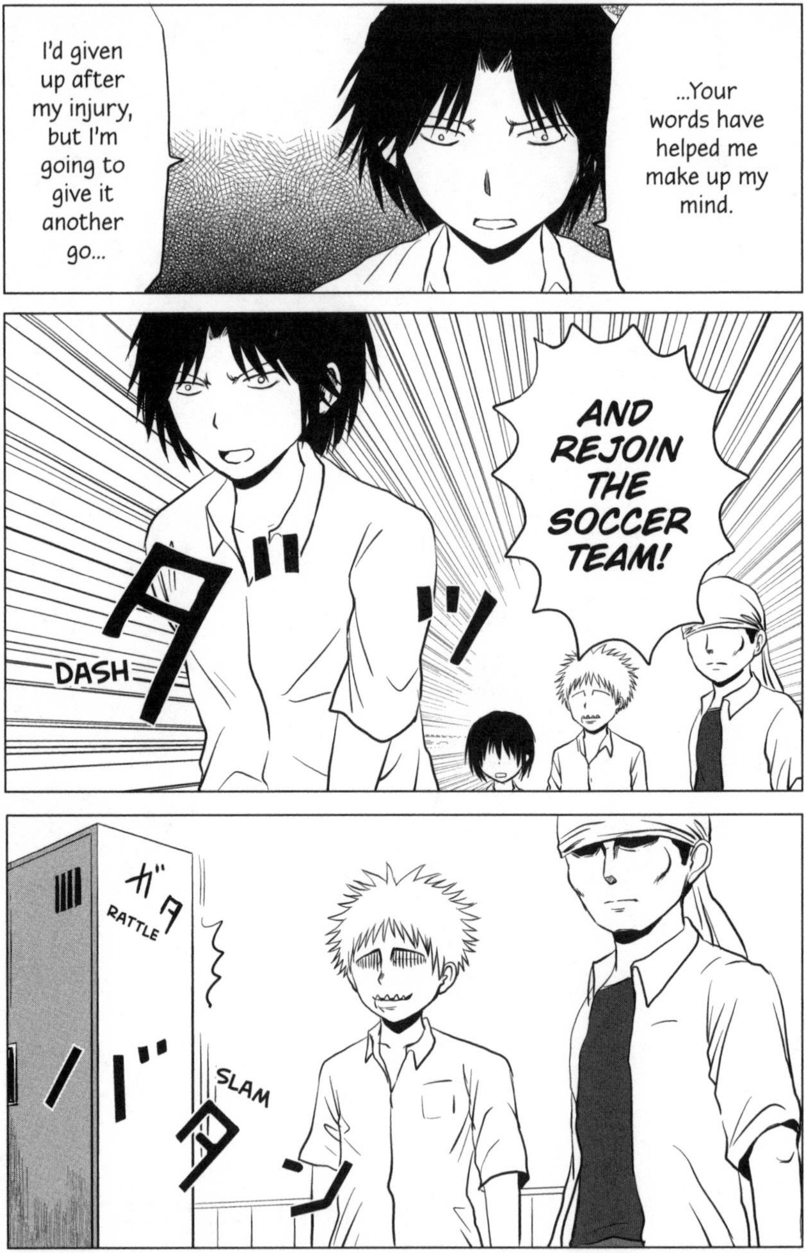
...Your words have helped me make up my mind.
I'd given up after my injury, but I'm going to give it another go...
AND REJOIN THE SOCCER TEAM!
ダッ
DASH
ガタ
RATTLE
バタン
SLAM

the

daily

lives

of

5 high school boys

chapter 81:
high school boys and annoyances

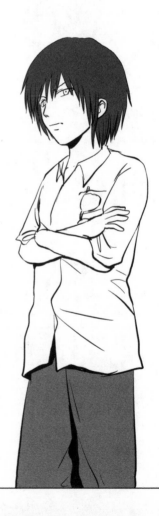

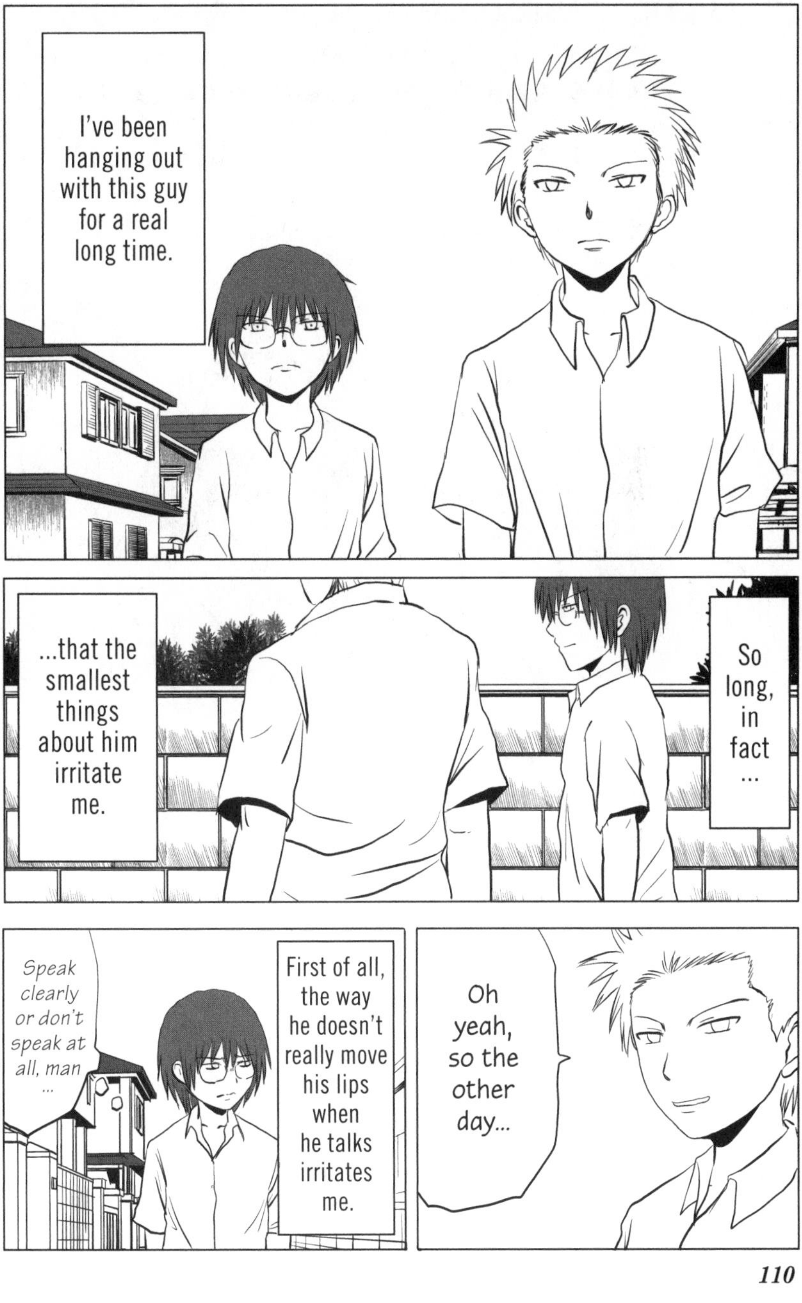
I've been hanging out with this guy for a real long time.
So long, in fact...
...that the smallest things about him irritate me.
Oh yeah, so the other day...
First of all, the way he doesn't really move his lips when he talks irritates me.
Speak clearly or don't speak at all, man...

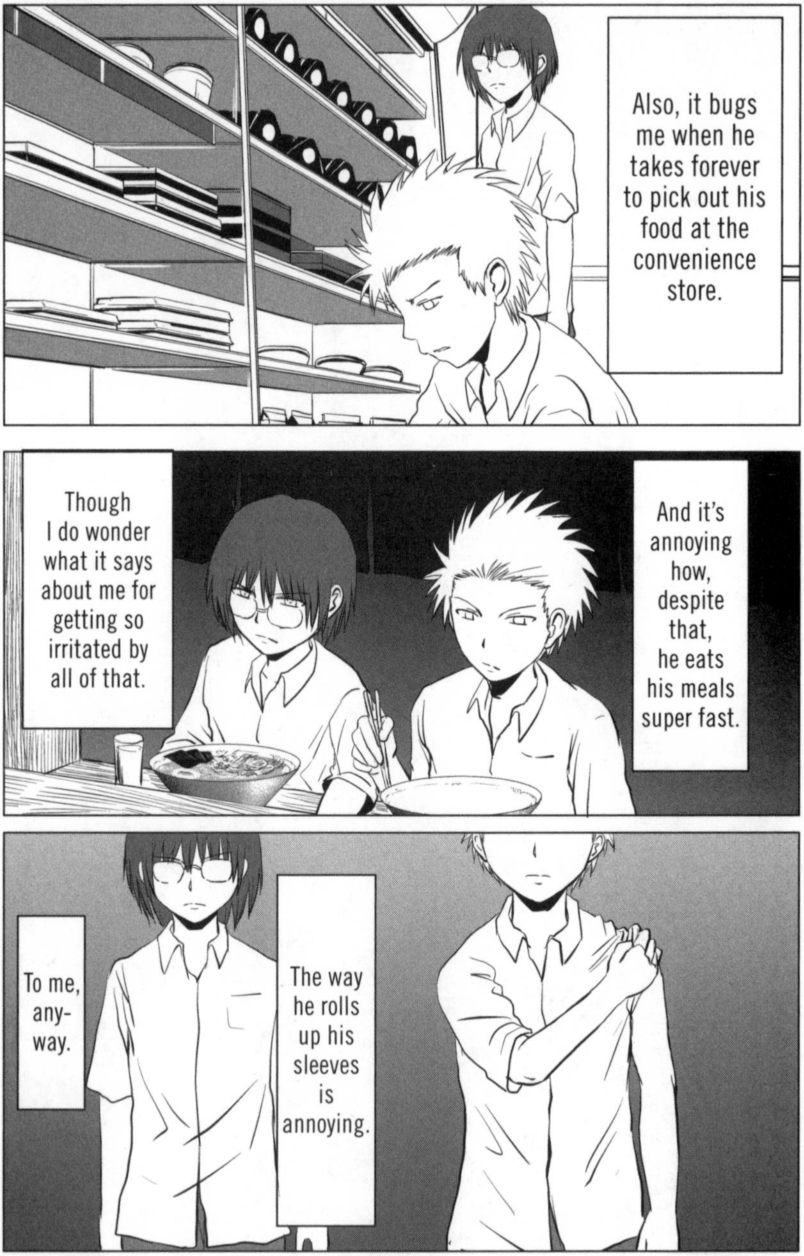
Also, it bugs me when he takes forever to pick out his food at the convenience store.
And it's annoying how, despite that, he eats his meals super fast.
Though I do wonder what it says about me for getting so irritated by all of that.
The way he rolls up his sleeves is annoying.
To me, anyway.

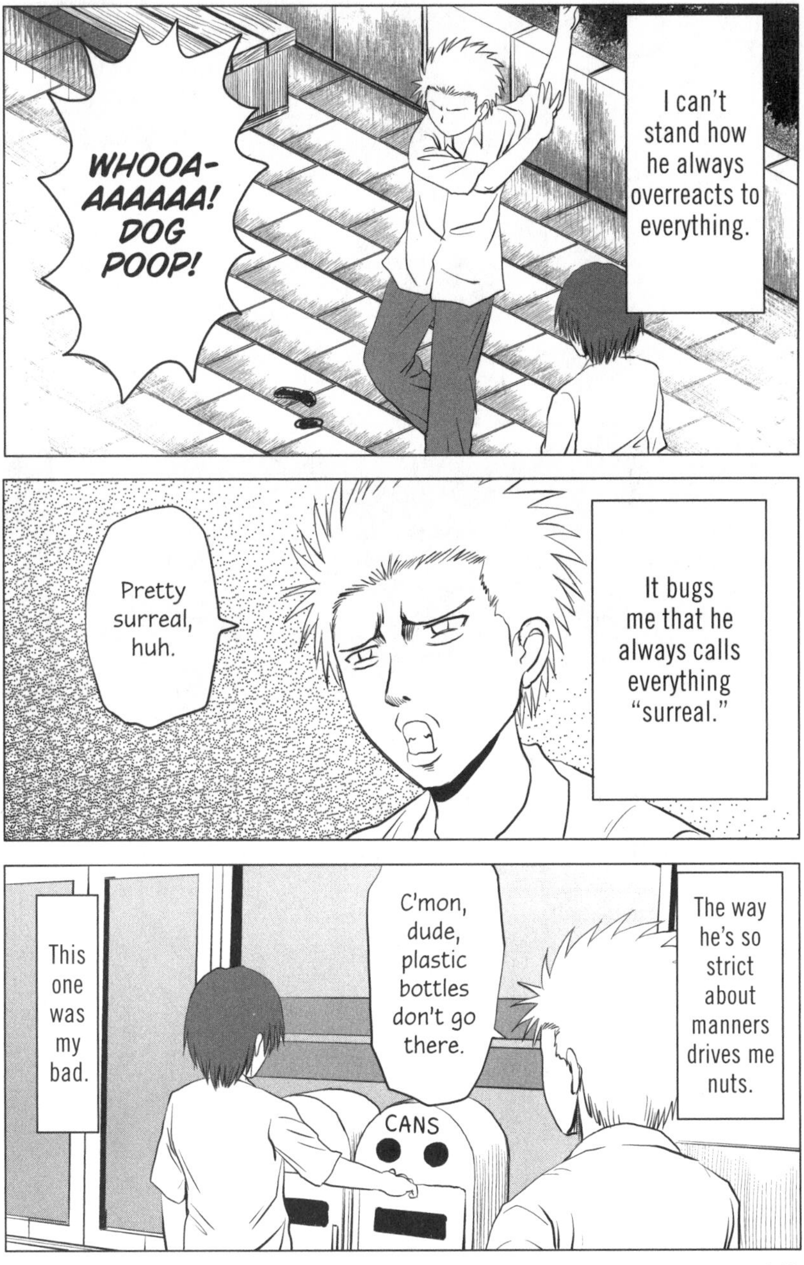
I can't stand how he always overreacts to everything.
WHOOA-AAAAAA! DOG POOP!
It bugs me that he always calls everything "surreal."
Pretty surreal, huh.
The way he's so strict about manners drives me nuts.
C'mon, dude, plastic bottles don't go there.
CANS
This one was my bad.

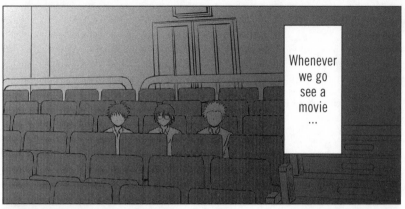

Whenever we go see a movie ...

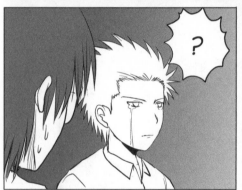

?

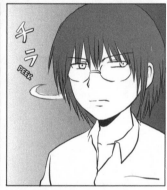

PEEK

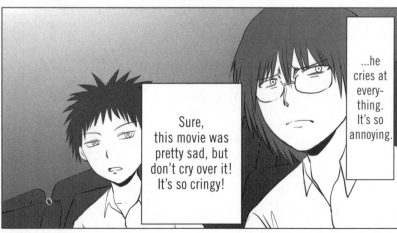

Sure, this movie was pretty sad, but don't cry over it! It's so cringy!

...he cries at everything. It's so annoying.

113

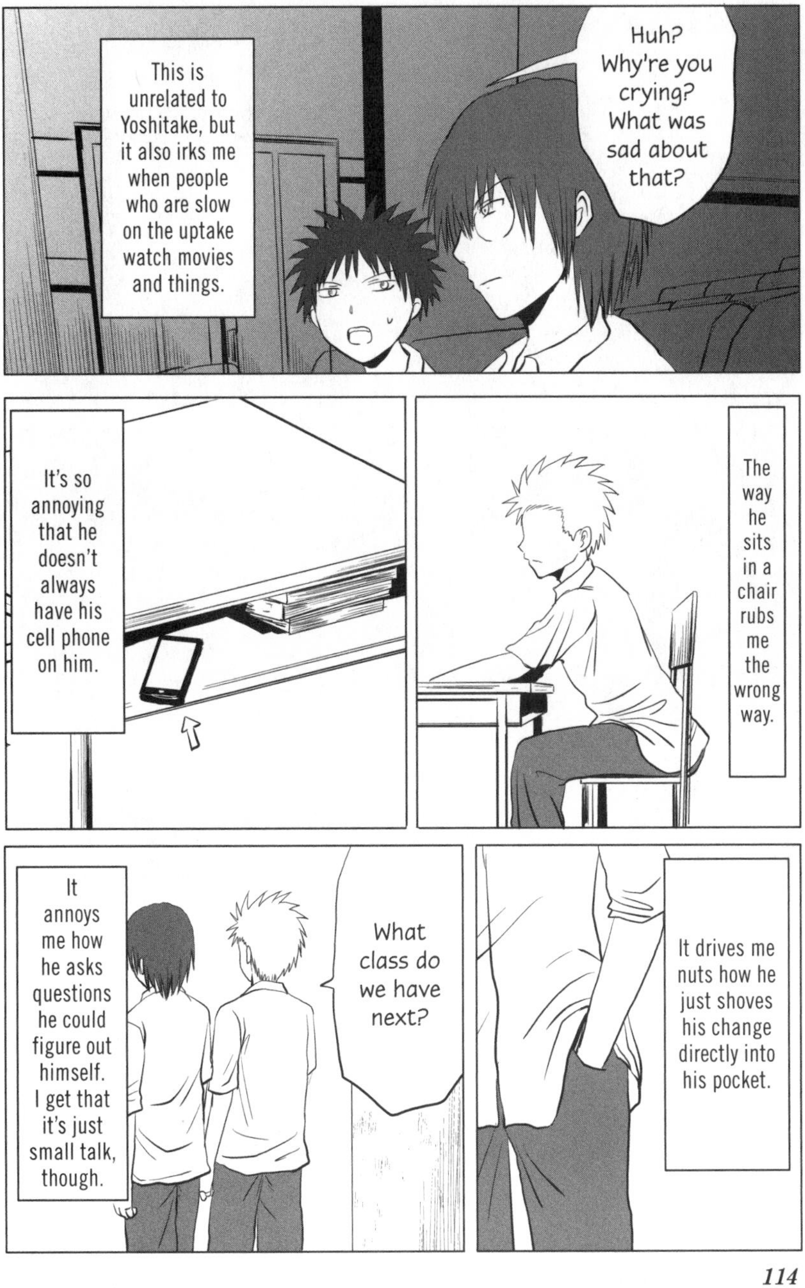
Huh? Why're you crying? What was sad about that?
This is unrelated to Yoshitake, but it also irks me when people who are slow on the uptake watch movies and things.
The way he sits in a chair rubs me the wrong way.
It's so annoying that he doesn't always have his cell phone on him.
It drives me nuts how he just shoves his change directly into his pocket.
What class do we have next?
It annoys me how he asks questions he could figure out himself. I get that it's just small talk, though.

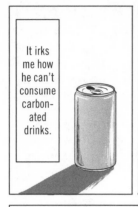

It bugs me when he acts stupid and waits for me to call him out.
It irks me how he can't consume carbon-ated drinks.
It's annoying how he goes to the bathroom an awful lot.
It gets on my nerves when I stay home from school, and he'll already have his notes ready for me to copy the following day.
The way he always brings canned coffee with him whenever he comes over is annoying.

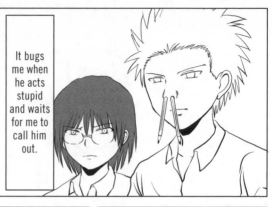

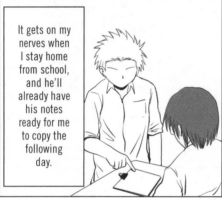

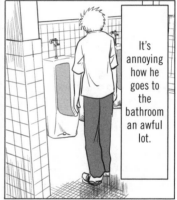

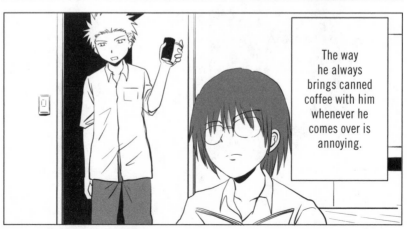

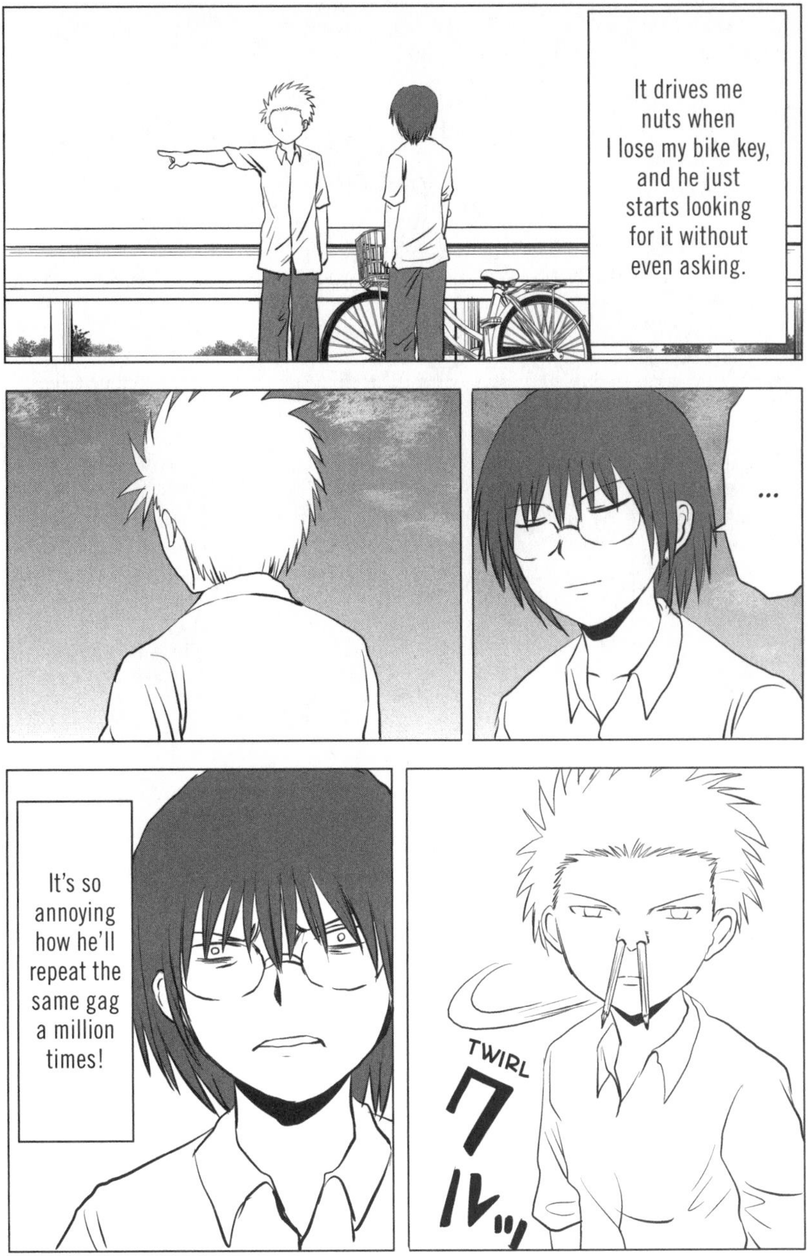
It drives me nuts when I lose my bike key, and he just starts looking for it without even asking.
...
TWIRL
クルッ
It's so annoying how he'll repeat the same gag a million times!

the

daily

lives

of

high school boys 5

special one-shot: ***high school girls are bizarre***

Main Characters:

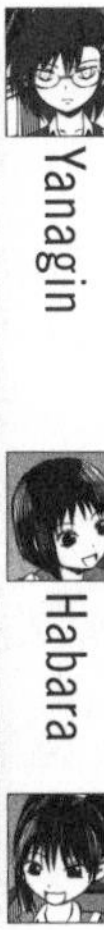

Yanagin

Habara

Ikushima

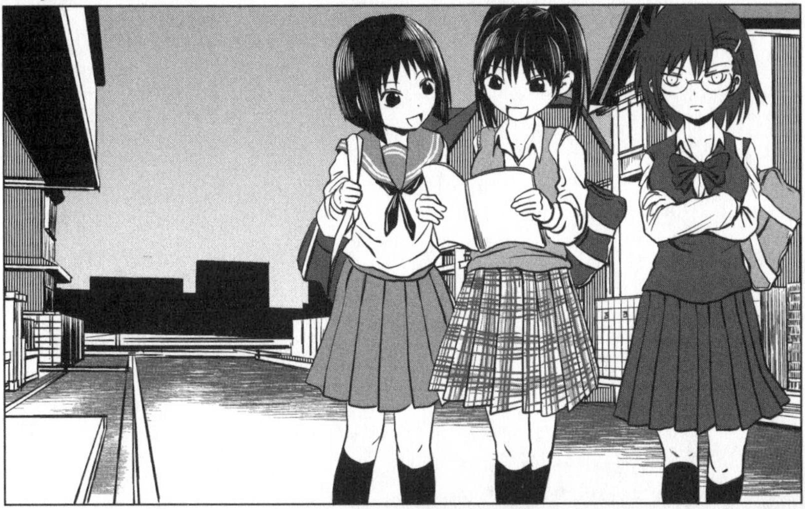

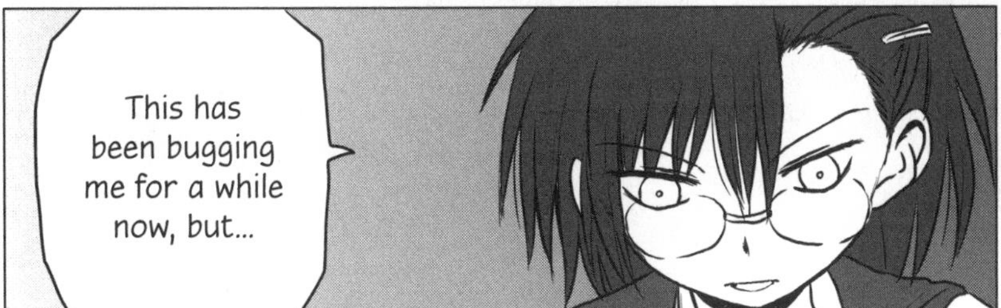
This has been bugging me for a while now, but...

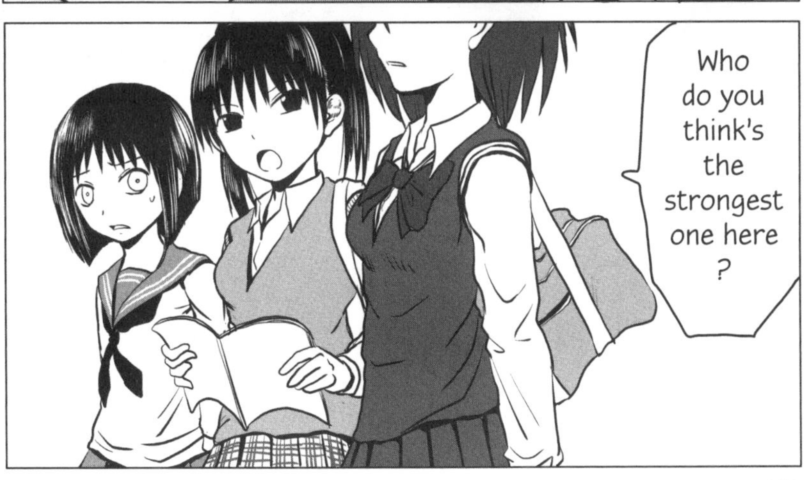
Who do you think's the strongest one here ?

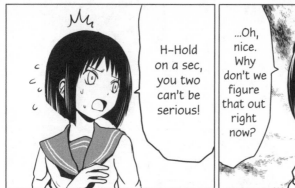

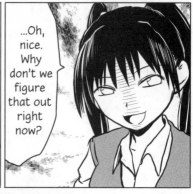

...Oh, nice. Why don't we figure that out right now?
H-Hold on a sec, you two can't be serious!
We can't pretend to be all buddy-buddy forever...
Wait, why not, though ...?
Let's not do this. It's stupid. Who cares who's strong or not?
Feelin' confident, eh, you monster?
What, scared of losing?
Ugh, c'mon ...

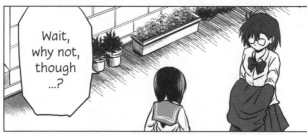

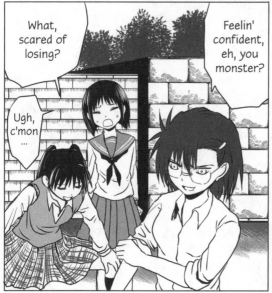

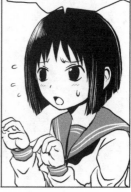

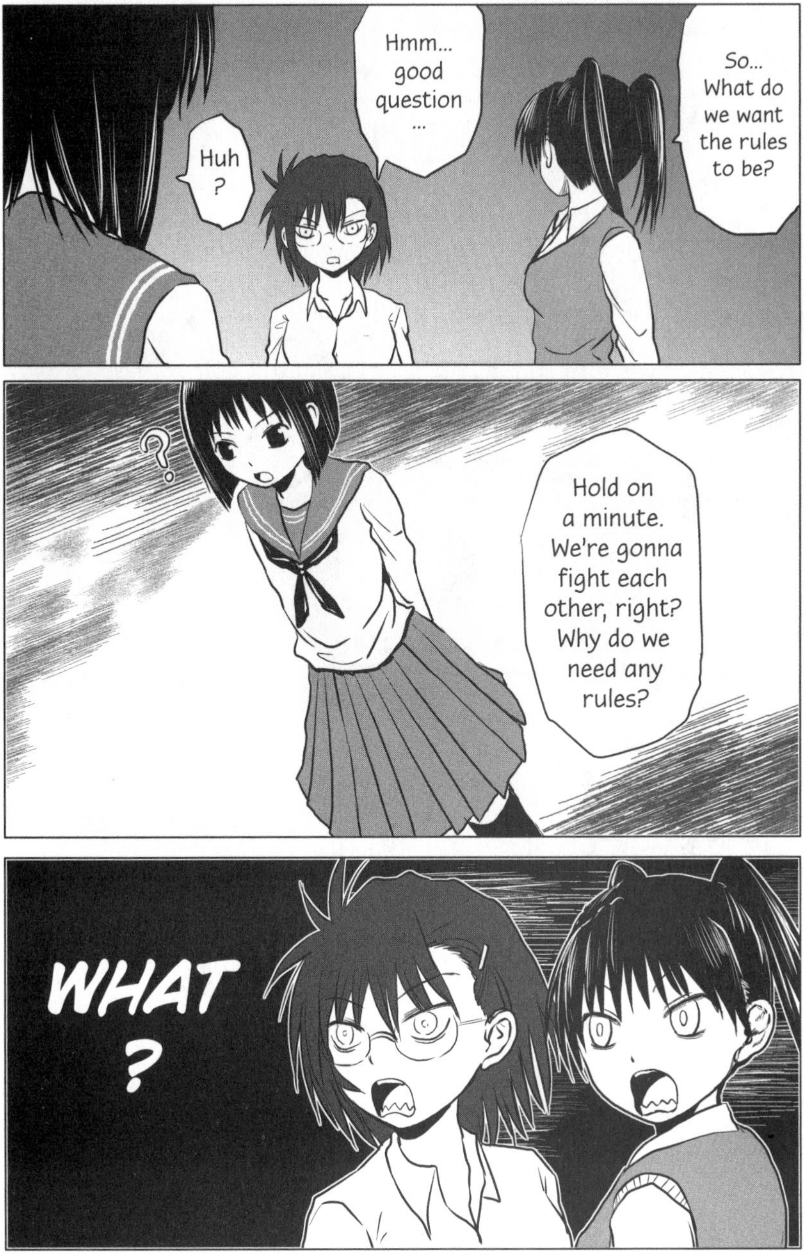
So... What do we want the rules to be?
Hmm... good question ...
Huh ?
Hold on a minute. We're gonna fight each other, right? Why do we need any rules?
?
WHAT ?

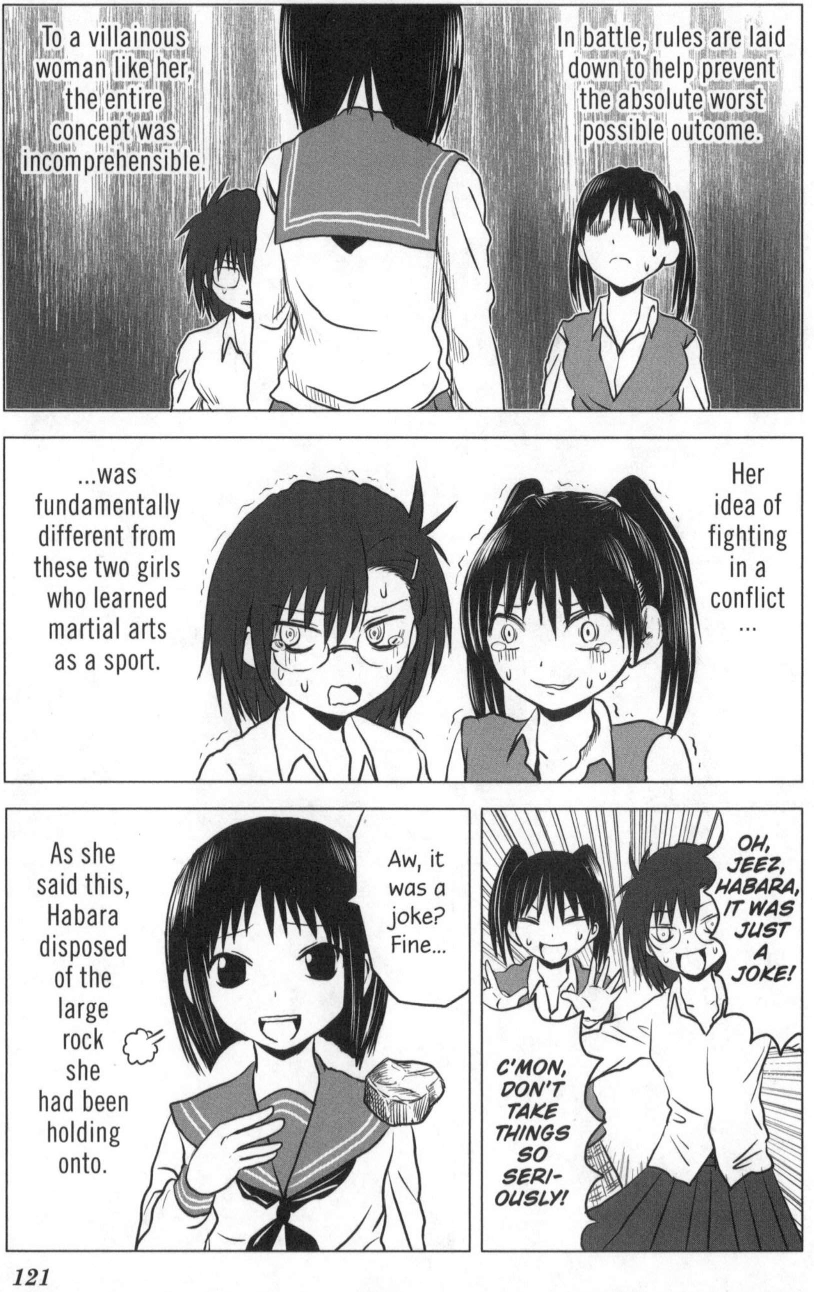
In battle, rules are laid down to help prevent the absolute worst possible outcome.
To a villainous woman like her, the entire concept was incomprehensible.
Her idea of fighting in a conflict ...
...was fundamentally different from these two girls who learned martial arts as a sport.
OH, JEEZ, HABARA, IT WAS JUST A JOKE!
C'MON, DON'T TAKE THINGS SO SERI-OUSLY!
Aw, it was a joke? Fine...
As she said this, Habara disposed of the large rock she had been holding onto.

chapter 12: antagonistic upperclassmen

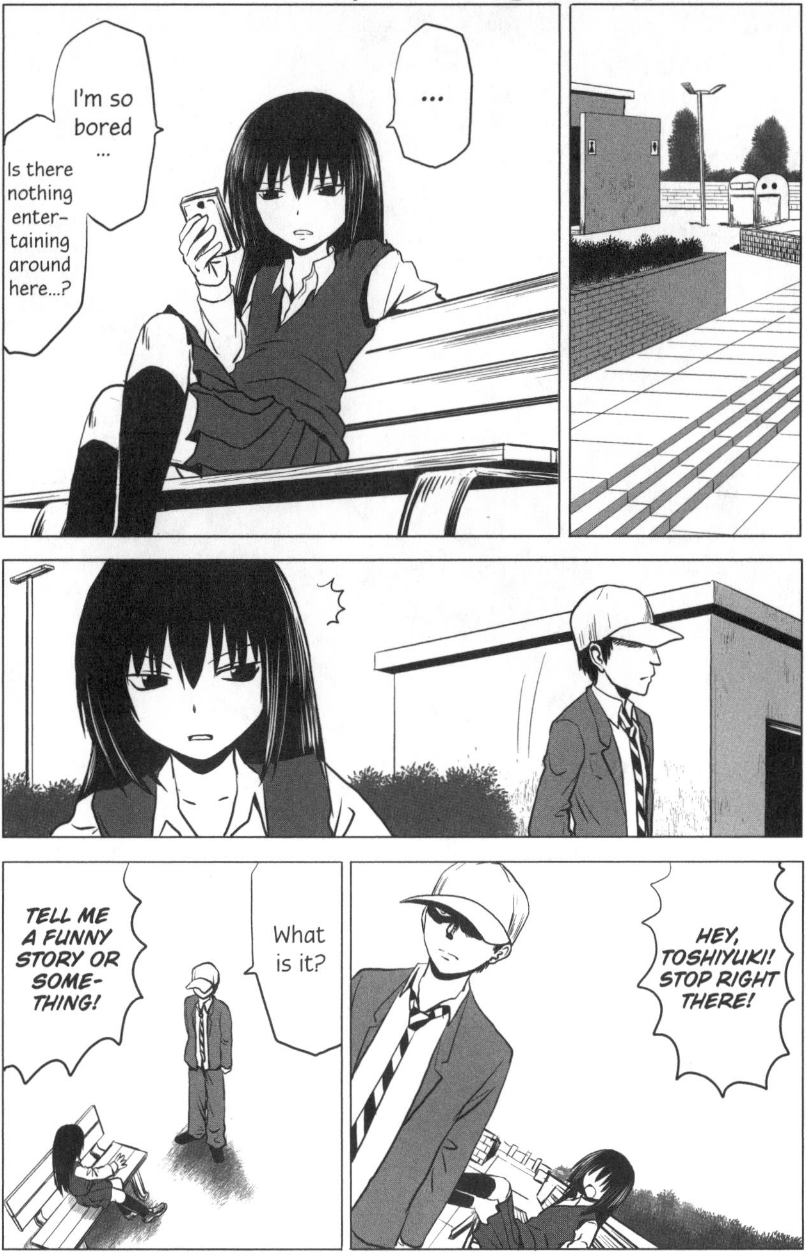
...
I'm so bored ...
Is there nothing entertaining around here...?
HEY, TOSHIYUKI! STOP RIGHT THERE!
What is it?
TELL ME A FUNNY STORY OR SOMETHING!

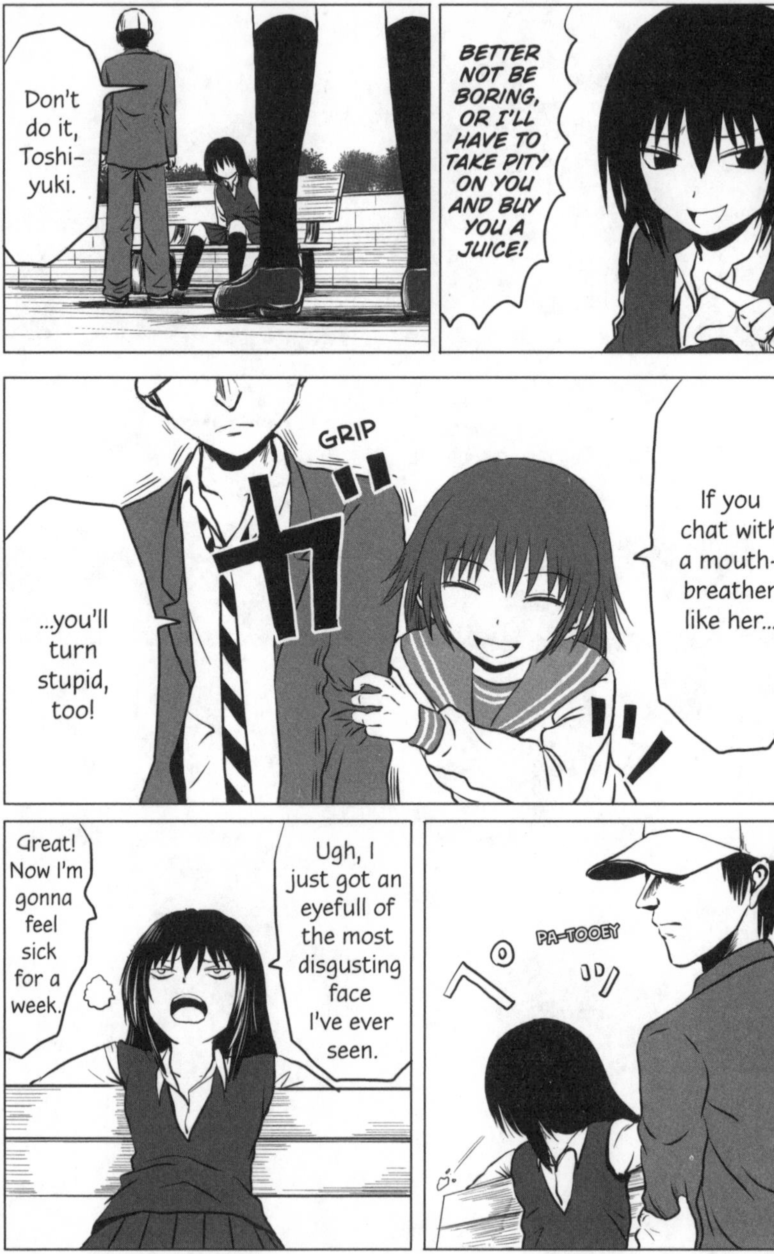

BETTER NOT BE BORING, OR I'LL HAVE TO TAKE PITY ON YOU AND BUY YOU A JUICE!
Don't do it, Toshi-yuki.
If you chat with a mouth-breather like her...
GRIP
...you'll turn stupid, too!
PA-TOOEY
Ugh, I just got an eyefull of the most disgusting face I've ever seen.
Great! Now I'm gonna feel sick for a week.

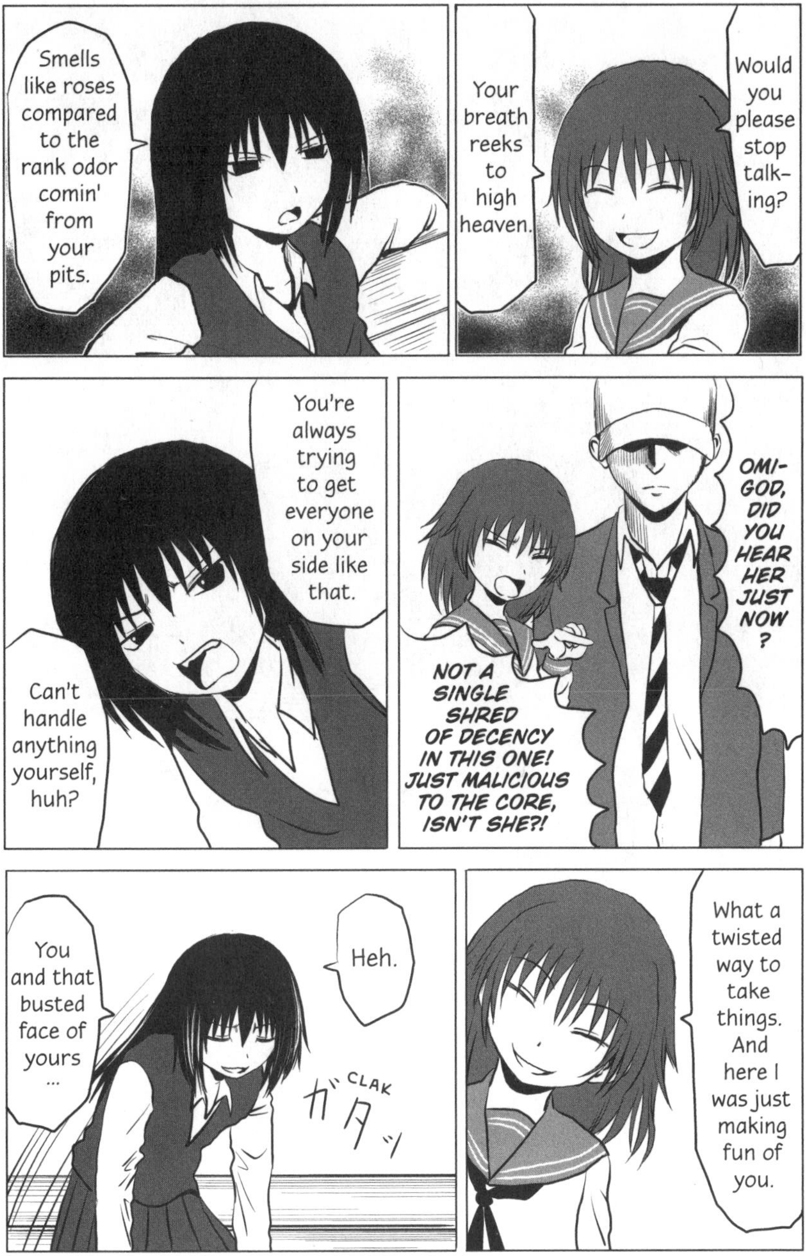
Would you please stop talk-ing?
Your breath reeks to high heaven.
Smells like roses compared to the rank odor comin' from your pits.
OMI-GOD, DID YOU HEAR HER JUST NOW?
NOT A SINGLE SHRED OF DECENCY IN THIS ONE! JUST MALICIOUS TO THE CORE, ISN'T SHE?!
You're always trying to get everyone on your side like that.
Can't handle anything yourself, huh?
What a twisted way to take things. And here I was just making fun of you.
Heh.
You and that busted face of yours ...
ガタッ
CLAK

MM
MMM
MM
MM
RMMM
FLASH
FWOOSH
?!

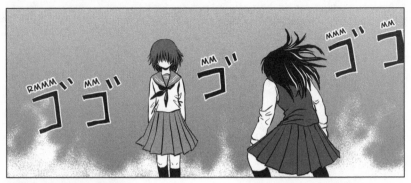

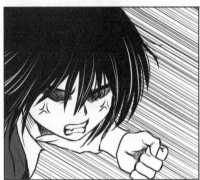

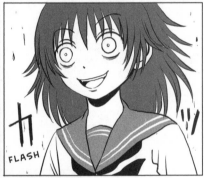

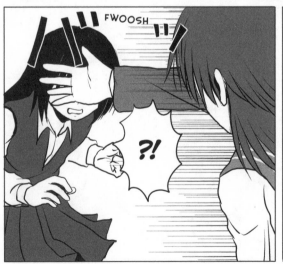

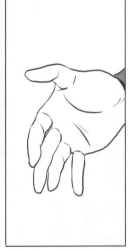

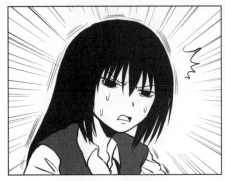
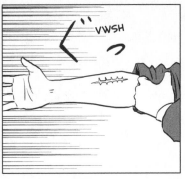

VWSH

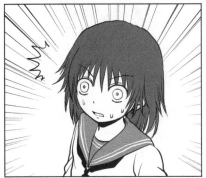
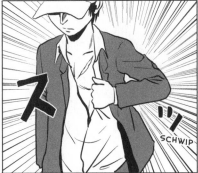

SCHWIP

ス

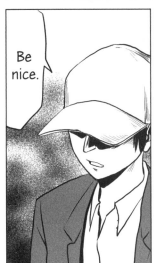

Be
nice.

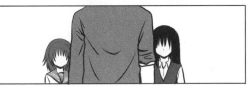

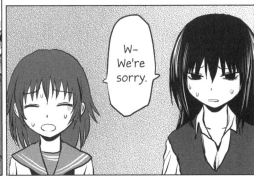

W–
We're
sorry.

126

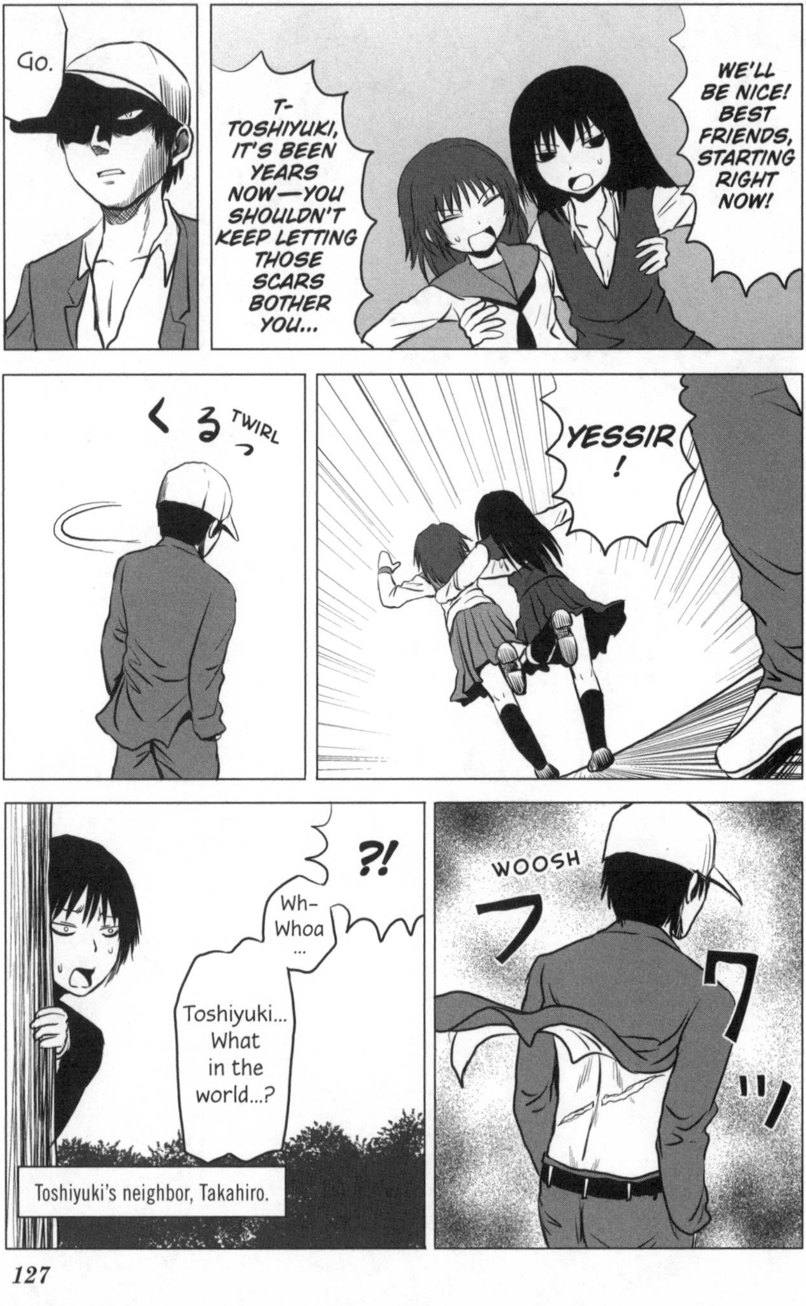
WE'LL BE NICE! BEST FRIENDS, STARTING RIGHT NOW!
T- TOSHIYUKI, IT'S BEEN YEARS NOW—YOU SHOULDN'T KEEP LETTING THOSE SCARS BOTHER YOU...
Go.
YESSIR!
くる TWIRL
WOOSH
フワッ
?!
Wh- Whoa ...
Toshiyuki... What in the world...?
Toshiyuki's neighbor, Takahiro.

chapter 13: friends

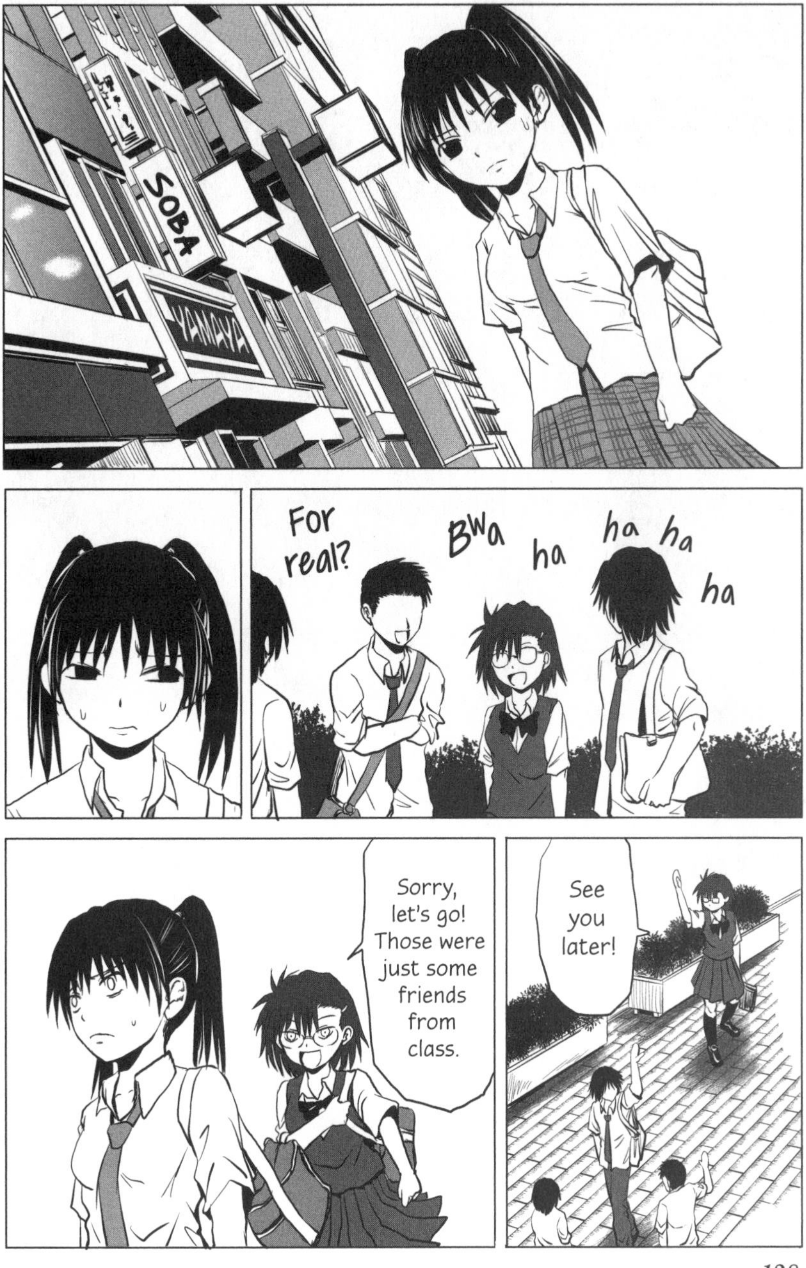
SOBA
Bwa ha ha ha ha
For real?
See you later!
Sorry, let's go! Those were just some friends from class.

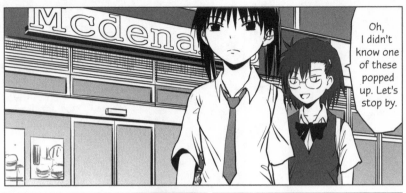

Mcdena
Oh, I didn't know one of these popped up. Let's stop by.
Hey, what's up, Toshiyuki.
Cool if we join you?
That reminds me, I wanted to ask you something.
What kinda fetish you got?
You're real gross, you know that?

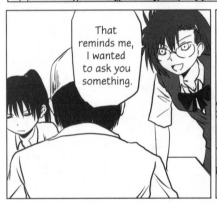

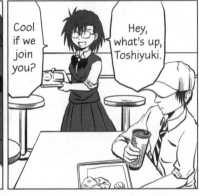

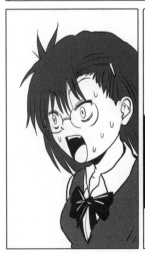

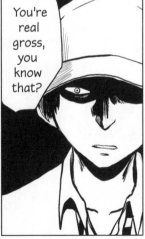

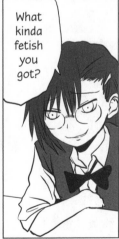

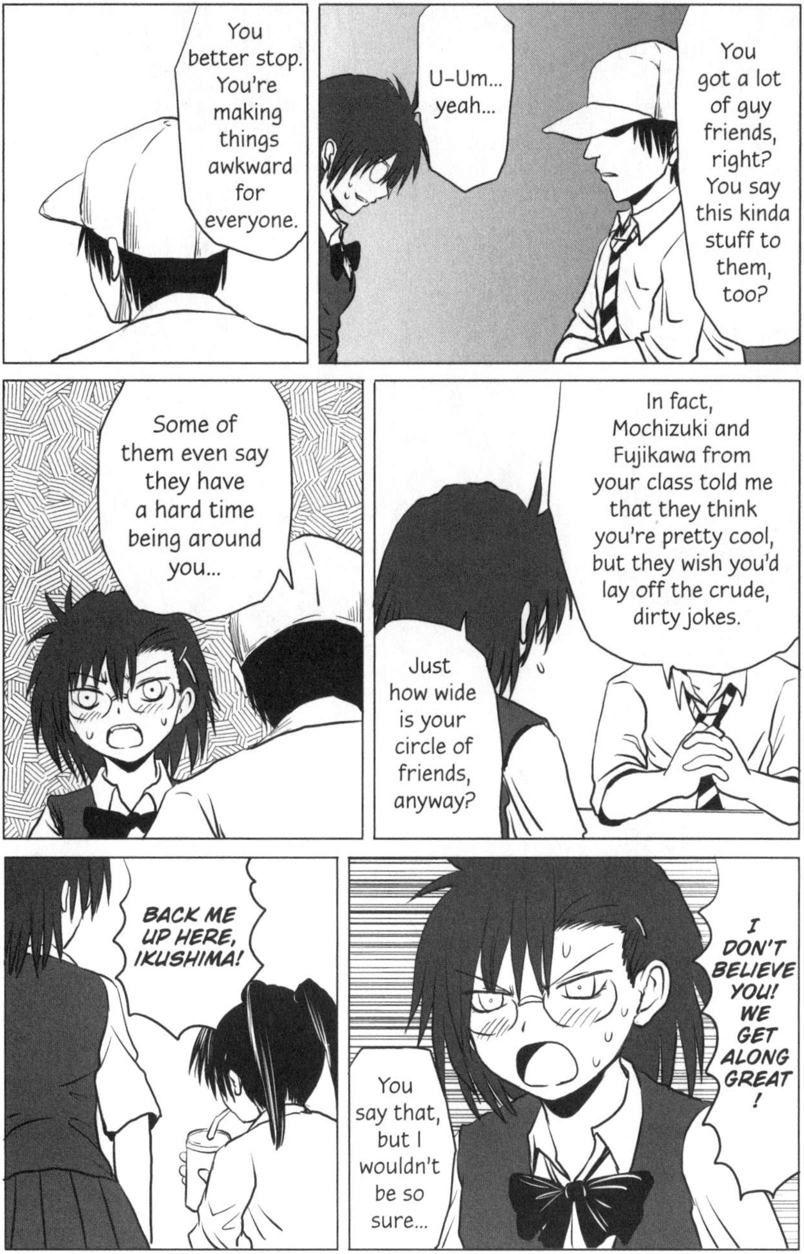
You got a lot of guy friends, right? You say this kinda stuff to them, too?
U-Um... yeah...
You better stop. You're making things awkward for everyone.
In fact, Mochizuki and Fujikawa from your class told me that they think you're pretty cool, but they wish you'd lay off the crude, dirty jokes.
Just how wide is your circle of friends, anyway?
Some of them even say they have a hard time being around you...
I DON'T BELIEVE YOU! WE GET ALONG GREAT!
You say that, but I wouldn't be so sure...
BACK ME UP HERE, IKUSHIMA!

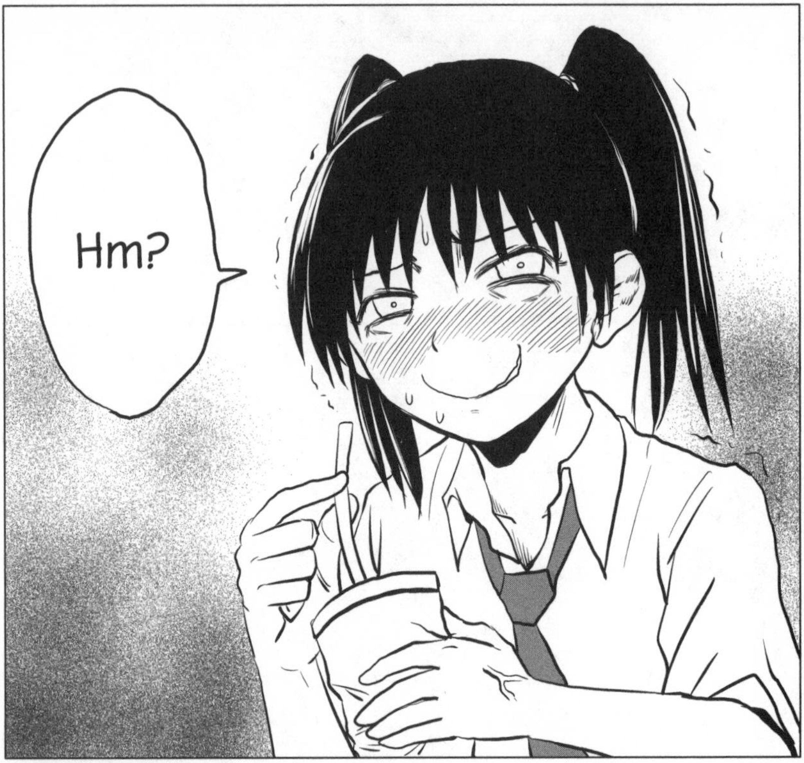
Hm?

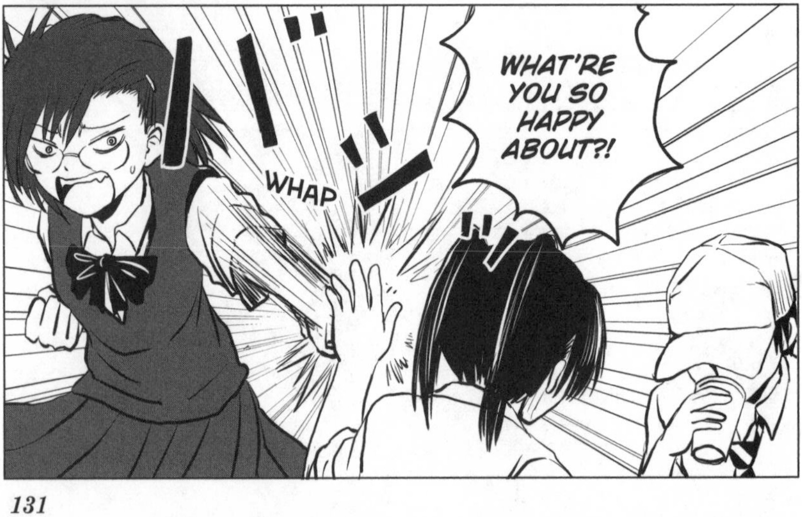
WHAT'RE YOU SO HAPPY ABOUT?!
WHAP

chapter 14: perseverance

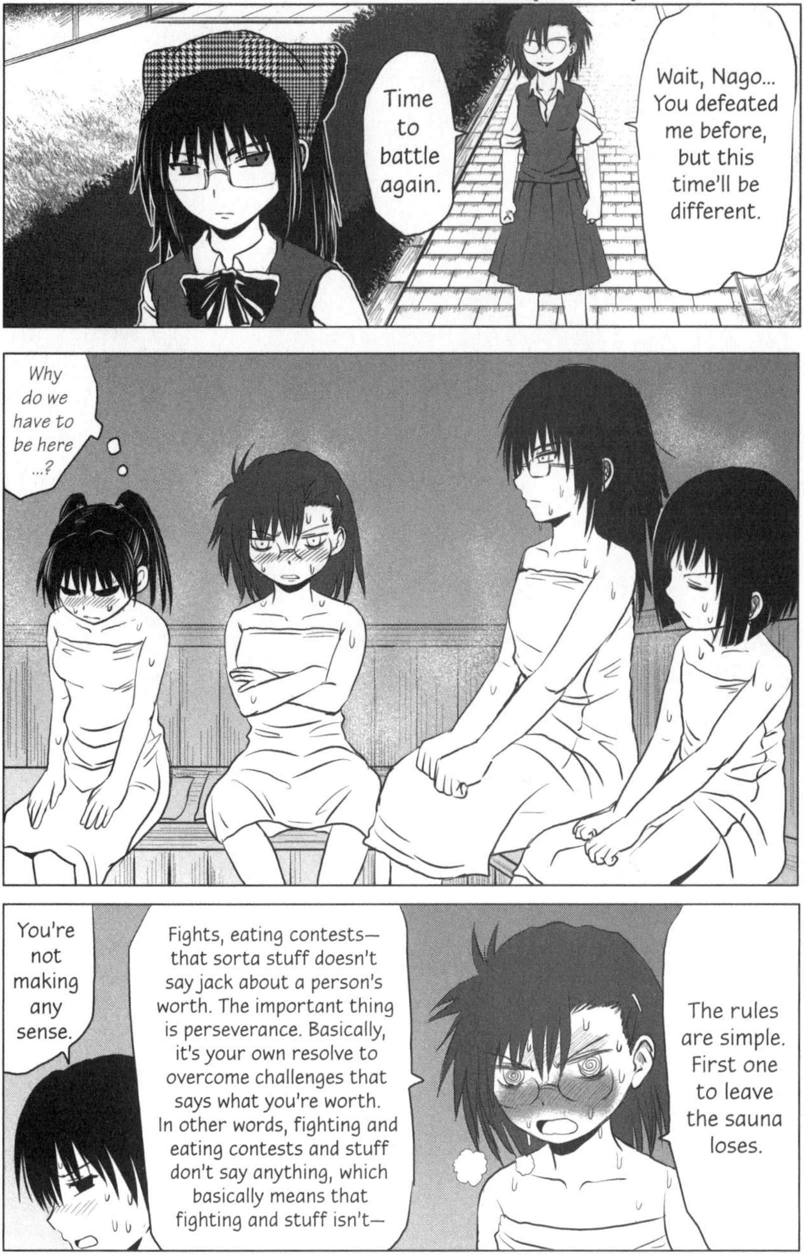
Wait, Nago... You defeated me before, but this time'll be different.
Time to battle again.
Why do we have to be here ...?
The rules are simple. First one to leave the sauna loses.
Fights, eating contests—that sorta stuff doesn't say jack about a person's worth. The important thing is perseverance. Basically, it's your own resolve to overcome challenges that says what you're worth. In other words, fighting and eating contests and stuff don't say anything, which basically means that fighting and stuff isn't—
You're not making any sense.

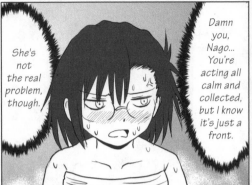

Damn you, Nago... You're acting all calm and collected, but I know it's just a front.
She's not the real problem, though.
Right now, the most danger-ous one here is Habara.
I bet this sorta heat's nothing to her.
I can't take it anymore, it's too hot!
Huh? I thought she'd have more grit.
BSSHT

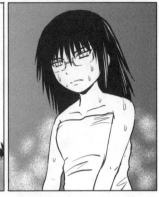

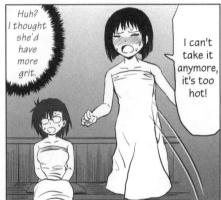

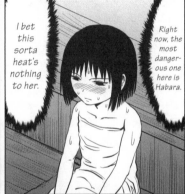

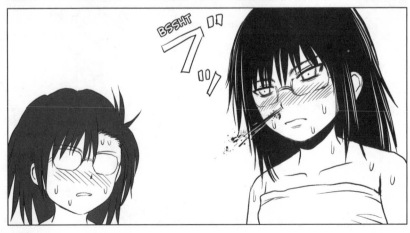

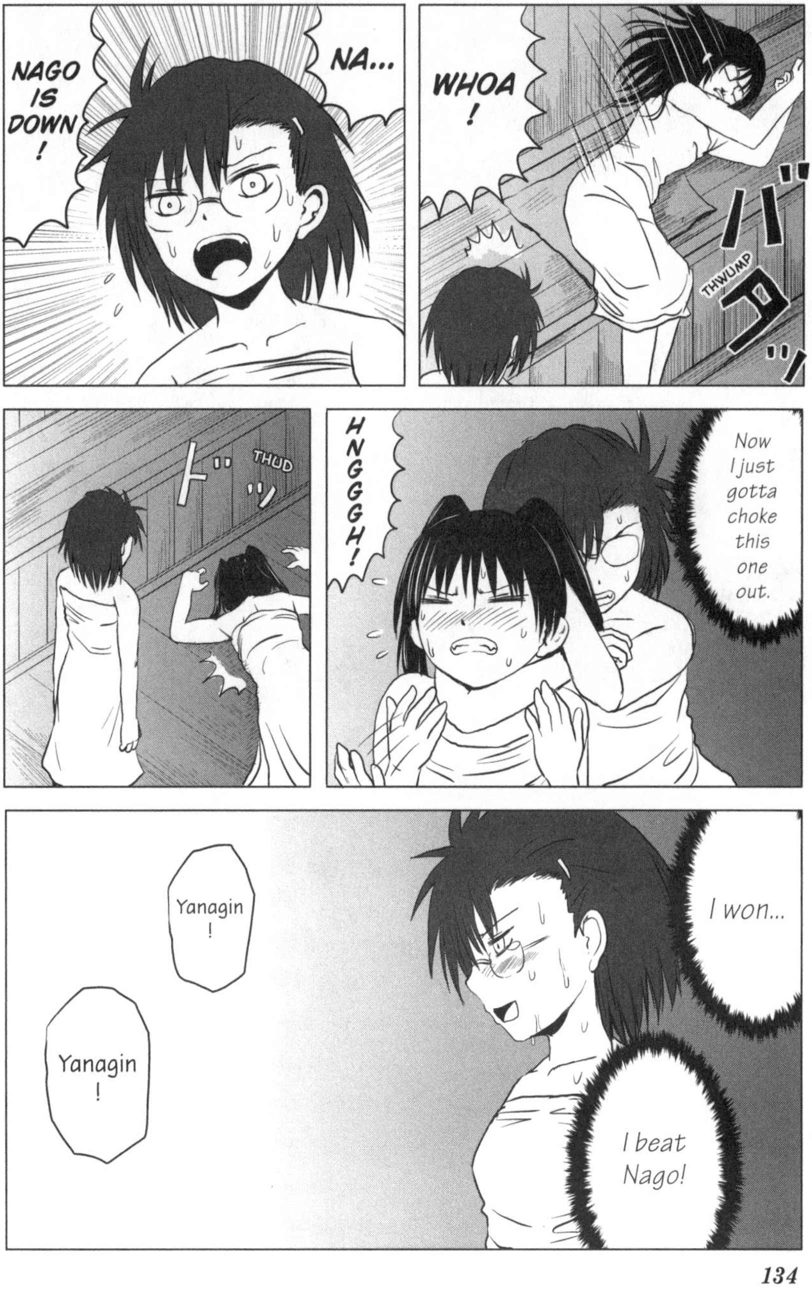
WHOA!
バタッ
THWUMP
NA...
NAGO IS DOWN!
Now I just gotta choke this one out.
HNGGGH!
ドッ
THUD
I won...
I beat Nago!
Yanagin!
Yanagin!

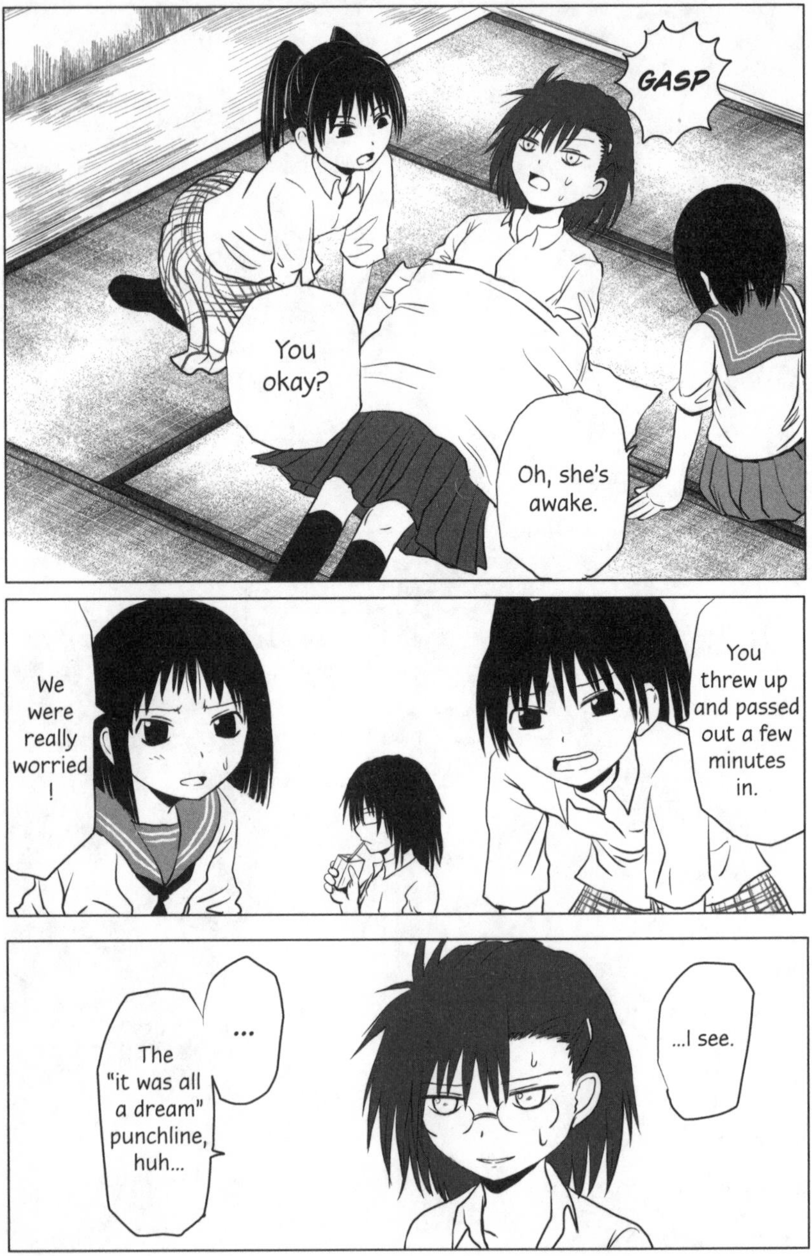
GASP
Oh, she's awake.
You okay?
You threw up and passed out a few minutes in.
We were really worried!
...I see.
...
The "it was all a dream" punchline, huh...

chapter 15: demon

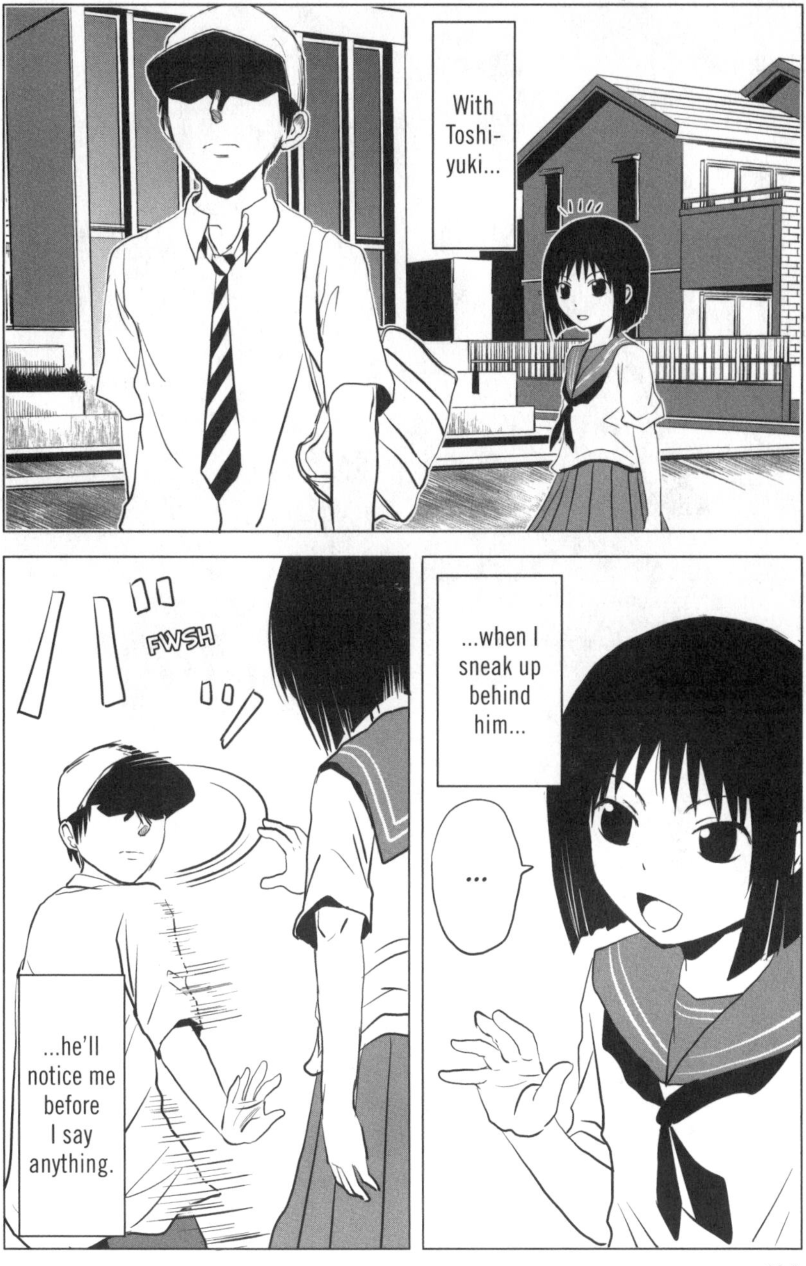

With Toshi-yuki...
...when I sneak up behind him...
...
FWSH
...he'll notice me before I say anything.

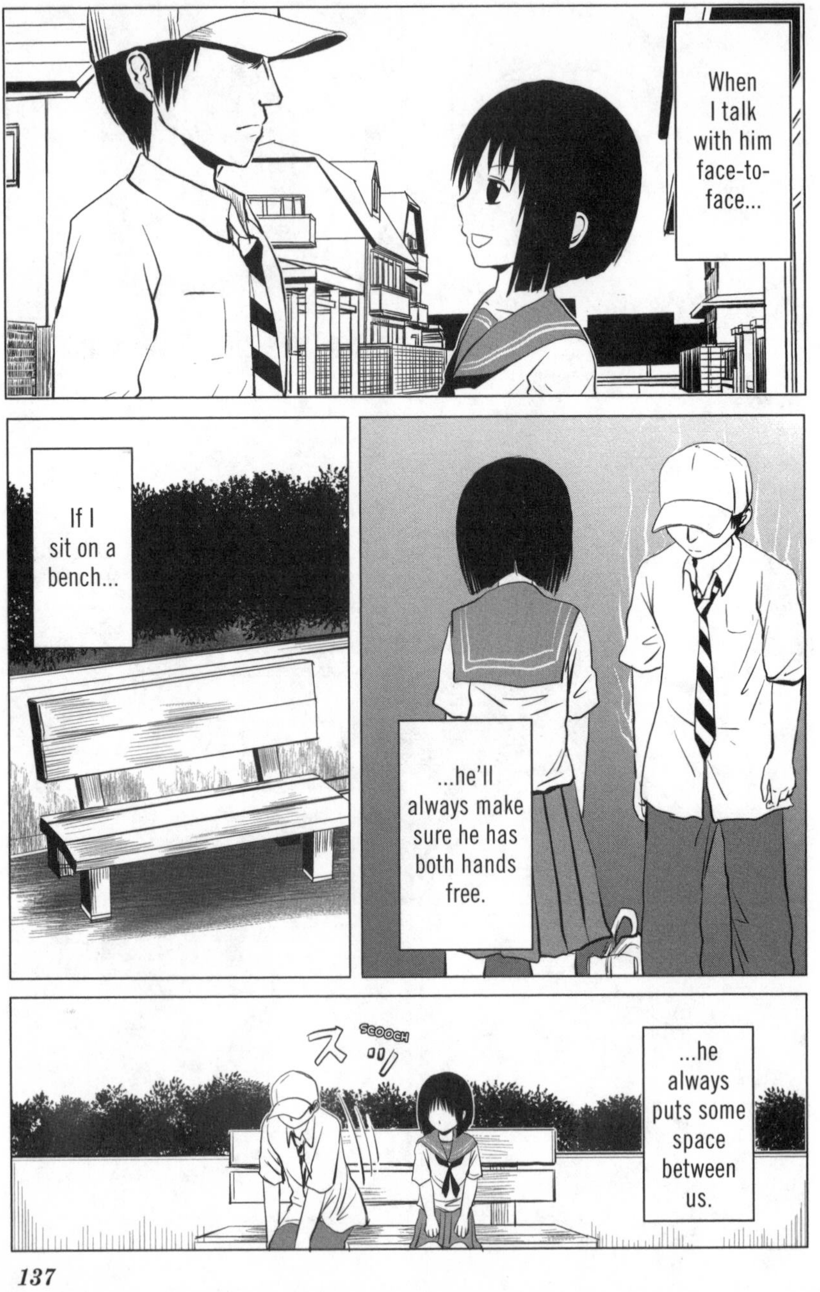
When I talk with him face-to-face...
...he'll always make sure he has both hands free.
If I sit on a bench...
スッ
SCOOCH
...he always puts some space between us.

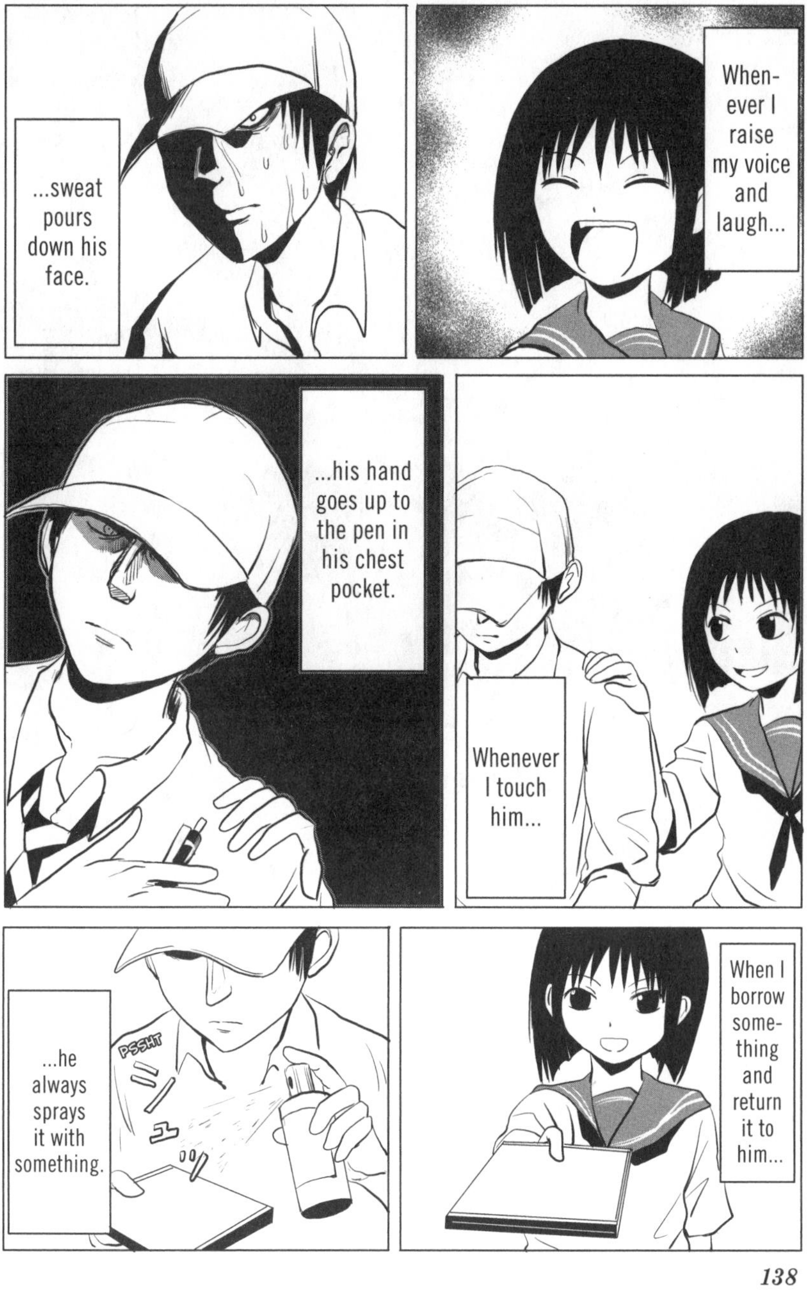
When-ever I raise my voice and laugh...
...sweat pours down his face.
Whenever I touch him...
...his hand goes up to the pen in his chest pocket.
When I borrow some-thing and return it to him...
...he always sprays it with something.
PSSHT

Consid-ering all of the above...
Maybe ...
Just maybe ...
Toshiyuki has some special feelings...
No, forget it. I must have the wrong idea...
IN A WAY, YOU'RE SPOT ON.
Yeah, in a way.

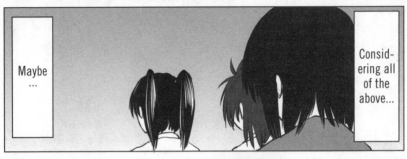

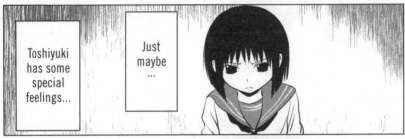

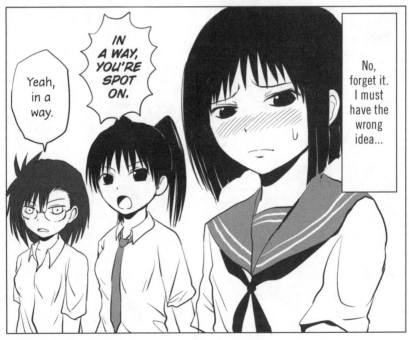

extra chapter: antagonism continues

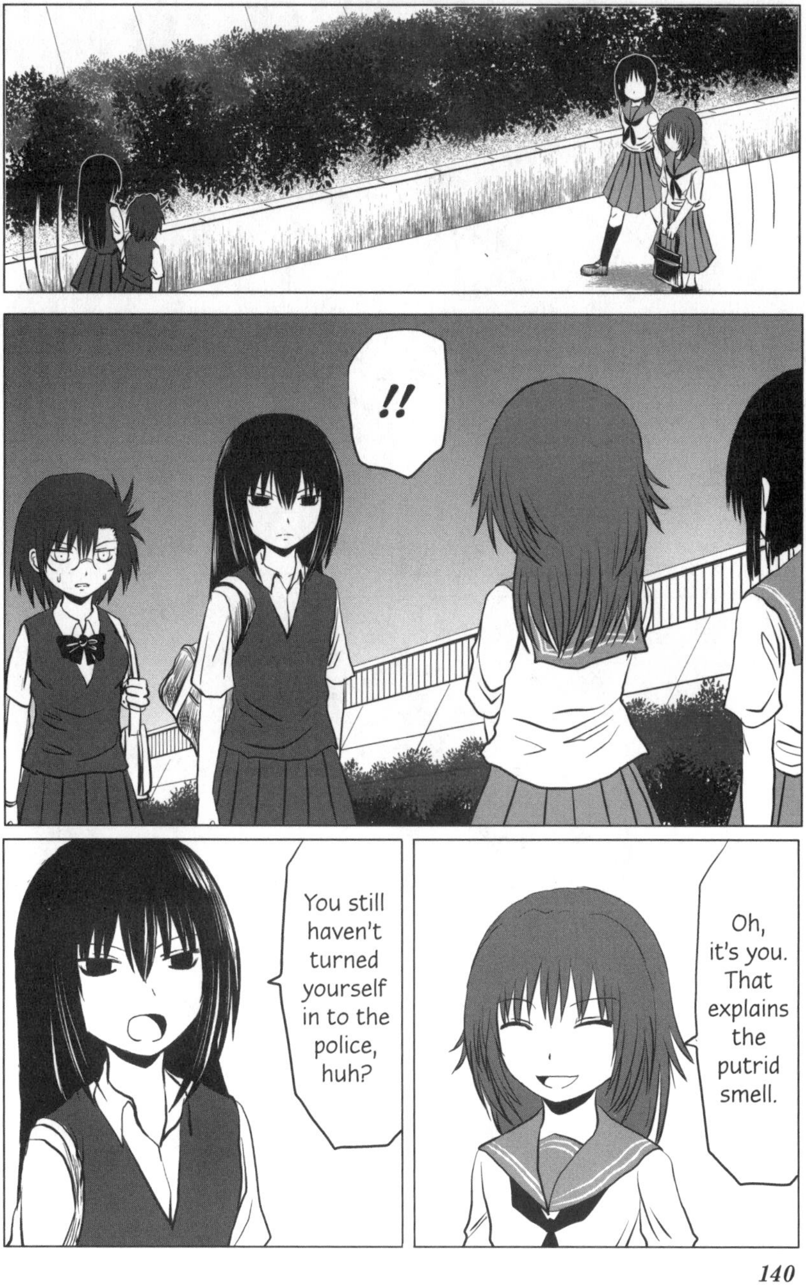
!!
Oh, it's you. That explains the putrid smell.
You still haven't turned yourself in to the police, huh?

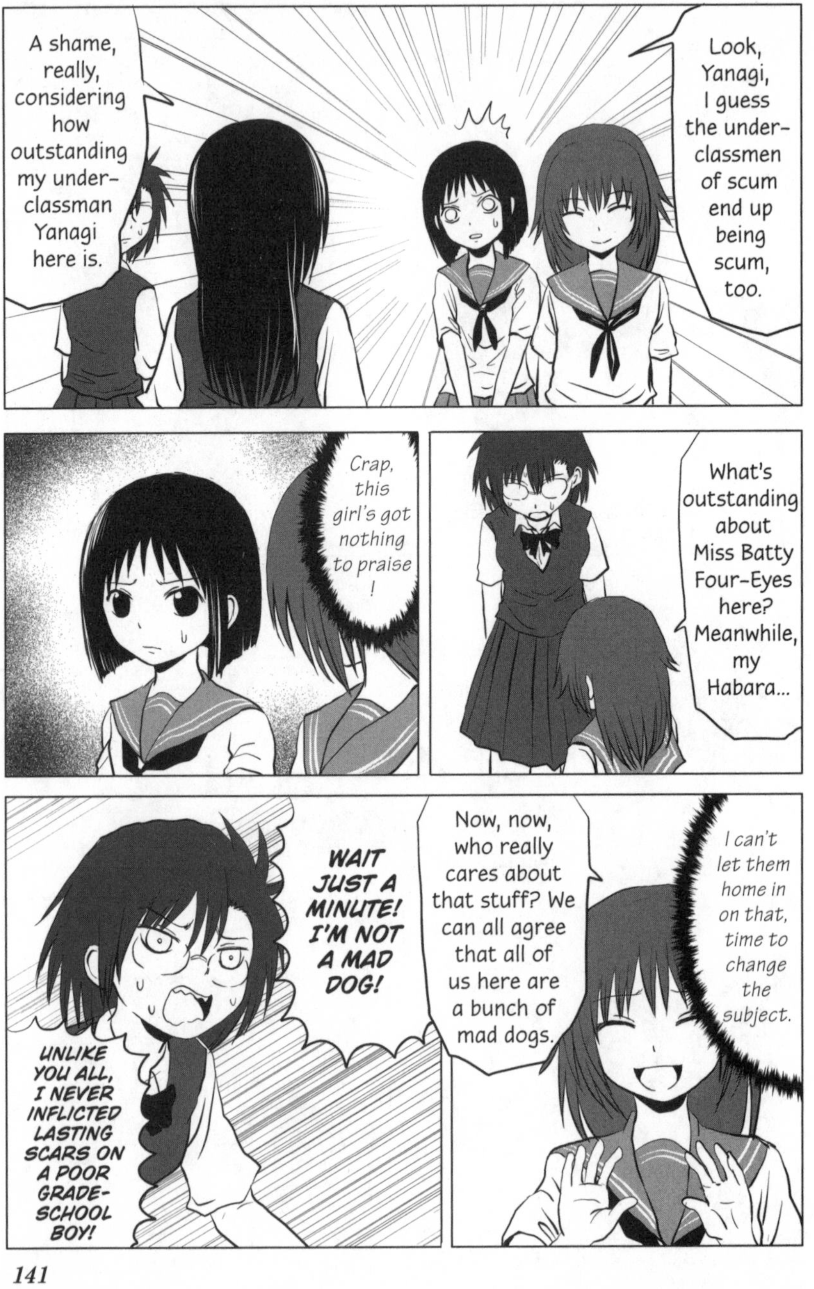
Look, Yanagi, I guess the under-classmen of scum end up being scum, too.
A shame, really, considering how outstanding my under-classman Yanagi here is.
What's outstanding about Miss Batty Four-Eyes here? Meanwhile, my Habara...
Crap, this girl's got nothing to praise!
I can't let them home in on that, time to change the subject.
Now, now, who really cares about that stuff? We can all agree that all of us here are a bunch of mad dogs.
WAIT JUST A MINUTE! I'M NOT A MAD DOG!
UNLIKE YOU ALL, I NEVER INFLICTED LASTING SCARS ON A POOR GRADE-SCHOOL BOY!

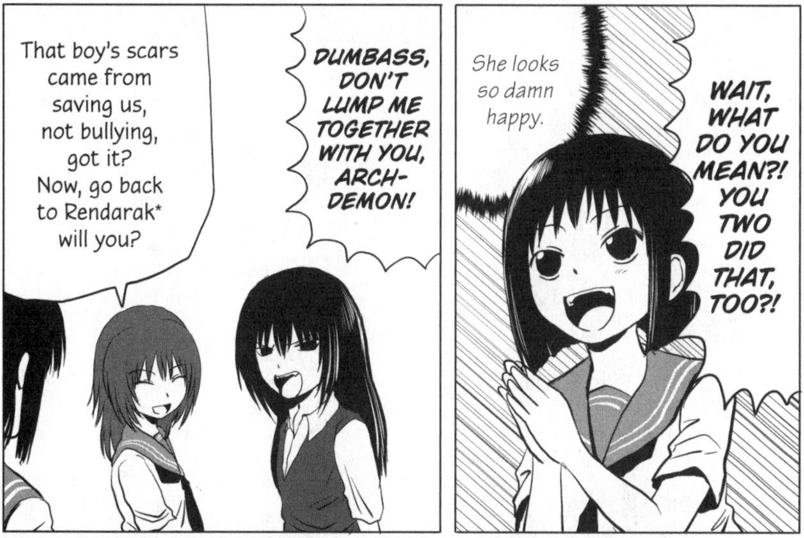
WAIT, WHAT DO YOU MEAN?! YOU TWO DID THAT, TOO?!
She looks so damn happy.
DUMBASS, DON'T LUMP ME TOGETHER WITH YOU, ARCH-DEMON!
That boy's scars came from saving us, not bullying, got it? Now, go back to Rendarak* will you?

*An area in *Dragon Quest II* near the end of the game where Archdemons are one of the enemies players can encounter.

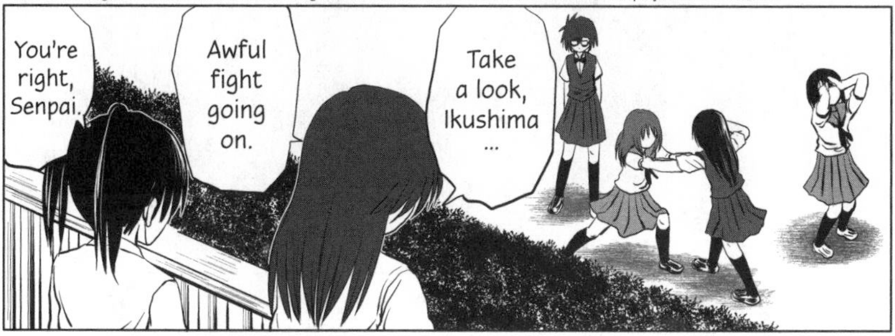
Take a look, Ikushima ...
Awful fight going on.
You're right, Senpai.

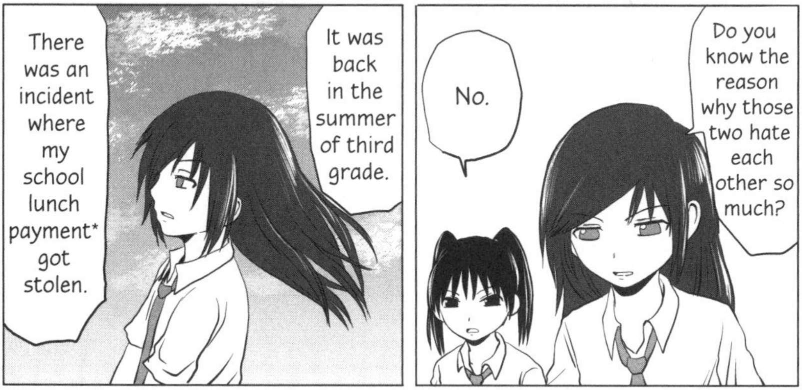
Do you know the reason why those two hate each other so much?
No.
It was back in the summer of third grade.
There was an incident where my school lunch payment* got stolen.

*When students in Japan pay for their lunch, they usually bring money in on a regular basis (like once a month).

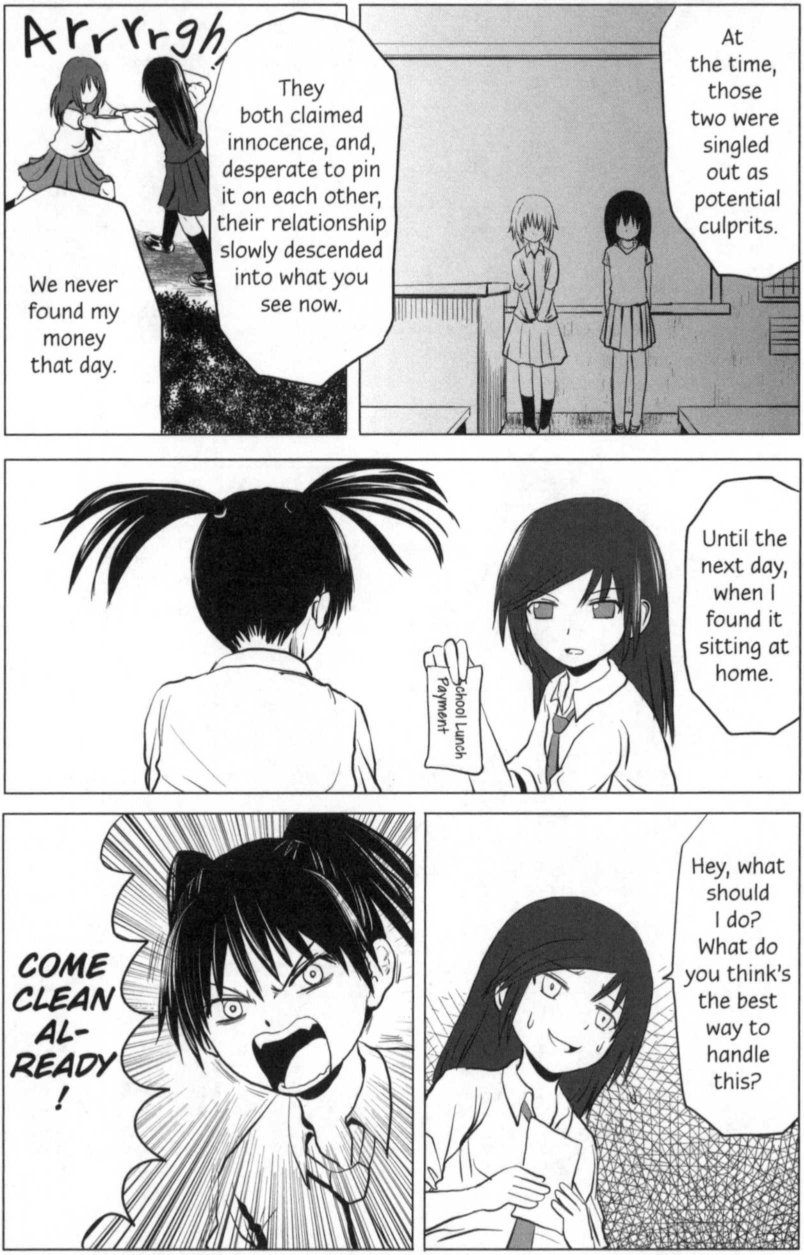
At the time, those two were singled out as potential culprits.
They both claimed innocence, and, desperate to pin it on each other, their relationship slowly descended into what you see now.
Arrrrgh!
We never found my money that day.
Until the next day, when I found it sitting at home.
School Lunch Payment
Hey, what should I do? What do you think's the best way to handle this?
COME CLEAN AL-READY!

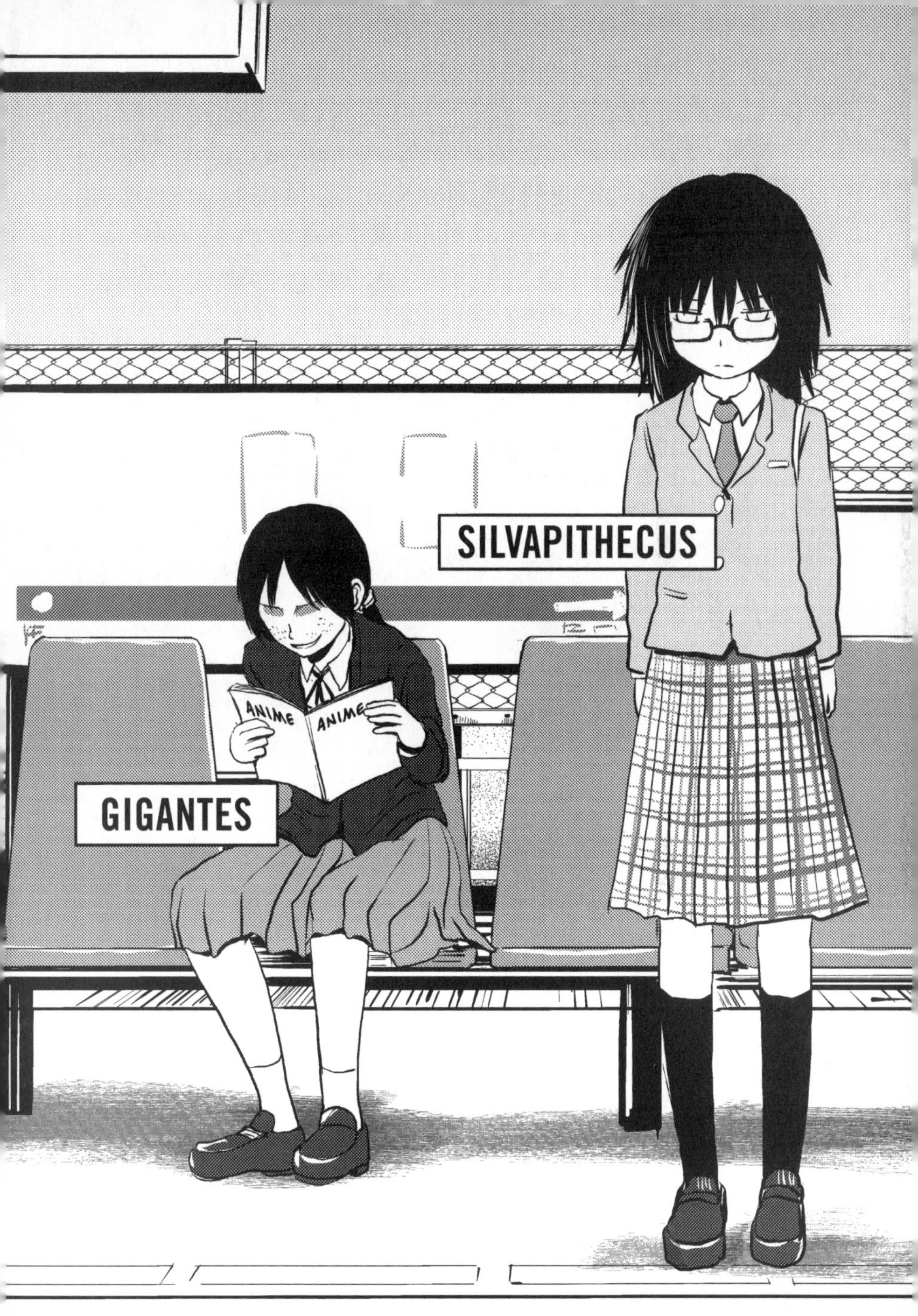
SILVAPITHECUS
ANIME
ANIME
GIGANTES

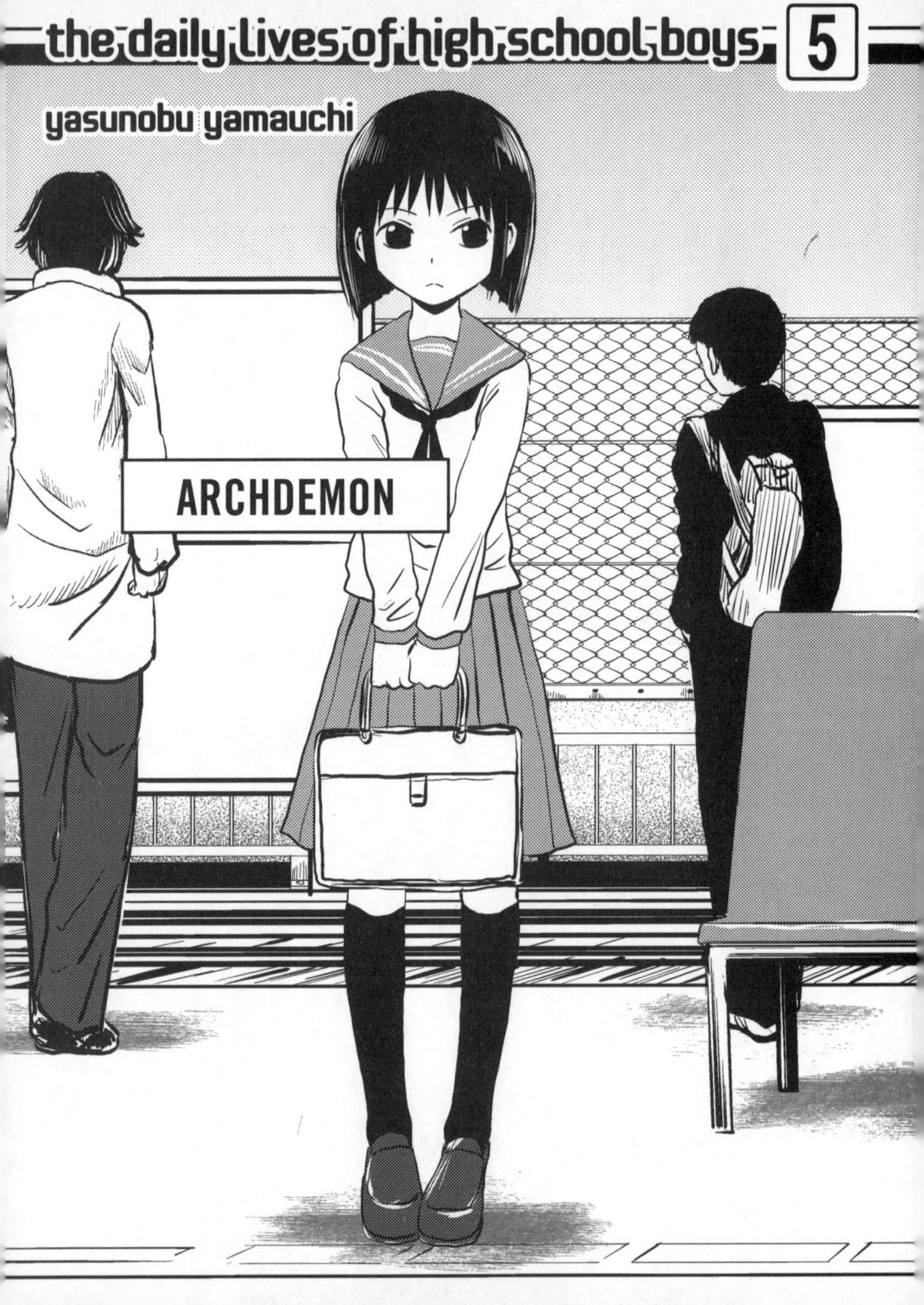
the daily lives of high school boys 5
yasunobu yamauchi
ARCHDEMON

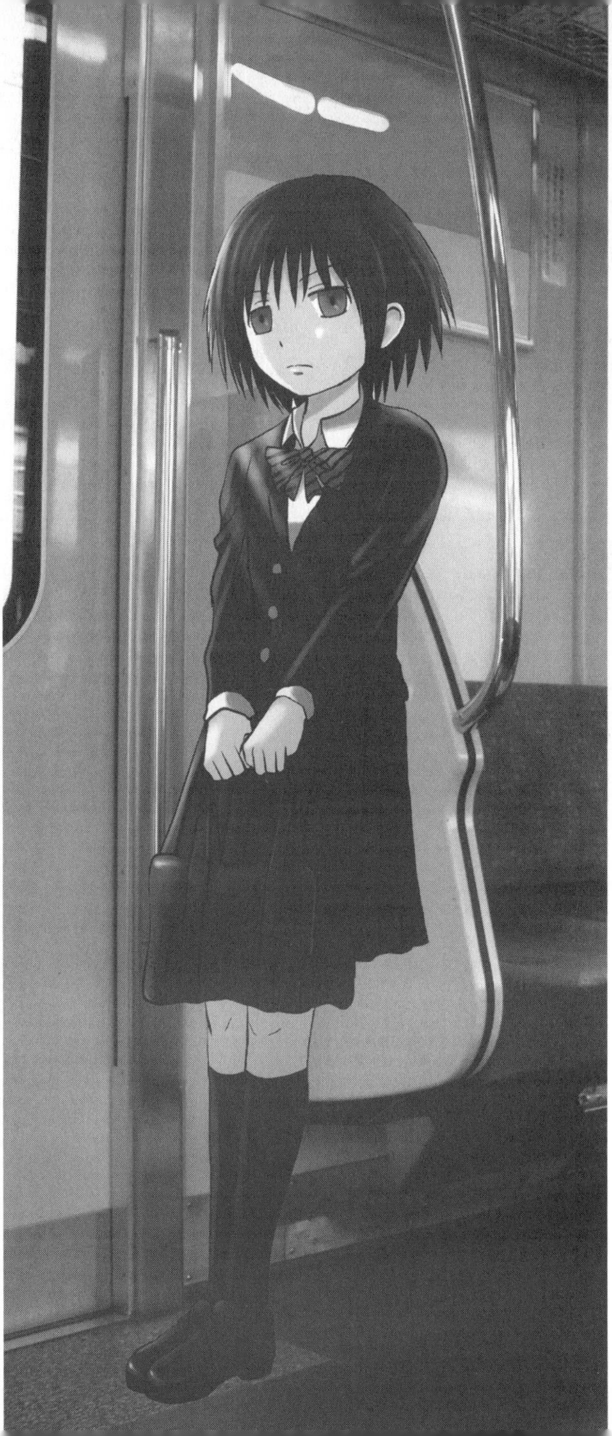

yasunobu yamauchi

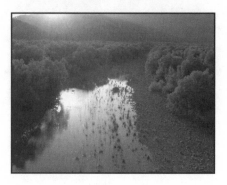

This is a short two-minute
walk away from my home.

the

daily

lives

of

5 high school boys

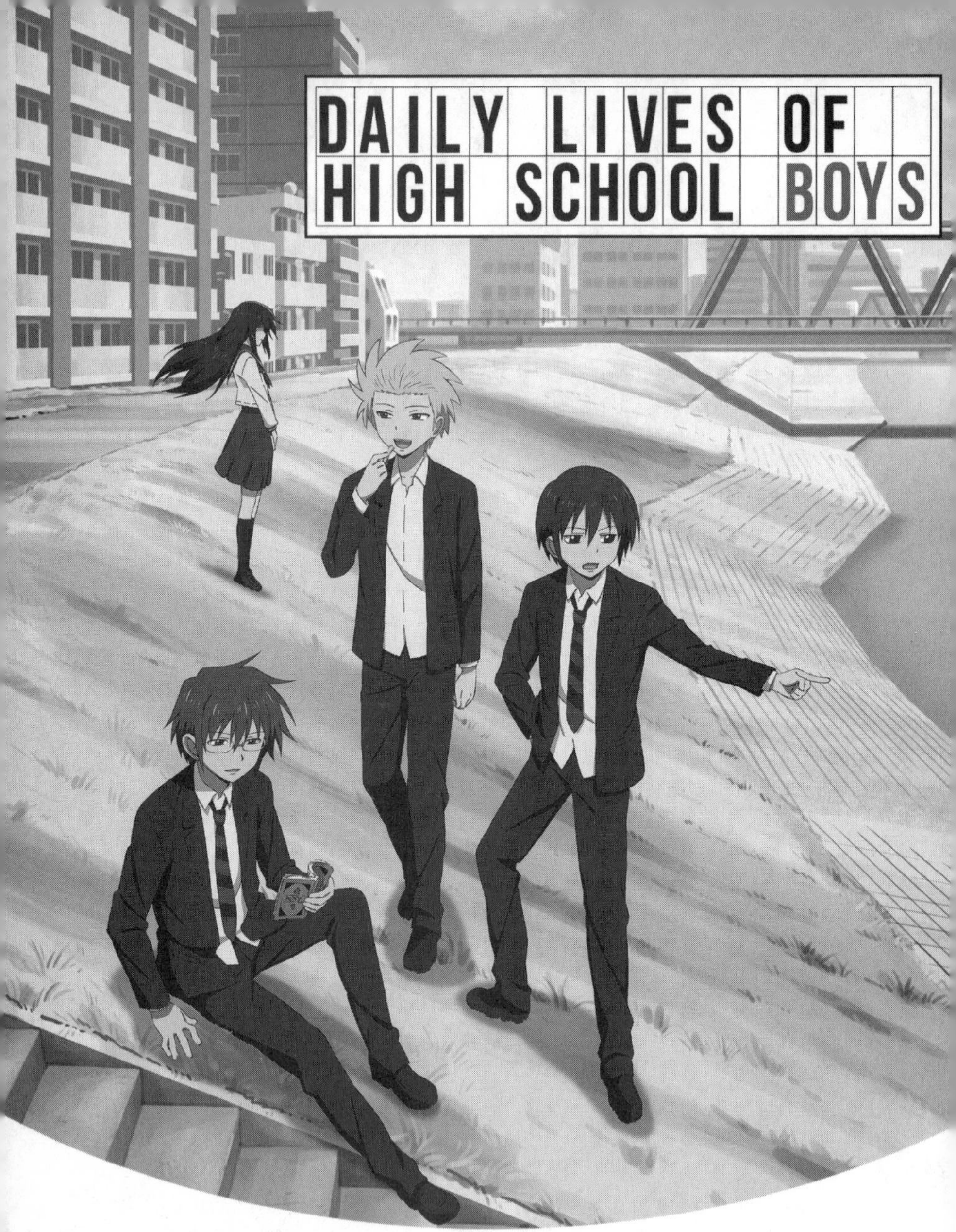
DAILY LIVES OF
HIGH SCHOOL BOYS

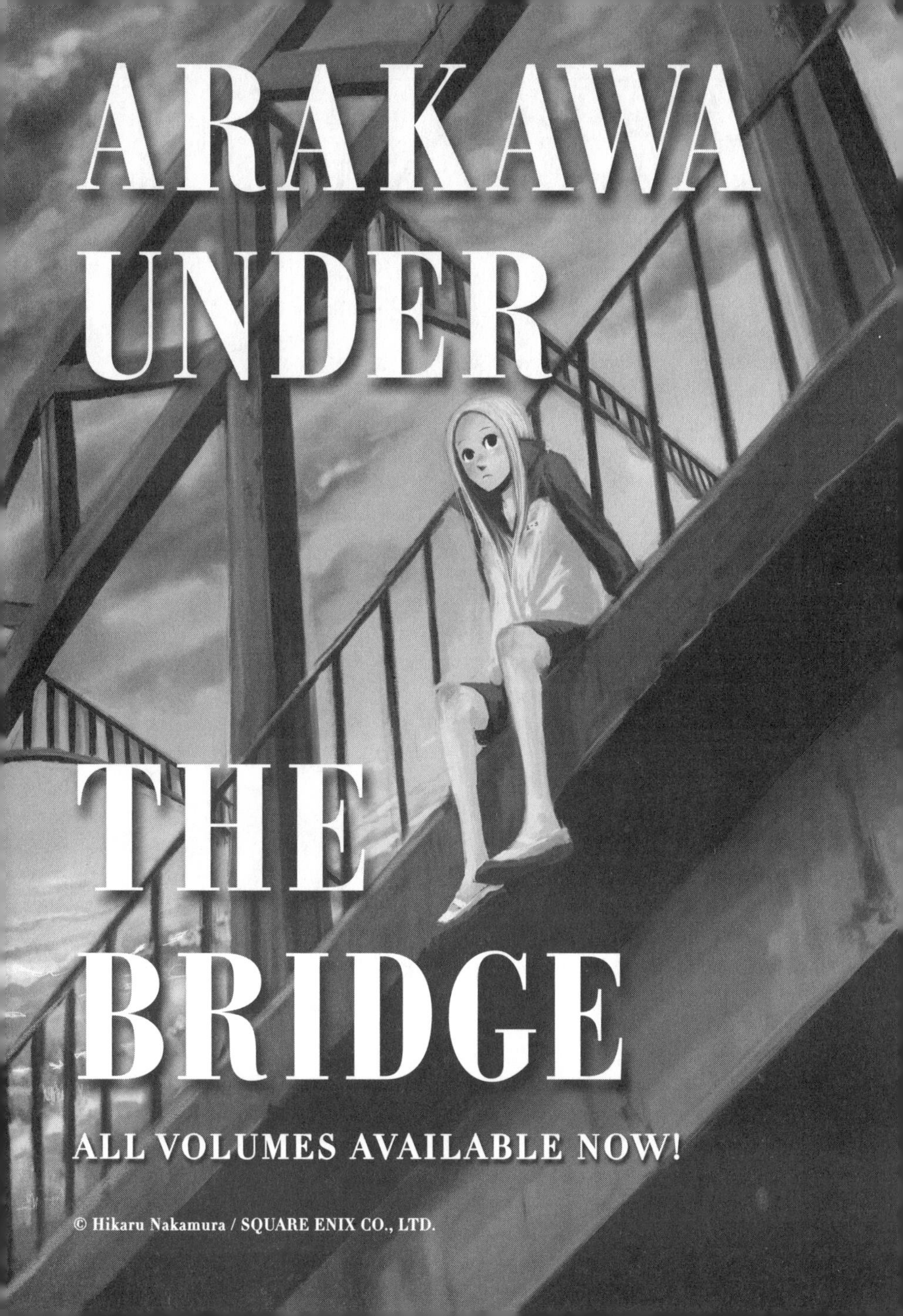
ARAKAWA
UNDER
THE
BRIDGE
ALL VOLUMES AVAILABLE NOW!
© Hikaru Nakamura / SQUARE ENIX CO., LTD.

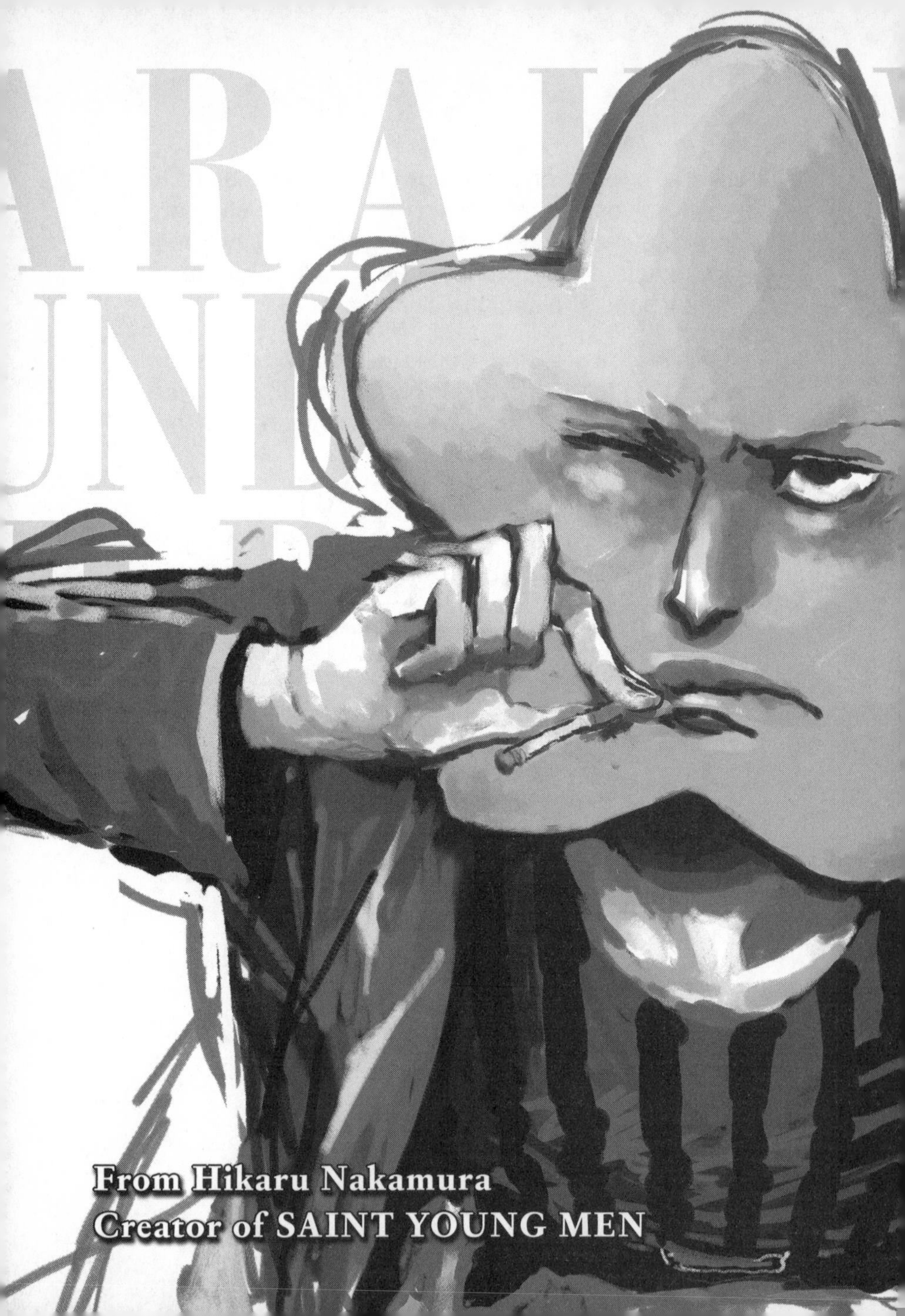
From Hikaru Nakamura
Creator of SAINT YOUNG MEN

From the creator of ***nichijou***, this surreal-slapstick series revolves around a penniless college student, Midori Nagumo, who lives in an ordinary city filled with not-quite-ordinary people. And as this reckless girl runs about, she sets the city in motion.

Midori is in a bit of a bind. She is in debt, and her land-lady is trying to shake her down for unpaid rent. Her best friend refuses to loan her cash since she's wised up to her tricks.

Maybe some bullying would help. Or a bit of pet-ty theft? Neither is sustainable. Maybe getting a job would settle things… But working means less time for fun adventures in the big city…

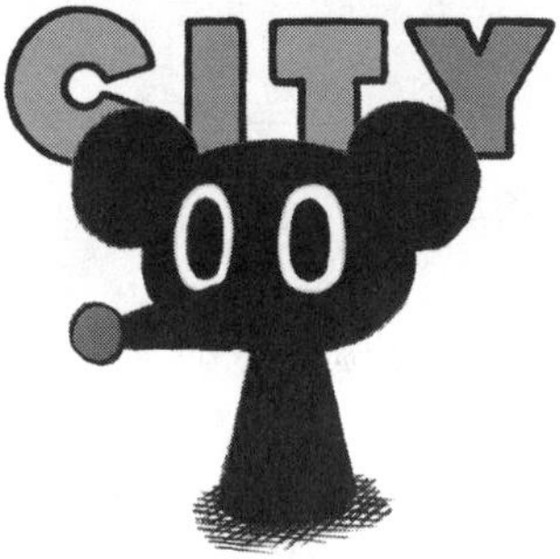
CITY

Volumes 1-10 Available Now!

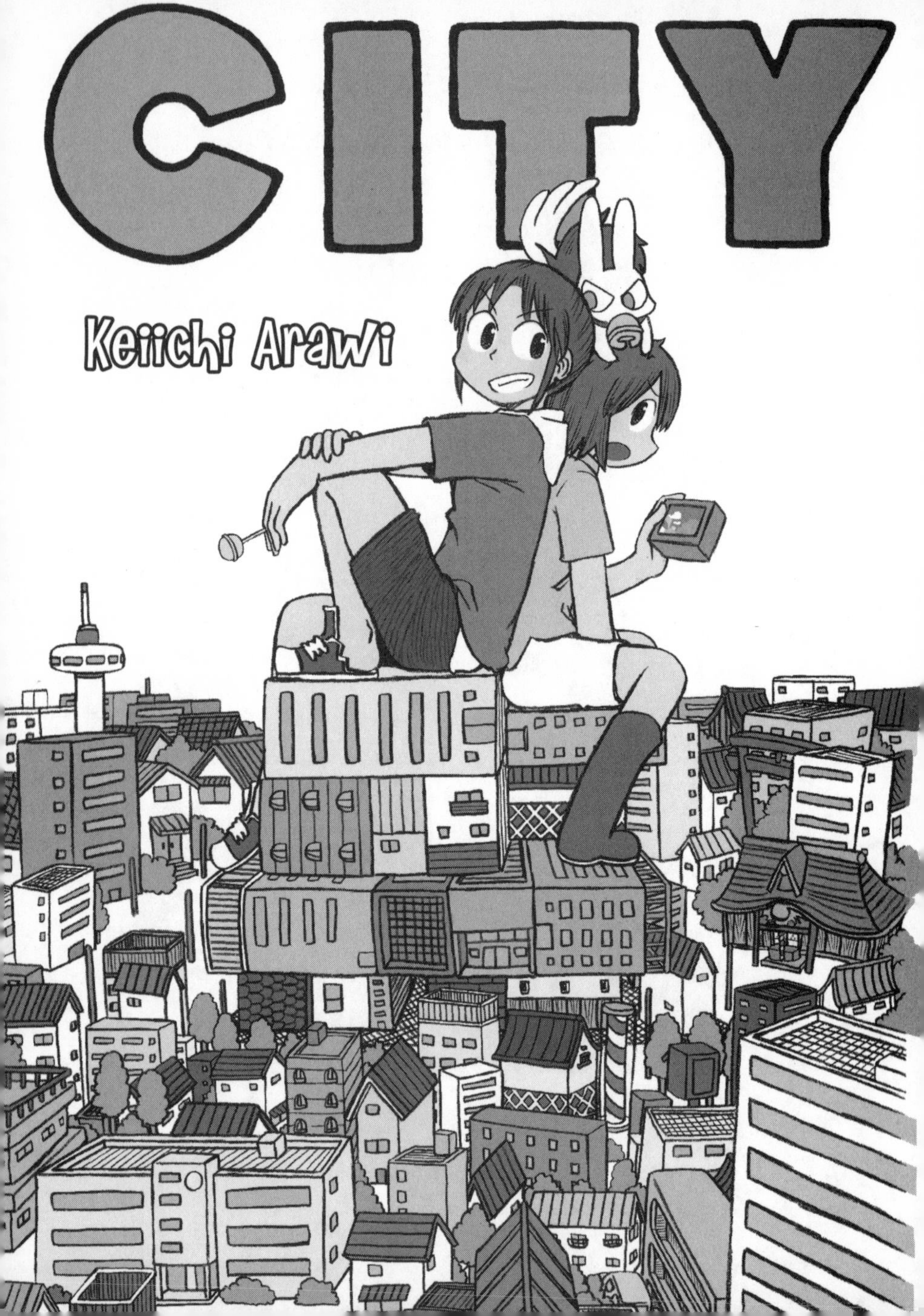
CITY
Keiichi Arawi

Prepare to be Bewitched!

Makoto Kowata, a novice witch, packs up her belongings (including a black cat familiar) and moves in with her distant cousins in rural Aomori to complete her training and become a full-fledged witch.

"*Flying Witch* emphasizes that while actual magic is nice, there is ultimately magic in everything." —*Anime News Network*

The Basis for the Hit Anime from Sentai Filmworks!

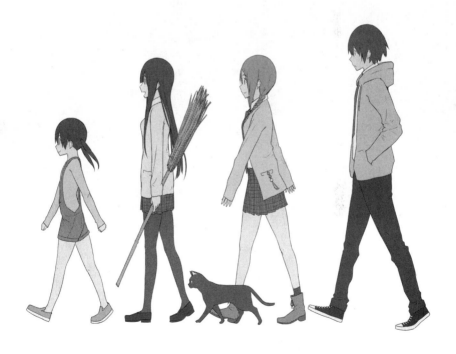

Volumes 1-9 Available Now!

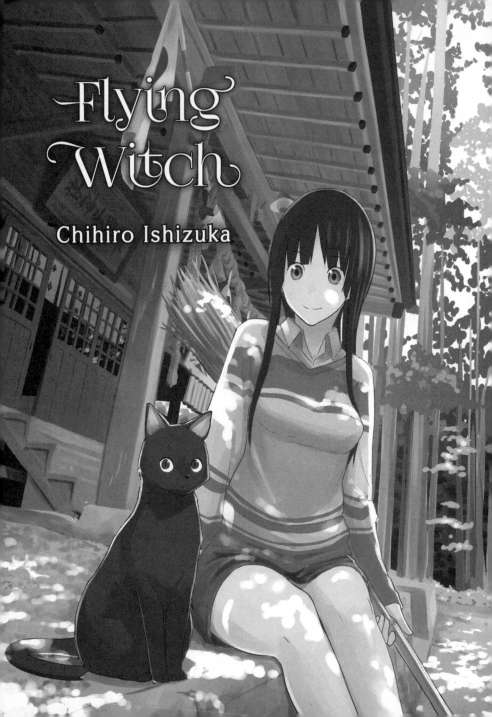

Flying Witch

Chihiro Ishizuka

The Delinquent Housewife!
by Nemu Yoko

Tohru Komukai and his bride-to-be, Komugi, move in with his family just until they find a place of their own. Or, that was the plan, until Tohru suddenly leaves for a long-term business trip overseas, leaving Komugi to fend for herself on her in-laws' turf. While Komugi is pretty, considerate and appears to be an ideal housewife, the truth is she doesn't know how to do a lick of housework, and can't cook at all. Also, she has a secret past as a member of an all-girls *bosozoku* biker gang! The only member of the family to learn these secrets is Dai, Tohru's younger brother, and he helps Komugi keep up appearances until she can learn how to hold her own as a domestic goddess...

ALL VOLUMES AVAILABLE NOW!

FUTSUTSUKA NA YOME DESUGA! © 2016 Nemu Yoko / SHOGAKUKAN

The Delinquent HOUSEWIFE! 1

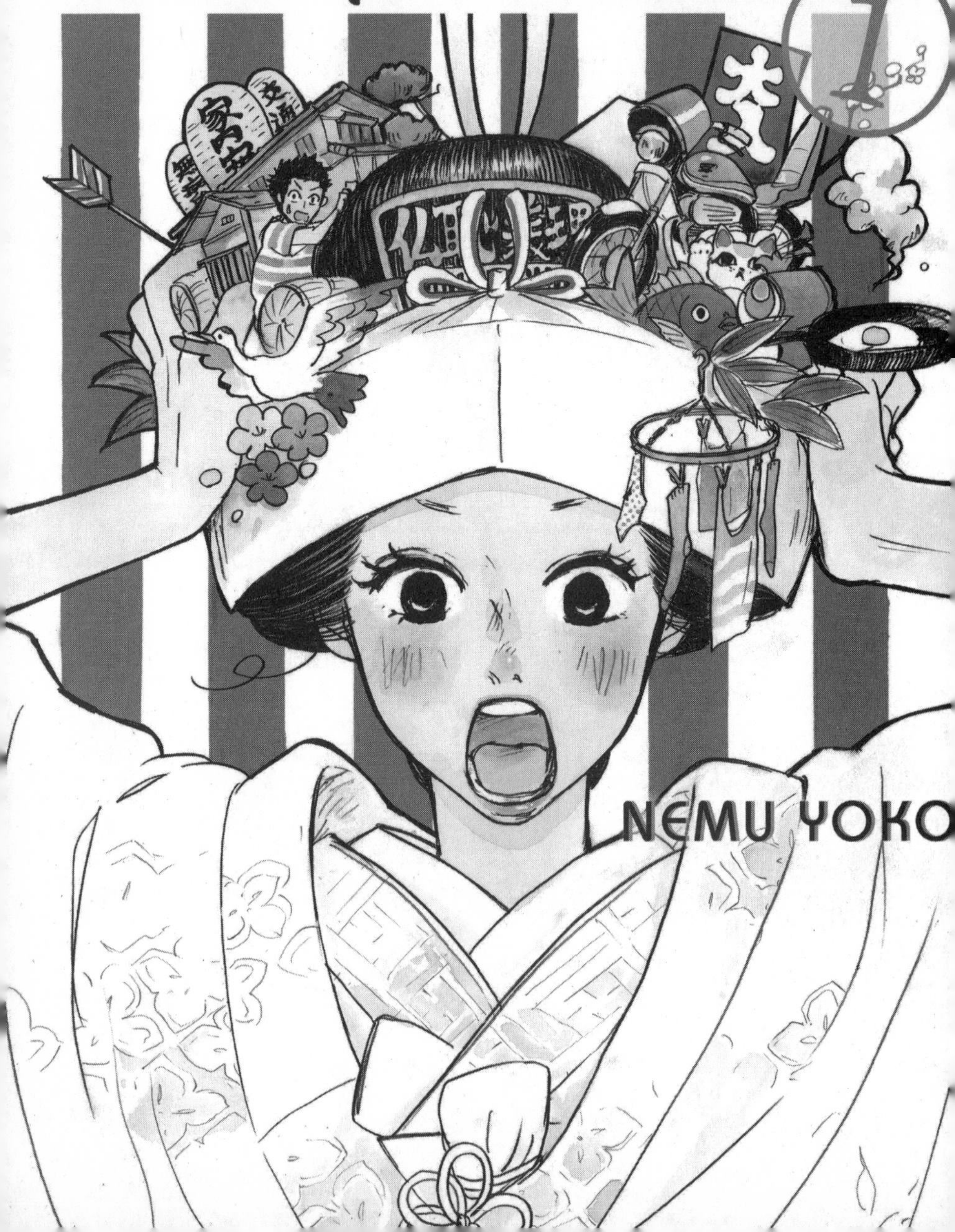

NEMU YOKO

OWN THE *&#@ MANGA THAT INSPIRED THE ANIME!

Get volumes 1 and 2 NOW!

POP TEAM EPIC

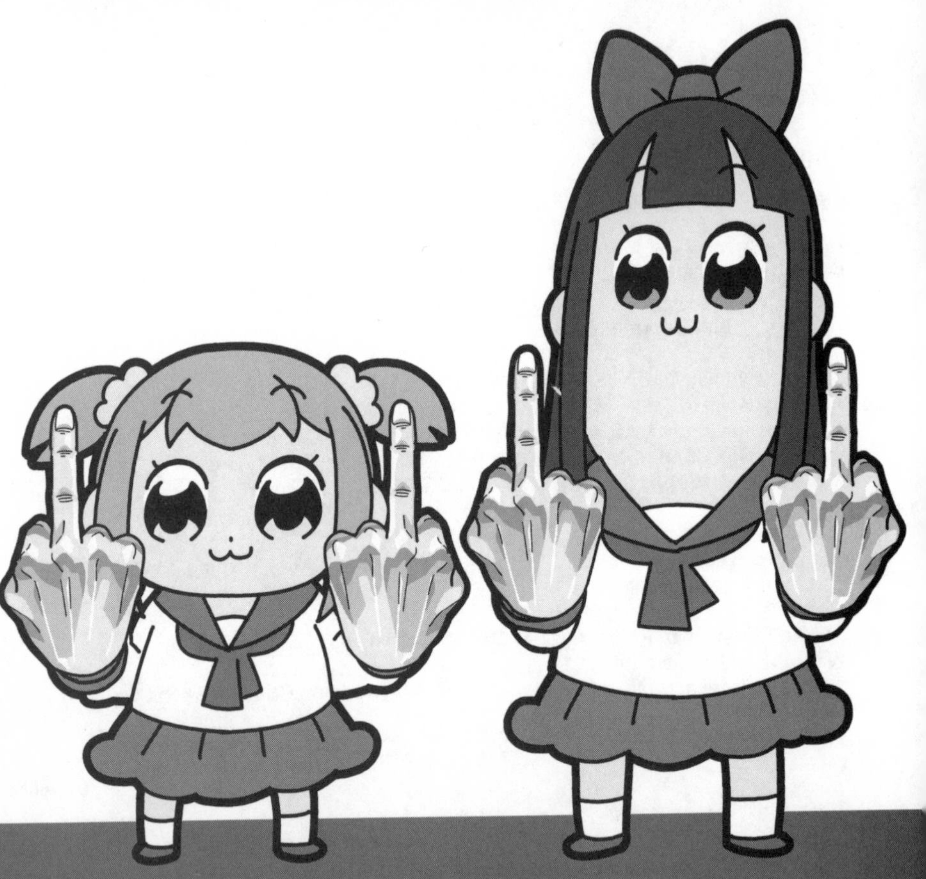

Bkub Okawa

THE DAILY LIVES OF
HIGH SCHOOL BOYS 5
Yasunobu Yamauchi

A Vertical Comics Edition

Editor: Ajani Oloye
Translation: David Musto
Production: Grace Lu
             Anthony Quintessenza

Translation provided by Vertical Comics, 2021
Published by Vertical Comics, an imprint of Kodansha USA Publishing, LLC,
New York

Originally published in Japanese as *Danshi Kokosei no Nichijo 5*
by SQUARE ENIX Co., Ltd., 2011
Danshi Kokosei no Nichijo first serialized in *Gangan Online*, SQUARE ENIX Co.,
Ltd., 2009-2012

This is a work of fiction.

ISBN: 978-1-949980-82-0

Manufactured in the United States of America

First Edition

Kodansha USA Publishing, LLC
451 Park Avenue South
7th Floor
New York, NY 10016
www.readvertical.com

Vertical books are distributed through Penguin-Random House Publisher Services.